# THE DOCTRINE OF GOD

# THE
# DOCTRINE OF GOD

## IN THE JEWISH APOCRYPHAL
## AND APOCALYPTIC LITERATURE

BY

HENRY J. WICKS, B.A., D.D. (LOND.)

WITH INTRODUCTION BY

### R. H. CHARLES, D.D., D.Litt.
CANON OF WESTMINSTER

*THESIS APPROVED FOR THE DEGREE OF DOCTOR
OF DIVINITY IN THE UNIVERSITY OF LONDON*

## KTAV PUBLISHING HOUSE, Inc.

### NEW YORK

### 1971

FIRST PUBLISHED 1915

SBN 87068-149-4

LIBRARY OF CONGRESS CATALOG CARD NUMBER: 77-78502
MANUFACTURED IN THE UNITED STATES OF AMERICA

2-28-74

# PREFACE

No attempt has been made in this work to classify the authors of the apocryphal and apocalyptic literature according to various religious sects, for this cannot be done with any confidence. As Dr. M. Gaster says: "The claim put up by some modern scholars to determine exactly whether a writer belonged to the Sadducees or the Pharisees rests on a very slender basis. . . . We cannot dogmatise on these questions, which are thus far only postulates and lack scientific proof." * The various books of the literature are here discussed, as far as that is possible, in their chronological order. It does not come within the scope of this work to attempt anything like a full treatment of questions of "Introduction," but it seems necessary to state briefly the reasons which have led the present writer to adopt certain critical theories as to the composition of the books under discussion and as to the dates to which they should be assigned. This has accordingly been done in a short introductory chapter. Attention is called in the summaries and conclusions to points of resemblance and dissimilarity in the doctrine of Palestinian and non-Palestinian writings, but in some cases it is impossible to be certain whether a writer lived in Palestine or amongst

* I.J.A., January 1910, pp. 17, 19.

v

the Dispersion. The author, like all students of this literature, is under deep obligation to those who have edited apocalyptic and other works, especially to Dr. R. H. Charles. He would also make grateful acknowledgment of the kindness of his friend, Mr. F. A. Freer, who has allowed him to use his English translation of the Apocalypse of Abraham, of which work there is as yet no published edition in this country. In citations from the literature use has been made of the following works : Messrs. Ryle and James's edition of the Psalms of Solomon and Dr. R. Harris's rendering of the Syriac version of that Psalter, Mr. Hart's "Ecclesiasticus in Greek" (with his references to MSS.), Cotton's translation of Macca-bees (for the 3rd and 4th Books), "The Speaker's Com-mentary" (for renderings of the Vulgate of Judith), and Dr. Tennant's "The Fall and Original Sin" (for the Syriac version of Ecclesiasticus). The rendering of one passage in the Apocalypse of Abraham has been borrowed from the last-named work. In citations from the Hebrew of Ecclesiasticus use has, of course, been made of the work of Messrs. Shechter and Taylor, G. Margoliouth, Cowley and Neubauer, and Israel Lévi. Studious endeavour has been made to acknowledge all help derived from previous workers in the same field of investigation. If in any case this has been omitted it arises from an inadvertence on the part of the author.

HENRY J. WICKS.

# ABBREVIATIONS USED

| | | |
|---|---|---|
| D.B | . | Hastings' Dictionary of the Bible |
| E.B. | . | Encyclopædia Biblica |
| J.Q.R. | . | Jewish Quarterly Review |
| J.E. | . | Jewish Encyclopædia |
| I.J.A. | . | International Journal of Apocrypha |

# CONTENTS

## CHAPTER III

# INTRODUCTION

SOME months ago I was asked by the Board of Studies in Theology of the University of London to examine a Thesis written by Mr. Wicks for the London D.D.

With this Thesis I was so favourably impressed that in my report to the Board of Studies I advised that Mr. Wicks should be encouraged to publish his Thesis, since it formed a good contribution on the subject he had chosen, and one which I should like to possess in a permanent form.

Dr. Wicks has now acted on the advice tendered, and it is the hope of the present writer that his work will meet with all due appreciation.

R. H. CHARLES, D.D., D.LITT.

4 LITTLE CLOISTERS,
WESTMINSTER ABBEY, S.W.

# THE DOCTRINE OF GOD

## INTRODUCTION TO THE LITERATURE

### THE SECOND CENTURY B.C.

#### ECCLESIASTICUS

UNFORTUNATELY, the data at our command do not enable us to be certain of the period at which this book was written and translated. Since it is doubtful whether Ben Sira praises the first or the second Simon, the original work may have been composed soon after the period 310–290 B.C., or not until after 219–199 B.C. Equal uncertainty hangs over the translator's statement in the Prologue as to the year when he arrived in Egypt. If we could be sure that it was in the reign of Euergetes the Second, it would be clear that the Greek version was made after 132 B.C. But Mr. H. J. A. Hart argues that the translation may have been made in the thirty-eighth year of Ptolemy Philadelphus, the year in which he died, which would be the first year of the reign of Euergetes the First, i.e. 247 B.C.* Since, however, we cannot be certain that the work is earlier than the second century B.C., and since it is clear that it cannot be later than that

---

* " Ecclesiasticus in Greek." See especially pp. 251 f., 254, 257.

I

century, we may include it within this period for the
purpose of our inquiry.

## THE ADDITIONS TO ECCLESIASTICUS

The English Revised Version has rejected a considerable number of ancient readings in this book on
the ground that they are not found in Greek Uncials
of the fourth century A.D. These, in the opinion of
H. J. A. Hart, are fragments of Pharisaic wisdom.
" Differences of attestation suggest, they do not prove,
that probably this author is a school and succession
of Scribes rather than a single Rabbi-Missionary of the
Dispersion. . . . But all belong to the period when
the Scribes of the Pharisees emerged from the Sages
of Israel and went out into the world as friendly rivals
of the Stoics. There is no external evidence to
decide these questions of date and authorship. It is
possible that the grandson himself supplemented this
Wisdom." * One important MS., 248, was regarded
by Edersheim as revised by a Christian hand, but a
review of its peculiarities shows nothing of a distinctively Christian character. Note will accordingly be
taken in the following pages of a number of passages
which the English R.V. has rejected and of some not
found in the A.V.

## TOBIT

The most various views have prevailed as to the date
of Tobit. Some have assigned it to the seventh century B.C., but others would place it eight or nine centuries later. If the reference to the Temple in 14⁴ᶠ· be
an allusion, as Hitzig supposed, to its destruction in
A.D. 70, that gives us, of course, a *terminus a quo.*

* " Ecclesiasticus in Greek," p. 318 f.

But it is more probable that 14⁵ refers to Zerubbabel's temple, and that in 14⁴ the author is speaking of the destruction of the house by Nebuchadnezzar. The fact that the two principal persons in the book bear the names of Tobit and Tobias points to a period when the odium attaching to Tobias the Ammonite had been obliterated, and, as J. M. Fuller suggests, makes it probable that the book was written after the career of the Tobias who redeemed the reputation of the name (223–187 B.C.).* Parallels with Ecclesiasticus suggest " a community of origin and date with that work." † The absence of any allusion to the cruelties of Epiphanes makes it unlikely that it was composed after those troublous times had begun, and the Angelology seems to indicate a date earlier than that of any part of the book of Enoch.

## THE ETHIOPIC ENOCH

It is generally recognised that this is a composite work, and it will be convenient here to discuss its teaching according to the arrangement adopted by R. H. Charles in his edition. Since chapters 1–36 contain no allusion to the troubles under Antiochus Epiphanes, they are held to be earlier than 170 B.C. In 83–90, " the great horn," who is described as still fighting, is considered by Charles to represent Judas Maccabæus. Accordingly, he dates this section 166–1 B.C. De Faye would put it later, as he considers that the great horn is one of the Hasmonæan princes, perhaps John Hyrcanus.‡ Chapters 91–104 possibly contain an allusion in 103¹⁵ to the cruelties of Jannæus,

* Cf. J. M. Fuller, Speaker's Comm., " Tobit."
† Ibid.
‡ " Les Apocalypses Juives," p. 30.

and may therefore have been written between 134 and 95 B.C. If, however, 102² refers to the murder of Antigonus by Aristobulus, the date will be 104–95 B.C., and Charles concedes the possibility of a still later date. In chapters 37–70 the oppressive rulers, in his judgment, are Maccabæan princes. He therefore dates this section 95–64 B.C. F. C. Porter argues that these rulers are Augustus with Herod and other vassal kings of Rome.\* As we shall show later, there is reason for giving a wider interpretation to the phrase " the kings and the mighty " than that which Charles adopts. Possibly these " Similitudes " were not written till late in the first century B.C., and it may be that the work was not composed until early in the first Christian century. It seems impossible to date chapters 72–82. The two chapters 80 f. are, in the opinion of Charles, the work of the editors, who gave the whole book the present shape before the dawn of the Christian era. The book has many interpolations. The following is Charles's list : 6³⁻⁸, 8¹⁻³, 9⁷, 10¹⁻³, ¹¹, 17–19, 39¹, ²ᵃ, 41³⁻⁸, 43 f., 54⁷⁻55², 56⁵⁻57³ᵃ, 59 f., 65–69²⁵, with 50, 71, 80 f., 90¹⁵, 91¹¹ 93¹¹⁻¹⁴, 96², 105–8.†

### JUBILEES

This book gives the High-priest the title " Priest of the Most High God," and, since this title was only borne by the Maccabees, the date of the work cannot be earlier than 135 B.C. Charles holds that the book is the work of one author, though based largely on earlier literature and traditions. The editors of the

\* " Messages of the Apocalyptic Writers," p. 318 f.
† See note on Dr. Charles's second edition of the book, p. 347.

Temple Bible Dictionary consider that the special animus of the writer against Edom seems to point to a date coincident with the beginning of the Herodian rule.* But the writer's approval of the pontificate of the Maccabees appears to indicate that he must have written before the great quarrel of the Pharisees with Hyrcanus, i.e. some years before the death of that prince (105 B.C.).

### THE TESTAMENTS OF THE TWELVE PATRIARCHS

In T. Levi 8$^{14 f.}$, there is a prophecy of the uprising of one who shall be Priest, King, and Prophet. Josephus, in the "Antiquities" and in "The Wars of the Jews," dwells on the uniqueness of Hyrcanus in this respect. Charles concludes that he is the man alluded to, and accordingly dates the book 137–105 B.C. Since, in T. Levi 7$^2$, Shechem is called a "city of imbeciles," and since, moreover, Hyrcanus captured that city within ten years of his accession, while about four years before his death he became master of Samaria, a date between 109–106 B.C. is probable. There are numerous interpolations of a clearly Christian character, and these are disregarded in our treatment of the work. There are also passages in which an attack is made on the Maccabæan dynasty. These cannot have been written by the original writer, who warmly supports the reigning house. They belong probably to a writer of the first century B.C. In the following pages, therefore, we distinguish the teaching of this interpolator from that of the original work.

### THE SIBYLLINE ORACLES

Book 3$^{97-829}$, the Proemium fragments, and Book 4 are generally regarded as of Jewish authorship.

* Page xxxiv.

Charles, while maintaining that the lines 3$^{97-829}$ are an aggregation of Oracles, agrees with Schurer that these lines are in the main from one author,, and date from the latter part of the reign of Ptolemy Physcon, which is referred to in each of the three sections, namely, 97–294, 295–488, 489–828. Since in ll. 520–72 there is a prophecy of the subjection of all Hellas, Charles and others conclude that the book cannot have been written before the fall of Corinth (146 B.C.).* A. C. Zenos dates it about 140 B.C., and regards it as the work of an Alexandrian Jew.† Bleek, who also assigns the work to a Jew of Alexandria, considers lines 350–80 as Christian in origin, but an examination of these lines discloses no distinctively Christian elements.‡ Alexandre, who regards the first and third sections as of the second century B.C., thinks that section 2 proceeds from the age of the Antonines.§ Alexandre thinks the fragments of the Proemium are of Christian authorship, but Charles is of opinion that they " probably formed the introduction " to 3$^{97ᵃ}$ and that " they contain nothing of an essentially Christian cast." ‖ Of Book 4 he says that the date and place are determined by three allusions. The lines 115–27 refer to the fall of Jerusalem in 70 A.D. The eruption of Vesuvius in 79 A.D. is referred to in ll. 130–6. The naive eschatology in ll. 179–282 shows that the author cannot have been an Alexandrian Jew, and the book was probably written in Palestine. Charles disagrees with Ewald

* E.B., art. " Apocalpytic Literature," 245–50.
† Dictionary of Christ and the Gospels, art. " Apocalyptic Literature," p. 84.
‡ E.B., art. " Apocalyptic Literature," 245–50.
§ Ibid.
‖ Ibid.

and Hilgenfeld, who thought that Book 4 was Essenic in origin. He considers that the reference to ablutions in ll. 163-5 should be understood of the baptism of proselytes, and that nothing else in the book points to Essenic ideas.* A. C. Zenos, who dates the work *circ.* 80 A.D., thinks that the author may have been a Christian or a Jew, and that the probability is largely in favour of the former alternative.† But examination of the work reveals no distinctively Christian ideas.

## The First Century B.C.

### I MACCABEES

The early origin of this book seems to be probable, since its author warmly approved of the transfer of the high-priesthood to the Maccabæan house (13⁴⁸). Since he makes no allusion to the death of Hyrcanus, and only briefly refers to his career, it is possible that his work was finished before 106 B.C. His jubilant style shows that it cannot have been much later. The passage 16²³ ᶠ· has been regarded as showing that the work was completed after the death of Hyrcanus; but, as C. C. Torrey suggests, that may be due simply to the writer's desire to conclude his work with some complimentary reference to his king.‡ We cannot, however, be sure that the book does not belong to the first century B.C., and the author's praise of the Romans shows that it cannot have been written after 63 B.C.

* E.B., art. " Apocalyptic Literature," 248.
† Dictionary of Christ and the Gospels, art. " Apocalyptic Literature," p. 84.
‡ E.B., art. " Maccabees," 2860.

## THE PSALMS OF SOLOMON

In their edition of this Psalter, Ryle and James show that the capture of Jerusalem by Pompey is, in all probability, alluded to in this work. The invader comes from " the uttermost parts of the earth," and is a " mighty striker " (8¹⁶). Though resisted in some quarters, and obliged to use a battering-ram (2¹), he is welcomed by the princes (8¹⁸⁻²⁰). His death is described in 2³⁰⁻³⁵. The description seems to suit neither Epiphanes, nor Herod the Great, nor Titus. Pompey seems to be the man here described. If so, the collection is probably to be dated after 63 B.C., and not very long after, since the great event of that year is still vividly present to the mind of the author or authors. Ryle and James " have no hesitation in assuming that the whole collection springs from the literary activity, if not of a single writer, at any rate of a single generation." * Psalm 2, if Pompey is referred to, must have been written after 48 B.C., and the editors ascribe the whole book to the period 70–40 B.C.

## JUDITH

C. J. Ball, in the Speaker's Commentary, observes after Fritzsche that " the advance in ceremonial strictness, the cry for vengeance, the long oppression which constitutes the background of the piece," with " the references to the Sanhedrin, undoubtedly point us to the latest pre-Christian centuries for the date of the story." †

The Hasmonæan period is indicated by the fact that the whole land is under the High-priest and the

---

* Ryle and James, " The Psalms of Solomon," p. xliii.
† Pp. 244 f.

Sanhedrin (4⁴˙⁶, 15⁵˙ ⁸). Jewish tradition, moreover, called " Judith the daughter of John the brother or of Mattathias the father of Judas Maccabæus" (Ball). Dr. Gaster dates the book *circ.* 50 B.C.* But, since the picture of the High-priest's supreme authority and the independence of the Hellenic towns agrees better with the period preceding the Roman domination, some argue for a date prior to 63 B.C. rather than later. F. C. Porter, however, observes that a writer may attempt to describe past conditions, and that this author professes to tell of a time long past (14¹⁰, 16²⁵). He thinks it quite probable that he wrote in the late Maccabæan period or in the time of Roman rule.†

### 3 (OR I) ESDRAS

There is a resemblance between the story of the three youths in this book and the tale of Jewish elders at the court of Ptolemy Philadelphus in the so-called " History of Aristeas." Lupton thinks that our book is " a composition of the same class and probably of the same time," and " Aristeas," he says, is " not considered to be earlier than the first century B.C." The allusion in 4²³ may point to an Egyptian origin for the book, but this may be due to the originator of the tale, not to the author of the book. Lupton thinks the book may have been written to encourage the builders of the temple at Leontopolis, and he argues that this is the more probable from the fact that the description of the rejoicings is more suggestive of Egyptian festivals than of the return from Babylon.‡ Most scholars, however, regard the book as having been composed in the first century B.C., and P. Volz thinks

* E.B., art. " Judith," 2645.
† D.B., art. " Judith," p. 823.
‡ Speaker's Comm., Introduction to 3 Esdras.

that Lupton's view is insufficiently supported.* Volz expresses the opinion that the praise of truth in this book discloses contact with the religious philosophy of Alexandria.†

## 2 MACCABEES

The victory of Judas over Nicanor with which this book closes was won in 161 B.C. The marvellous narratives contained in it point to the probability of its having been written at a period somewhat distant from the actual events. From the statement in 15³⁷ one would infer that the book must have been written before 63 B.C., though C. C. Torrey dismisses this as a mere flourish.‡ Torrey dates the work in the latter half of the first century B.C. There are no data to determine the age of the work of Jason on which this writer professes to base himself. The letters addressed to Jews in Egypt and the fact that the earliest allusions to the book come directly from Alexandria indicate that probably the author was a Jew of Egypt.

## THE ADDITIONS TO DANIEL

There are no data on which a decisive judgment may be formed as to the date of these additions. C. J. Ball's theory is that the " History of Susanna " was written in the time of Ben Shetach, President of the Sanhedrin, *circ.* 100 B.C.§ A. Kamphausen says : " We may safely assume that the additions to the Greek Daniel had been made before the beginning of the Christian Era. The balance of probability is that

* E.B., art. " 3 Esdras," 1493.
† Ibid.
‡ E.B., art. " 2 Maccabees," 2874.
§ Speaker's Comm., p. 330.

they were not translated from any Semitic source, but were originally written in Greek." *

## THE EPISTLE OF JEREMY

Attempts have been made to find a date for this epistle by the aid of a supposed allusion to it in 2 Maccabees, $2^{1\,t.}$; but, as verse 4 in that chapter shows, there is no such allusion. Ewald finds in verses 18, 34, 53, 56, 59, 66, indications of the times of the later Seleucidæ and Ptolemies, and so concludes that it was written about the beginning of the first century B.C.† André thinks that the author is " vraisemblablement un Juif d'Égypte." ‡

## THE FIRST CENTURY A.D.

### WISDOM

No conclusion as to the date of this book can be drawn from the picture of the author's suffering compatriots, or the hostility to the Egyptians manifested in the later chapters, or the references to the apotheosis of kings. These might indicate any one of several periods. Nor can we date the work from its doctrine of ethical immortality, for we do not know at what period the Egyptian Jews began to formulate that doctrine. It is a moot point whether the authors or author ever read Ecclesiasticus, but apparently the Greek version of Isaiah and Job has left its impress on our book. This use of the Septuagint makes it improbable that its date is earlier than the beginning of the second century B.C., but a *terminus ad*

---

* E.B., art. " Daniel," 1013.

† Cf. Speaker's Comm. in loc. on which this account of the Epistle is based.

‡ " Les Apocryphes de L'Ancien Testament," p. 268.

*quem* is a matter about which it seems impossible to speak with any confidence. Kohler argues that, since St. Paul and the writer of the Epistle to the Hebrews draw on Wisdom, the first part at least must have been written in the first century B.C.* Toy, from internal evidence, thinks it might have been written in 145–117 or 47–30 B.C., but adds that the writer would know his people's story and might write in a quiet time.† Farrar, on the other hand, is of opinion that Philo's influence is to be seen in our book, and, in that case, it cannot have been composed earlier than A.D. 40. " It is," he says, " certainly possible, and in my opinion probable, that it was written in the decade after the death of Christ." ‡ Charles also places it in the first century A.D.§ We treat it in this work under that period because it is impossible to be certain that it was written earlier.

Scholars are as much divided on the question of the unity of the book as on that of its date. Wisdom is very differently regarded in the earlier and later chapters. God's grace to Gentiles is strikingly brought out only in the latter part, and sections here are so mutually inconsistent on this matter as to create doubt whether they proceed from one author. Immortality is taught only in the earlier part, although it might well have been in evidence in the later portion, where the writer designs to comfort the troubled. Hughes emphasises the fact that in the first part punishment is merely retributive, whereas in the second it is remedial; but the point is of less importance than he thinks, because Part 1 deals mainly,

---

* J.E., art. " Wisdom of Solomon," p. 540.
† E.B., art. " Wisdom (Book)," 5347.
‡ Speaker's Comm., p. 421 f.
§ E.B., art. " Eschatology," 1366.

if not exclusively, with penalties beyond the grave, while Part 2 tells of punishment in this life.* The facts mentioned above militate, however, against the idea that the book is a unity. Kohler is led to the conclusion that " it consists of three independent parts which have no real connection, and which treat of subjects altogether different." " It is evident," he says, " that these three parts, or at least the first two (1–9, 10–19), cannot have emanated from the same author." † This view is now supported by C. H. Toy, but Gregg and Farrar reject it. It will be convenient in our discussion of the book to consider the teaching of the two main sections independently. There is general agreement that the work proceeds from an Egyptian Jew or Jews.

### THE BOOK OF BARUCH

This book, as A. A. Bevan says, is " very far from presenting the appearance of an organic unity." ‡ $1^{15}$–$3^8$ is evidently a distinct work from the later portion of the book, and possibly $1^{1-14}$ does not belong to the writer of this section. Schurer, however, regards $1^1$–$3^8$ as from the same hand, and Ewald agrees.§ Marshall considers that $3^9$–$4^4$ and $4^5$–$5^9$ are the work of two writers.‖ Part 1 is possibly dependent on the book of Daniel, and, if so, its *terminus a quo* will probably be *circ.* 167 B.C. But our book may be the source and not the copy. Textual resemblances to Theodotion's version suggest that the work in its Greek form cannot have appeared till the latter half

* " Ethics of Jewish Apocryphal Literature," p. 8.
† J.E., art. " Wisdom of Solomon," pp. 538, 540.
‡ E.B., " Baruch," 492–4.
§ Ibid.
‖ D.B., " Baruch."

of the second century A.D. But these may be due to a correcting copyist. Ewald assigned it to a Jew of Babylon or Persia, under a late Achæmenian king.* André and others suggest a date after A.D. 70. Parts 2 and 3 are, in the opinion of Ewald, to be dated soon after 320 B.C. But, as A. A. Bevan says, few would now put it so early. On the ground that $4^3$, in his opinion, refers to Gentile Christians, Marshall thinks $3^9$–$4^4$ was written about the year A.D. 70; $4^5$–$5^9$ he places after A.D. 70, and from the hopeful tone he thinks it was not written soon after that date.† There is close verbal resemblance between $4^{36}$–$5^9$ and Psalms of Solomon 11, and it may be that this writer used that Psalter. Possibly, however, both borrowed independently from the Septuagint.‡ It is then impossible to say definitely to what period the various strata in this composite book should be assigned, and we cannot be sure that any of it was written before the Christian era. We treat it, therefore, under the heading of the first Christian century, as Dr. Charles has done in his article on Eschatology in the Encyclopædia Biblica.

### THE ASSUMPTION OF MOSES

In this work Herod is apparently spoken of as already dead. If this is a correct interpretation of the writer's meaning, it could not have been written until after 3 B.C. Further, if this is so, there is an erroneous prophecy as to the duration of the reign of the sons

* D.B., art. " Baruch."
† Ibid.
‡ This is the view of Kneucker—cf. Ryle and James, " The Psalms of Solomon," p. lxxii; but these editors consider it untenable.

of Herod. Consequently, the book must have been composed before these rulers had reigned thirty-four years, i.e. before A.D. 30. Perhaps the death of Archelaus in A.D. 6 gave rise to the prophecy of the brief reign of Philip and Antipas. If so, the book must be dated between A.D. 7 and A.D. 30.* Some scholars, however, regard it as a production of the second century A.D.

## THE APOCALYPSE OF BARUCH

There are clear indications of the fact that this apocalypse is the work of several writers. The legend of the destruction of Jerusalem by angels recorded in 6–8 and 80 was obviously unknown to the author of chapter 67, or disallowed by him. The most striking fact, however, is that in some sections the greatest optimism prevails as to the earthly future, whereas in others there is the most intense pessimism on the subject. Kabisch, Charles, and De Faye independently arrive at the conclusion that the work is of a composite character, though they differ in their views as to the details.

(1) An outstanding fact is that in some sections the Messiah is expected, i.e. 27–30, 36–40, and 53–74, while in the rest this hope is conspicuously absent. Charles and De Faye agree that the two last-named are pieces of separate authorship from the rest of the book. Charles thinks it possible that they proceed from one author, but inclines on the whole to regard them as the work of two. De Faye expresses the opinion that 6–32* may be one original whole, but admits that it may be composite, and the dis-

* See Charles's " Assumption of Moses," Introduction. The statement in the text is a summary of his views.

tinctive characteristics of 27–30 constitute strong reasons for regarding these chapters as a fragment of an originally separate work. It will be convenient in our discussion to treat these three writings as independent, and to use the headings suggested by Dr. Charles—A$^1$, A$^2$, A$^3$.

(2) With regard to the remainder of the book, it is plain that we have still the work of several writers. De Faye argues that 1–5 is probably a distinct piece, and that 6–32$^6$ may be a unity, though it is possibly the work of two or more writers. Charles, however, shows that, in some sections in this part of the book, the hope of a national restoration is inculcated, while in others it is abandoned. He distinguishes these differing sections as B$^1$ and B$^2$ and rejects De Faye's idea as to chapters 1–5. De Faye's main reasons for his view of these chapters are (1) that in them Jeremiah is ordered to withdraw from the city, while 9$^1$ implies that he is still in it when the city is captured, and (2) that in 6$^9$ the restoration of Jerusalem is foretold, while in 4$^{2-7}$ that notion is derided. It is not, however, at all clear that De Faye is correct in his idea of what is implied in 9$^1$, and Charles solves the difficulty of 4$^{2-7}$ by the theory of an interpolation. The despairing passage in 10$^6$–12$^4$ is possibly another interpolation. If, then, we eliminate from this whole section the three passages 4$^{2-7}$, 10$^6$–12$^4$, and 27–30, there remain two strata, the one optimistic and the other pessimistic. There seems to be no reason why we should attribute 32$^7$–35 to any other authors than these two.

(3) With regard to 41–52, De Faye would assign 43$^3$–47 for the most part to the final editor of the book, and he considers that 41–43$^2$, 48–52, with 76$^{1-4}$, are the work of a new author. He gives to this the

title "L'Assomption de Baruch." His main ground for distinguishing between this "Assumption," the work of the editor, and the chapters 1–32⁶ is that in the first Baruch is to go to heaven without dying (43², 48³⁰, 76²), while in the second he is to die (44⁸, 78⁵, 84¹, 77¹²), and in the third he is to continue living on the earth until the consummation of all things (13³, 25¹). But 13³, 25¹, do not imply this, and are therefore quite in harmony with the "Assumption." De Faye also maintains that 1–32⁷ and 48–52 are not mutually compatible, for in the first Baruch is absorbed in the fate of the city, while in the second he is calmly discussing speculations as to bodily resurrection. To this there is the obvious reply that the same writer may be occupied with different subjects at different times, and the pessimism in this fragment inclines one, with Charles, to regard it as probably part of the work of B². There is nothing in 41–43², 43³–47, to lead us to differ from the view of Charles that they belong to B¹ or B², as they are respectively optimistic and pessimistic in character.

(4) Chapters 75–87 are, in the opinion of De Faye, the work of the editor in the main, but they contain nothing which is inconsistent with the theory of Charles that they are for the most part the work of B¹. Chapter 80 certainly appears to bear his impress, for it refers to his story of the angelic destruction of Jerusalem. Charles, however, assigns 75 f. and 83 to B²; 76 contains B²'s view of the fate of Baruch; 83 has his pessimism; 75 may belong to B¹, for its doctrine of God's grace agrees better with his views than with those of B². Chapter 85 is probably the work of another author, for in B² Jeremiah is with the exiles in Babylon, while here the exiles are said to be bereft of the prophets by death. On the whole,

2

while it is impossible to be sure of the entire correct-
ness of any critical reconstruction, it seems that that
which Charles suggests is strongly supported. We
shall, accordingly, treat of the theology of the non-A
sections under the titles which he suggests—B[1], B[2],
B[3]. De Faye thinks that there are Christian interpolations in the work, e.g. in 41 f., 44[9-18]. " L'on n'est
plus dans le monde, des idées purement juives." *
Kabisch regards 28[5], 30[1], 32[2-4], 35, 76[1], as of Christian
origin. Examination, however, reveals nothing in
these passages that could not have come from the
pen of a non-Christian Jew. Drummond says: " I
have not observed a single expression which betrays
a Christian hand." †

(5) The A sections must have been written prior
to A.D. 70, because of the view in each of them as to
the theatre of the Messianic kingdom and the peculiar
privileges of the inhabitants of the holy land at its
establishment. The allusions in 39 show that A[2]
was written at the time of the Roman government of
Palestine. If the " last leader " in 40[1] be Pompey—
and the reference to his impieties favours that view—
the date of A[2] is determined within narrow limits.
As Charles suggests, the glorification of Moses at the
expense of Enoch in A[3] appears to be a sign of hostility
to nascent Christianity, and, if so, A[3] must be dated
after A.D. 50. As for A[1], we can only say that it was
composed before A.D. 70. S was probably written on
the morrow of the great disaster of A.D. 70. B[2], by
the transfer of Enoch's functions to Baruch, appears
to be within the Christian era, and by its pessimism
after A.D. 70. B[3] is probably of a later date. It is
more difficult to form an opinion in the case of B[1].

* Op. cit. p. 198.
† " The Jewish Messiah," p. 125.

Charles regards it as after A.D. 70 by its references
to the destruction of Jerusalem, and from its optimism
he infers that it must have been soon after that date.
Since, however, the destruction referred to is that
which occurred in Baruch's time, it is a moot point
whether the date of B$^1$ is not earlier. The authors
of the Temple Bible Dictionary think that the
book originated in the last pre-Christian century, or
that at least its nucleus was written then.* Our
review shows that there is some justification for the
latter view. A$^1$, A$^2$, and B$^1$ may belong to that time.
But it is quite possible that the whole was written
in the first century A.D., and 32$^{2-4}$, which may be the
work of the final editor, shows conclusively that the
whole work was not put into its present form until
after A.D. 70.†

The following are the divisions of the book in the
arrangement of Charles: A$^1$, 27–30$^1$; A$^2$, 36–40 ;
A$^3$, 53–74 ; B$^1$, 1–4$^1$, 5–9$^1$, 43–44$^7$, 45–46$^6$ ; 77–82, 84,
86, 87 ; B$^2$, 4$^{2-7}$ (?), 13–25, 30$^2$–35, 41 f., 44$^{8-15}$, 47–
52, 75, 76, 83 ; B$^3$, 85 ; E and B$^2$, 9$^2$–10$^5$ ; B$^2$ or S
10$^6$–12$^4$.

## 4 (or 2) ESDRAS

There are strong reasons for regarding this book as
a composition derived from a variety of sources.
Kabisch propounds the theory that it consists of a
Salathiel Apocalypse (S), an Esdras Apocalypse (E),
an Eagle vision (A), a Vision of the Son of Man (M),
and a second Esdras Apocalypse (E$^2$). These have
been joined into one by an editor who has made some
additions of his own. G. H. Box, the latest commen-

---

* Page xxxiii.

† For De Faye see op. cit., chiefly Appendix 3. For Charles
see his edition of the Apocalypse.

tator on the work, agrees in the main with the views of Kabisch, but would assign more than he does to the pen of the editor. Gunkel, however, does not endorse these views, but Kabisch has the support of R. H. Charles. The following are the divisions of the book according to Kabisch:

S $3^{1-31}$, $4^{1-51}$, $5^{13\,f.}$–$6^{10}$, $6^{30}$–$7^{25}$, $7^{45}$–$8^{62}$, $9^{13}$–$10^{57}$, $12^{40-48}$, $14^{28-35}$.

E $4^{52}$–$5^{13a}$, $6^{13-25,\,28}$, $7^{26-45}$, $8^{63}$–$9^{12}$.

A $10^{60}$–$12^{40}$. M 13, with interpolations by the editor.

E². $14^{1-17a\;\;18-27\;\;36-47}$. R, the editor $1^{32-36}$, $6^{11\,f.}$, $^{26\,f,\,29}$, $10^{58\,f}$, $12^{9,\,34,\,37-9,\,49-51}$, $13^{13b-15}$, $^{16-24,\,25b,\,29-32,\,54-8}$, $14^{8,\,17b,\,48-50}$, etc.

In S the idea of a Messiah or a Messianic kingdom on earth is categorically dismissed. God Himself will visit His creature, and no other ($5^{56}$–$6^{6}$). The writer of S sets himself to replace the popular and political aspirations of his people by the conception of the great consummation in the unseen world, which is, according to him, imminent. But the notion of a Messianic kingdom on earth appears in the E sections, and these accordingly cannot have proceeded from the pen of the man who wrote S. Moreover, the question in $4^{52}$ is introduced in such a way as to make it clear that $4^{52}$–$5^{13}$ is a fragment of another work. In $6^{11\,ff.}$ the question is taken up where it is left in $4^{52}$–$5^{13}$, and this section has no connection with that which now immediately precedes it. $7^{26-44}$ and $8^{63}$–$9^{12}$ manifestly do not belong to S, by reason of their teaching as to the coming kingdom of God on earth; but there seems no good reason for differing from the view of Kabisch, who assigns them to the author of E. A is marked out as a distinct piece of work by its characteristic conceptions. " The outstanding fact that engages and obsesses the apocalyp-

tist's thought is the overwhelming might and extent
of the Roman Empire." * M is a piece of writing
distinct from A, for there is no one world-power in the
writer's view, and he, unlike A, conceives of Messiah
as the pre-existent and supernatural Son of Man.
E² is like S in that the writing is pessimistic with
regard to the world, but unlike S because in it the
Messiah appears. It may, however, be a part of E,
especially as 14⁹ (cf. 7²⁸) not improbably implies the
idea of a Messianic kingdom. Kabisch thinks that
S was written about A.D. 100, and Charles would date
it A.D. 70–100. The abandonment of the idea of a
Messianic kingdom probably points to the fact that
it was not written on the morrow of the catastrophe
of A.D. 70. In E the conception of the salvation of
those living in Palestine in the last time suggests a
date prior to A.D. 70, and the allusion to the land
that now has rule and "that which is after the third
(kingdom)" probably indicates the composition of
the work in Roman times.

Beyond this it is impossible to go with any confidence. Perhaps E belongs to the first century B.C.
A is of the period of Domitian or Vespasian. M, where
the world is pictured as in an anarchic condition, possibly dates from a period before the battle of Actium
(B.C. 31). Kabisch regards it as of about that date,
but Charles will only say that it was written before
A.D. 70. Kabisch supposed that S was written in
Rome, but, as Box points out, it was natural to represent Salathiel as living in Babylon, since the historical
framework of the apocalypse is the Babylonian exile.
Box thinks that E² clearly implies a date subsequent
to A.D. 70. The emphasis laid upon the restoration of
the law that has been burnt (14²¹) points, he thinks,

* Box, " The Ezra Apocalypse," p. 246.

unmistakably to this.* Chapters 1, 2, 15, and 16 are here left out of account, as it is matter of general agreement that they are manifestly of Christian authorship.

### 3 MACCABEES

It is generally agreed that we cannot be sure of the exact period in which this book was written, and " to look for an ' historical occasion ' for the writing of an edifying story such as this is quite useless." † Since, however, the author makes use of Daniel with apocryphal additions, it is improbable that he lived earlier than the first century B.C. Language, style, and knowledge of Egyptian affairs probably indicate that he was a Jew of Alexandria, and he may have lived there as late as the first century A.D.

### 4 MACCABEES

This author's acquaintance with Greek rhetorical schools and his apparent interest in the study of philosophy are indications, as Dr. C. C. Torrey says, of the fact that he lived in some Hellenised city.‡ Nothing definite, however, can be said as to the date. In the opinion of Mr. Israel Abrahams, the work probably belongs to the period shortly before the fall of Jerusalem.§

### SLAVONIC ENOCH

It seems a fair inference from the allusion in this work to sacrifices as still being offered ($59^2$) that it

---

* Op. cit., p. xxxii. For views of Charles, see E.B., " Eschatology," 1369 f.
† E.B., art. " Maccabees (Books)," 2881.
‡ Ibid. 2883.
§ J.E., art., " Books of Maccabees," p. 244.

was written before the destruction of the Temple. It appears to be probable that the author had read Ecclesiasticus, and his teaching about the eighth day seems to be expounded in the " Epistle of Barnabas." Charles considers that he used Ethiopic Enoch in its latest form and would accordingly date it in the first half of the earliest Christian century. He admits, however, that it may have been written at any time after 30 B.C. It is argued that the agreement of the writer in speculation with Philo and writings of a Hellenistic character points to an Egyptian origin of the work. Tennant finds in it " Egyptian local colouring." He is of opinion that the work is possibly influenced by the Christian Scriptures, and therefore considers that it may perhaps be of a later date than that which Charles assigns to it. He also suggests that the longer version of the book—A— has perhaps suffered interpolation from some Christian hand or that of a Jew influenced by Christianity.*
On this point, however, Torrey entirely disagrees with him.†

### THE APOCALYPSE OF ABRAHAM

Louis Ginzberg says of this work : " It clearly cannot have been written before the destruction of the Temple, as it contains Abraham's lamentations over that catastrophe. The emphasis laid on the freedom of the will, notwithstanding the fall of man, presupposes a knowledge of the Christian doctrine of sin, against which this passage seems to be directed. But this very opposition to Christian dogma shows that at the time the apocalypse was written Chris-

* " The Fall and Original Sin," p. 295.
† J.E., art. " Apocalyptic Literature," p. 674.

tianity was not far removed from Judaism, at least, not in Palestine, where, since he used a Semitic language, the author must have lived. The last decades of the first (Christian) century appear to be the period in which the apocalypse was written." * It is clear, however, that the original work has suffered from Christian interpolation. The insulted and beaten man in chapter 29, who is the hope of the Gentiles, is manifestly the Lord Jesus Christ, and it is therefore evident that some Christian was the author of this passage. Ginzberg thinks that there are Gnostic interpolations in the work. The statement that Azazel shares with God the power over Israel is, in his judgment, " the Gnostic doctrine of the God of the Jews as Kakodaimon."†

### THE ASCENSION OF ISAIAH

In its present form, this work may not be earlier than A.D. 150–200. Its constituents were, however, in existence in the first century A.D. Only the section " The Martyrdom of Isaiah " is of Jewish origin, i.e. $1^{1, 2a, 6b, 13a}$, $2^{1-8}$, $2^{10}-3^{12}$, $5^{1b-14}$. In the opinion of Charles and other scholars, it is clear that this section circulated originally as an independent work.‡

### THE REST OF ESTHER

It is impossible to say which of the four Ptolemies is referred to in $11^1$, since "each had a wife or a mother named Cleopatra." Dositheus, who is also mentioned in that verse, was the bearer of a common name. Some argue that Ptolemy Philometor is meant. If so,

* J.E., art. " Apocalypse ot Abraham," p. 92.
† Ibid.
‡ See Charles, " The Ascension of Isaiah " (Introduction).

and if further, as some urge, the Epistle of Phurai is the whole Greek text of the book of Esther, the date of the work will be *circ.* 177 B.C.  Fuller thinks that the character and style of the Additions support this view, and he argues that "certain sentiments and expressions tend to point to a Jew of Persia as the author of some of the Additions." *  Since, how-ever, the suzerainty of the four Ptolemies ranged over the period 205 B.C. to A.D. 81, it is possible that these Additions belong to the last period of this litera-ture.  H. M. Hughes thinks that the similarity in some points of doctrine between the Additions and certain Alexandrian books, e.g. Part 2 of Wisdom, 2, 3, 4 Maccabees, "suggests the possibility that they were written about the beginning of the Christian era " and in Alexandria.†

## THE PRAYER OF MANASSES

The Chronicler (2 Chron. 33¹⁹) says that the prayer of Manasseh is "written in the history of Hozai " (LXX.—" of the seers ").  Evidently he meant that he had such a prayer before him, but it is argued by Fritzsche that our work is a later production based on this passage.  Ball, however, thinks that our author is possibly a Hellenistic Jew who has given us a free rendering of a lost Haggadic work.‡  Bissel and Fritzsche regard this prayer as of the period of the Maccabæan revolt.  Berthold assigned it to the second or third century A.D.  Ball thinks it may be of the time of the Maccabees.§  The exaggerated idea

* Speaker's Comm., p. 366.  Facts mentioned here are based on the Introduction in this Commentary.
† Op. cit., pp. 5, 9 f.
‡ Speaker's Comm., " Manasses."
§ Ibid.

of the merits of the three patriarchs has been held to be a sign of late origin, but Ball replies that these ideas have their roots in the Old Testament. F. C. Porter, against Swete, maintains that the prayer is doubtless Jewish and thinks that its eschatology points to an earlier rather than a later date.* We put it in this place in our study, because it is impossible from the data to assign it to an earlier century with any confidence.

* D.B., art. " Manasses," p. 233.

# CHAPTER I

## THE TRANSCENDENCE OF GOD

" THE word Transcendence," says Dr. W. Newton Clarke, " institutes the great comparison between God and the universe, and asserts the superiority of God. But this superiority or transcendence of God has sometimes been interpreted in ways that are impossible in the light of our present knowledge. Under a variety of influences, it has come to pass that the transcendent God was represented as a God outside the world and above it, separated from an order so inferior as to be unworthy of His immediate presence." * Elsewhere he speaks of " the false idea of transcendence according to which God's transcendence removed Him from contact with the world " and adds the affirmation that " between the actual transcendence of God over the universe, and His real indwelling, there is no shadow of incompatibility." †

Now, modern Jewish theologians take the gravest objection to the idea that this false notion of transcendence was ever held by their people. Thus Dr. J. Abelson, defining transcendence as the idea of God as One " sitting far from the world . . . surveying it unconcerned from some incomparable height," says : "There is nothing more harassing in reading the

---

* " The Christian Doctrine of God," p. 313.
† Ibid. p. 321.

opinions of the average Christian theologian than the ever recurring taunt that the Jewish theological teachers of Old Testament as well as New Testament times confined their horizon wholly and solely to the transcendence of God." * Similarly, Dr. Schechter says: "Among the many strange statements by which the Jewish student is surprised when reading modern divinity, there is none more puzzling to his mind than the assertion of the transcendentalism of the Rabbinic God and His remoteness from man." † We are concerned, then, in this chapter with a twofold inquiry : (1) Is the conception of God in this literature that of a Being of transcendent greatness ? and (2) Is He regarded as remote from this world and mankind ? But the two questions really run up into one. For, if God is conceived of as infinitely great, if He is the Omnipresent One in that " He is free from all limitations of space in His activities and can do everywhere all that He can do anywhere," so that " all that He is, is everywhere available for action at all times," then He is not the distant God.‡ He is rather " the Far and the Near." All expressions, on the other hand, which imply that He is remote, necessarily impair the conception of His greatness. We shall have to take account of the use of divine names implying greatness, and of passages in which omnipresence, omnipotence, or omniscience is predicated. Attention must be given to anthropomorphic representations and to the use of anthropopathisms. Inquiry must be made as to the doctrine of angels and spirits, in particular as to the conception of their functions as the ministers of God, or as intermediaries between

* " Hibbert Journal," January 1912, pp. 430, 432.
† J.Q.R., vol. vi., p. 417.
‡ " The Christian Doctrine of God," p. 327.

Him and man. It will be needful also to consider whether He is conceived of by any writers as dependent on these servants when He would act. Does He act, when He will, without their mediation on the world and on man? Is there direct communication between Him and man? Nor will our inquiry be complete without asking whether God is conceived of as really governing this world, and if so, to what extent.

## THE SECOND CENTURY B.C.

### ECCLESIASTICUS *

Ben Sira calls God "the Most High" (e.g. 23²³, 24²³, 29¹¹), "the Mighty One" (46⁶), "the Almighty" (42¹⁷, 50¹⁴, ¹⁷). He is "the King of the kings of the earth" (Hebrew text, 51¹² ᶜ ⁽¹⁴⁾). He "beholdeth from everlasting to everlasting, and there is nothing wonderful before Him" (39²⁰). † In the latter part of this sentence, the Hebrew gives us אין נפלא וחזק ממנו and Israel Lévi renders this: "Rien n'est pour lui impossible ni difficile," remarking that his rendering of נפלא by "impossible" is supported by Gen. 18¹⁴ and Jer. 32¹⁷, ²⁷. ‡

It is impossible to Ben Sira's thinking that men should speak of God adequately. Let them exalt Him as much as they can and put forth their full strength; they will still fall short in their attempt to utter His greatness (43³⁰). His "eyes are ten thousand times brighter than the sun, beholding all

---

* The references to chapters and verses are here given as in the English R.V.

† Ἀπὸ τοῦ αἰῶνος εἰς τὸν αἰῶνα ἐπέβλεψε. Hebrew: מעולם ועד עולם יביט

‡ "L'Ecclésiastique Hebreu," in loc.

the ways of men and looking into secret places. All things were known to Him or ever they were created" (23¹⁹ ᶠ·). He knows all the works, words, and thoughts of man (17¹⁹ ᶠ·, 39¹⁹, 42²⁰).

It is clear that God was to Ben Sira's mind purely spiritual. He does not abstain, indeed, from the use of anthropomorphic expressions. His language, for example, when he describes God's revelation to Moses, is modelled upon that of the O.T. Nicolas says : " L'Ecclésiastique se contente de faire mention de la nuée sans ajouter que Dieu y était caché." * But in 45⁵ we read that God caused Moses " to hear His voice, and led him into the thick darkness, and gave him commandments face to face." This resembles closely the O.T. statement : " Moses drew near to the thick darkness where God was " (Exod. 20²¹). In 17¹⁵ again, he says : " Their eyes saw the greatness of the glory and their ear heard the glory of their [or His] voice." Perhaps, as Edersheim thinks, we should accept the reading αὐτῶν in the latter part of this sentence, and understand that it was the voice of the commandments which they heard.†

But Ben Sira shows in 45⁵ that he did not object to speak of man as hearing the voice of God. Still, he does not say that Israel or Moses *saw* God, and, in his eulogy of the patriarchs (44 f.), he avoids any mention of a divine appearance to them even in dreams. As Edersheim justly remarks, Israel is said in 17¹³ to have seen " the greatness of glory," not God's glory itself, and in 45⁵, where it is said that God showed Moses " part of His glory," the partitive genitive, which is omitted in most versions, is " highly sig-

* " Des Doctrines Réligieuses des Juifs," p. 41.
† Speaker's Comm., in loc.

nificant." * Indeed, Ben Sira apparently protests against the idea that any man has ever seen God (43$^{31}$). On the whole, we may fairly say of Ben Sira what Kautzch says of the O.T. prophets : "The analogy of the human personality had still to be used, as indeed now. But there is not a single trace that they continued to share that naive belief in Jahweh's possession of a human bodily form." † Nicolas sums up the position of Ben Sira in these words : "Au point de vue de l'Ecclésiastique ce ne sont plus seulement les représentations anthropomorphiques qui donnent de fausses idées de la divinité ; les conceptions les plus élevées de l'esprit humain ne peuvent même la faire connaître telle qu'elle est . . . l'Eternel est incompréhensible dans son essence pour les facultés bornées de l'homme." ‡ It is, however, to be observed that, far as Ben Sira is from alluding in the manner of the Enoch books to the form of God, or to divine appearances, he clearly did not conceive that expressions in which God is spoken of as being like man convey false ideas of Him. He uses such expressions freely, though he safeguards himself against misapprehensions by other language in which he dwells on the infinite exaltation of God. Thus, he not only copies the Biblical statement that man was made in the image of God (17$^3$), but also, in the O.T. manner, he speaks frequently of the feelings of God—His wrath (5$^{6\ f.}$, 45$^{19}$), His hatred (10$^7$, 12$^6$, 15$^{13}$, 27$^{24}$, and (Hebrew) 31$^{13}$), His compassion and His love (2$^{11}$, 4$^{10,\ 14}$). According to the Hebrew, Ben Sira speaks also of God's "rage" (16$^{18}$). His God is high above man, but He is by no means absolutely unlike His creature.

* Speaker's Comm., in loc.
† D.B., " The Religion of Israel," p. 679.
‡ Op. cit., p. 160.

Ben Sira was, however, very far from thinking of God as separated by a chasm from His world. In one passage he appears, indeed, to affirm that angels rule the world as God's viceroys. " For every nation He appointed a ruler and Israel is the Lord's portion " (17¹⁷). This seems, at first sight, to be an echo of Deut. 32⁸ (LXX); but Edersheim points out that, according to the later Midrash, God assigned to the nations bounds according to the number of angels, and these angels are regarded as hostile to Israel. Since Ben Sira makes no allusion to such hostility, since, moreover, Michael was held to be Israel's angel-prince, he is inclined to think that the rulers in this passage are probably secular princes.* Omitting, then, this verse, we find scarcely any reference to angels in the work. In 48²¹ the Greek gives us : " He smote the camp of the Assyrians, and His angel destroyed them." But here the Hebrew substitutes for ἄγγελος the word מגפה (plague). Indeed, the Hebrew text does not contain the word "angel," and in the Greek version angels are only mentioned in citations from the O.T. Possibly, in 39²⁸, the πνεύματα are spirits ; but if so, it may be, as Edersheim says, that we must regard this passage " as embodying the same idea as in later Rabbinism which personified as angels certain natural phenomena and eventualities." † " In general," as C. H. Toy says, " Ecclesiasticus may be said to anticipate Sadduceeism in holding aloof from angels and spirits, whose agency in actual life it does not recognise." ‡ But Ben Sira strongly insists on God's personal administration of this world. In His hand is the authority of the earth (10⁴). He casts down the thrones of rulers and plucks up the roots of

* Speaker's Comm. in loc.          † Ibid.
‡ E.B., " Ecclesiasticus," 1175.

nations ($10^{14}$). He determines, also, the fortunes of individuals. It is He who sets up a poor man from his low estate ($11^{12}$). He can easily make a poor man suddenly rich ($11^{21}$). Edersheim, commenting on $11^{12}$, expresses the opinion that Fritszche is in error when he regards the person here spoken of as idle or wanting in energy. "Such a person," he says, "could not be represented as receiving divine help. The argument is not in support of fatalism, but intended to show the superiority of moral worth." * But it is to be noted that the man is described as sluggish ($11^{12}$), and, though the argument doubtless is not fatalistic in tendency, it *is* directed to show that God ordains individual success or failure at His own will. This is shown in ver. 14—"Good things and evil, life and death, poverty and riches, are from the Lord." It is not only true that prosperity comes to a man when you cannot find its explanation in his ability, and can only say that God has willed it, but also, more broadly and universally, it may be said that God absolutely determines the lot of the individual. We have the same teaching elsewhere. Some men God "blessed and exalted, some of them He hallowed and brought near to Himself, some of them He cursed and brought low, and overthrew them from their place. As the clay of the potter in his hand, all his ways are according to his good pleasure, so men are in the hand of Him that made them to render unto them according to His judgment" ($33^{12\,f.}$). And again : "Laugh not a man to scorn in the bitterness of his soul, for there is One who humbleth and exalteth" ($7^{11}$). Ben Sira teaches that God dwells in Zion as well as in heaven ($36^{13}$). In the tabernacle, "Wisdom ministered before Him" ($24^{10}$). He is

* Op. cit. in loc.

accessible to man. " The prayer of the humble pierceth
the clouds " (35¹⁷). God " will listen to the prayer
of him that is wronged " (Ibid. ¹³). Men are exhorted
not to justify themselves " in the presence of the
Lord " (7⁵). He directs the ways of a man who asks
His guidance (37¹⁵). " He that seeketh things pleasing to God shall receive instruction, and He will
answer him in his prayer " (Hebrew 32¹⁴ ⁽¹⁾). It is
thus abundantly clear that, to the mind of Ben Sira,
God was near to mankind. In one statement, we
have what looks like a pantheistic conception : " The
sum of our words is, He is all " (43²⁷). Edersheim very
naturally rejected this, as no part of Ben Sira's work.
" We have no hesitation in regarding this as a bold
later addition by the younger Siraicide." * But,
though the Syriac does not contain the sentence, it is
now known to be in the Hebrew, where we have :
" The conclusion of the matter is, He is all." As
C. H. Toy, however, suggests, the sentence may be
from the author himself, but possibly it is an addition
made by a Hebrew scribe, or it may have been made
first in Greek, and then transferred to Hebrew.† Be
this as it may, it is, of course, abundantly clear that
Ben Sira was no pantheist. To interpret the passage
in that sense is, as J. S. Clemens says, to give it a
meaning " completely at variance with the prevailing
presentment throughout the book." ‡ The old Latin
seems to be an attempt at explanation : " Ipse est
in omnibus."

### ADDITIONS TO ECCLESIASTICUS

In regard to our subject in the present chapter,
we have to note passages which show a desire on the

* Op. cit., p. 14 n.    ‡ I.J.A., July 1909, p. 61.
† E.B., " Ecclesiasticus," 1174.

part of the scribe or scribes who made the additions to emphasise Ben Sira's doctrine of the actuality of God's reign in this world. Thus in 18²⁴, after the words, "The Lord alone shall be justified," we have the following addition : "And there is none other save Him, He that steers the world with the span of His hand, and all things obey His will, for He is King of all in His might, dividing among them holy from profane" (MSS. 70, 106, and 248). Again, in 18²⁹, there is the sentence : "Better confidence in the only Master than to cling with dead heart to dead things" (MS. 248). And in 20³¹ we have : "Better inexorable persistence in seeking the Lord than a masterless charioteer of his own life" (MSS. 248–30). The manuscripts 70 and 253 and the Syro-Hexaplar (under asterisk) give us a sentence in which reference is made to those "to whom God appears" (1¹⁰), and L. after 13 is similar. The Additions thus lay stress on the doctrine of God as nigh to the world and man, and this is regarded as a doctrine of great practical importance, giving men confidence.

### TOBIT

The author calls God "the Most High" (1⁴, ¹³, 4¹¹), "the Holy One" (12¹², ¹⁵), the "King of Heaven," the "Great King," the "Everlasting King" (13⁷, ¹¹ ; 13¹⁵ ; 13⁶, ¹⁰). The doctrine of Omniscience is not expressly stated, but it is the clear implication of Sarah's prayer to the God who knows her perfect chastity (3¹⁴). The writer appears to have held the spirituality of God, for not only has he nothing inconsistent therewith, but also he almost completely avoids the use of anthropomorphic language. Moreover, he uses very sparingly expressions in which God is in any way likened to man. The love of God is, however, referred to in one passage, and in another He is described as turning to them that do truth and not hiding His face from them ($13^{10}$; $13^{6}$). The author teaches that God helps man by means of angelic agents ($3^{17}$, $5^{16, 21}$). Each of the principal characters of the book is described as approaching God in prayer, but it is said that the prayers of men are presented to God by seven privileged angels ($12^{12, 15}$). On the other hand, God is represented not only as dwelling in heaven, but also in Jerusalem, in " the temple of the habitation of the Most High " ($5^{16}$, $1^{4}$).

He punishes Israel for sin ($3^{4}$). Tobit discerns in his affliction the fact that God controls events ($11^{15}$). The wife of Tobias is foreordained for him ($6^{17}$). There is, moreover, recognition of a divine control of human fortune generally : " If thou doest the truth, thy doings shall prosperously succeed to thee and to all them that do righteousness " ($4^{6}$).

### ETHIOPIC ENOCH, 1–36

This apocalyptist marks his sense of the greatness of God by the titles which he uses. God is " the Lord of lords," the " God of gods," " King of kings." The throne of His " glory standeth unto all the generations of the ages " ($9^{4}$). He is the " Holy and Great One " ($1^{3}$, $14^{1}$, $25^{3}$), " the Lord of glory, the Eternal King" ($25^{3}$, $27^{3}$). Such names of honour are of frequent occurrence in these chapters. God is " the Honoured and Glorious One," " the Most High " ($9^{3}$), who liveth for ever ($5^{1}$). He is not styled the Almighty, but His power is described in a prophecy of the dread convulsions of nature, which are to take place when He appears " in the strength of His might "

($1^{4\cdot7}$).  He is the Omniscient.  " All things are naked,
and open in Thy sight, and Thou seest all things,
and nothing can hide itself from Thee" ($9^5$).
" Thou knowest all things before they come to pass "
(Ibid. [11]).  " Ten thousand times ten thousand were
before Him, but He stood in no need of counsel "
($14^{22}$).

Language of an anthropomorphic character is freely
used.  It is said that God " will come forth from His
dwelling, . . . and, going from thence, He will tread
on Mount Sinai, and appear with His hosts " ($1^{3\cdot4}$).
He will " come down to visit the earth with goodness " and will sit on a high mountain ($25^3$).  He
dwells in a wonderful house in the heavens ($14$).  He
speaks to Enoch with His own mouth ($14^{24}$).  The
author thus appears to teach the crudest anthro-
pomorphism.  But he gives us other statements which
somewhat modify first impressions.

(1) His account of the divine descent for judgment
is called a " parable " ($1^3$).

(2) He declares that Enoch saw the heavenly things
in sleep ($13^{7\cdot,\,10}$, $14^2$).

(3) God dwells, according to him, in a house whose
floors and ceilings are of fire (Ibid. [17]).  His raiment
shines more brightly than the sun, and it is " whiter
than any snow " (Ibid. [20]).  " Sans doute," says M.
de Faye, " cette lumière surnaturelle, qui resplendit
sur les sommets de l'Univers, n'est pas la faible clarté
du soleil.  Seul Enoch a le privilège de la percevoir.
Mais, quelque épurée qu'elle soit, cette lumière divine
renferme toujours un nescio quid qu'elle a en commun
avec la lumière que nos yeux contemplent. . . . On
y apprend que la δόξα θεοῦ, la gloire de Dieu, est
par essence de la lumière." *

* Op. cit., pp. 137, 139.

(4) According to the Ethiopic version, the God who reveals Himself to Enoch is the Invisible One.

" None of the angels could enter and could behold the face of the Honoured and Glorious One, and no flesh could behold Him " ($14^{21}$). Here, however, the Gizeh Greek fragment gives us not τοῦ ἐντιμοῦ καὶ ἐνδοξοῦ but διὰ τὸ ἔντιμον καὶ ἔνδοξον (" on account of the magnificence and glory "). It is, therefore, a moot point whether the writer meant to assert God's essential invisibility.

(5) A further fact to be observed is that, while the writer speaks of the face and the mouth of God, there is an avoidance of every sort of anthropopathism throughout the whole section 1–36.

Charles considers that this section is composite in character, apart from the interpolations which he names, because in " 12–16 the transcendence of God is pictured in an extreme degree . . . whereas, in 1–11, 20–36, the old Hebrew standpoint is fairly pre-served." " God will come down to judge on Sinai ($1^4$). . . . God Himself will come down to visit the earth with blessing, and will sit on His throne on earth." * This is, of course, a view which it is quite possible to take; but a study of closely similar language used in Enoch 83–90, Jubilees, and the Testaments makes it appear much more probable that the references to a divine descent are here to be understood in a poetic sense, and simply enshrine the idea that God will in the future judge the wicked and bless the righteous. The idea of a divine visitation of mankind is common. It appears even in such a work as Ecclesiasticus. Our author does but say in more highly coloured and imaginative fashion what others say in a less rhetorical manner.

* Edition of Ethiopic Enoch, p. 55.

Chapter 20 is treated by Charles as an interpolation in his general introduction to this work. But, in a note on page 91, he adds that it is " probably an original part of this section." If this is correct, our author teaches that six great angels watch over the universe, having Paradise, Tartarus, and the world under their government. Three of them are set over mankind. These angels, however, seek orders from God before they act (9¹¹). God also intervenes in the affairs of earth, using angels as His agents (e.g. 10⁴). They say to Him : " Over all things hast Thou dominion," and Enoch calls Him " the Great Lord and the King of the World " (9⁵, 12³). Angels are mediators between God and suppliant men. God Himself commands Enoch to tell the watchers that it is their duty to intercede for men (15²). This work also contains the singular teaching that the prayers of troubled men were of old addressed to angels. The cry of men comes to the gate of heaven, and the angels say to one another : " To you, ye holy ones, complain the souls of men, saying :  ' Procure us justice with the Most High ! ' " (9² ᶠ·). To the mind of this writer, then, God was one remote from men, dwelling in a distant heaven, governing by angelic lieutenants, intervening by their instrumentality, not accessible to the cry of man save by means of angelic intermediaries. God is even distant in this book from the angels, though they are described as " the holy ones who were nigh to Him," for it is added that " none of those who were around Him could draw nigh to Him " (Ibid. ²² ᶠ·). It is significant also that the watchers are not called sons of God, but " sons of the heavens " (6²). On the other hand, God speaks to Enoch, not only by angelic messengers, but also directly in a dream (14²⁴), and the basis of the whole work is that the writer is one who has an immediate divine inspiration.

ETHIOPIC ENOCH, 83–90

This apocalyptist describes God as the Lord, King both great and mighty in His greatness, Lord of the whole creation of the heaven, King of kings, and God of the whole world, whose power and kingship and greatness abide for ever and for ever and ever, and His dominion throughout all generations (84²). In one place, the writer appears to contradict the idea of Divine Omniscience. There, an angel scribe is ordered to write down all the transgressions of Israel's shepherds, and God says : " Read out before Me by number how many they destroy . . . that I may have this as a testimony against them and know every deed of the shepherds " (89⁶¹⁻³, ⁷⁰ᶠ·). But it is clear that this scene is only a dramatisation of the idea, which the author desires to emphasise, that God has withdrawn from sinful Israel. It is simply a part of the imagery of his parable, and the recording angel is manifestly a superfluous official. For in 84³ we have this sentence : " Thou knowest and seest and hearest everything, and there is nothing which is hidden from Thee ; for Thou seest everything."

God is described as descending from heaven to act on Israel's behalf at the Exodus. " The Lord of the sheep descended at the voice of the sheep from a lofty abode and came to them " (89¹⁶). He " went with them as their Leader. . . . His face was dazzling and glorious and terrible to behold " (Ibid. ²²). He placed Himself between the sheep and the wolves, and, when the wolves saw Him, they fled before His face (89²⁴⁻⁶). " And after that I saw the Lord of the sheep standing before them, and His appearance was great and terrible and majestic, and all those sheep saw Him and were afraid before His face " (89[30]).

All this is clearly a telling and vivid forthsetting in symbolic speech of the fact that God delivered His people from Egypt.  It is a dream of Enoch (85[1]) and gives us no information as to the writer's ideas of the divine essence.  Further, since this is symbolic, the writer's picture of the last things—a part of the same dream—must be similarly interpreted.  He sees a throne " erected in the pleasant land," and the Lord of the sheep sits thereon (90[20]).  He sees the Lord of the sheep bringing a new house, and He Himself is within it (90[29]).  These pictures evidently do not import a denial of the divine spirituality.  God, however, like man, rejoices (89[58], 90[33, 38]) and has wrath (84[4, 6] 89[33]).

Although this writer says, "Thou hast created and rulest all things " (84[3]), his mind is almost wholly occupied with God's dealings with Israel.  M. de Faye rightly says :  " Il ne connaît que l'histoire d'Israël.  Il ne fait allusion à celle des autres nations qu'en tant qu'elle touche à celle du peuple élu." *  He narrates the long story of God's providential government of His chosen race.  He brought Joseph's eleven brothers to Egypt (89[14]).  He intervened at the Exodus (Ibid. [16]).  He called Moses to be their leader (Ibid. [17]).  He raised up Saul and David (Ibid. [42, 45]).  He sent prophets (Ibid. [51]).  He delivered Elijah in the fiery chariot (Ibid. [52]).  He at last handed over Israel to Gentile oppressors and to the cruel shepherds (Ibid. [55, 59]).  Evidently, the writer had a strong faith in the controlling hand of God in the fortunes of Israel.  Moreover, while God is described as using angelic ambassadors in 87[26], 89[1], He

* Op. cit., p. 29.

is also said to have spoken to Moses Himself ($89^{17}$),
and He is in person Israel's Deliverer in the Exodus
($89^{16\,\text{ff.}}$). Enoch also prays directly to God ($83^{10}$), and
this is the privilege of a believer ($83^8$). The nation
cries to Him, not in vain, for deliverance from Pharaoh
($89^{15}$), and there is not in the writer's whole story of
the Exodus any such suggestion of angelic agents
and intermediaries as we have in Enoch 1–36. Israel's
redemption is regarded as God's own unmediated act.
But at last, according to our author, God becomes
remote from Israel. He is remote in the sense that
He commits the nation into the hands of seventy
angels (89), and does not act on behalf of His people.
Yet, even in this troublous time, He inspires His servant who writes this vision, and His withdrawal from
Israel is a temporary one. In a coming age, He will
be in close contact with Israel and the Gentiles
($90^{28\,\text{f.}}$). He will not make the Messiah His agent.
The Messiah in this apocalypse, though He appears,
has no function to discharge. As in the Exodus, so
in the future, God will Himself act. It is further to
be observed that, while this writer speaks of God's
heavenly abode ($89^{70,\ 76}$, $90^{14}$), he is also influenced
by Isaiah $66^1$. "All the heavens," he says, " are
Thy throne for ever, and the whole earth Thy foot-
stool for ever and for ever and ever " ($84^2$).

## JUBILEES

In a great number of passages, this writer speaks
of " the Most High God." There are places in the
work in which he seems to deny the omniscience of
God. Thus, it is said that angels announce, when
they come before the Lord, " all the sin which is committed in heaven, and on earth, and in light, and in

darkness, and everywhere " (4⁶). The Lord, we are told, "knew that Abraham was faithful . . . for He had tried him " (17¹⁷). Mastema (Satan) says that by trial God will know if Abraham is faithful (17¹⁶). But we have found such representations in Enoch 83–90, coupled with express assertions of omniscience, and so in Jubilees it is often said that God has fore-knowledge of man's action and even of man's nature. He foretells the future to Enoch, Abraham, Jacob, and Moses (1¹⁻²⁹, 4¹⁹, 16¹⁶, 32²¹). He sees what happens on earth. He "looked upon the earth . . . and all that were upon the earth had wrought all manner of evil before His eyes " (5³, cf. 1¹²). He takes knowledge of secret evil deeds (41³, ⁵ after Gen. 38⁷, ¹⁰). He knows the character and thoughts of men before they are born. At the creation, He says : " I have chosen the seed of Jacob from amongst all that I have seen " (2²⁰). Of Israel, He says : " I know their rebellion and their stiff neck before I bring them into the land " (1⁷). Again, " I know their contrariness and their thoughts " (1²²). It is clear, therefore, that this writer thought of God as the Omniscient One.

There are also a number of passages in which he employs anthropomorphic language. He uses great freedom in excising or revising statements in the Biblical record. All the more remarkable, therefore, is the inclusion of the statement from Genesis that at Babel the Lord descended to see the city and the tower (10²³, cf. Genesis 11⁵). He also says that " the Lord smelt the goodly savour " at the time of Noah's sacrifice (6⁴, cf. Genesis 8²¹). He declares that God will at last descend and dwell with a purified Israel throughout eternity (1²⁶), and that then "the Lord will appear to the eyes of all " (1²⁸). After Genesis 17, he reports an interview of God with Abraham and copies verse 22 in that chapter, when he says : " God went up from Abraham " (15²²). On the other hand, there is a notable absence of any attempt to describe the form of God or His heavenly abode. The writer also does not repeat the Bible story of the visit of the three men to Abraham, one of whom is God (Gen. 18¹). He refuses to say that God appeared in a human form to the patriarch, and substitutes these words : " We [angels] appeared to Abraham " (16¹). At times he changes Biblical statements in significant fashion. For example, where we read, " The Lord said unto Abram " (Gen. 12), he writes : " The word of the Lord was sent unto him through me," i.e. an angel (12²²). Again, where we have in Genesis : " The Lord made a covenant with Abram " (15¹⁸), Jubilees has : " We [the angels] made a covenant with him " (14²⁰). But this is not always the case. Our author frequently tells us that God Himself spake to the patriarchs (13¹⁹, 15⁵, 18¹˙ ¹⁴), and even that He appeared to them (15³˙ ²², 24⁹˙ ²², 32¹⁷, 44⁵). But he sometimes explains that this took place in dreams. Thus, he tells the story, after Genesis 35⁹, of the Lord's appearance to Jacob, but he adds that it was " by night " (32¹⁷). So again, when he says in 44⁵ that " the Lord appeared unto Jacob," it is explained that Jacob waited " if perchance he should see a vision as to whether he should remain or go down " to Egypt (44³, cf. Gen. 46²). The language in 10²³˙ ²⁶˙ ²⁸ is strikingly similar to that of Enoch 83–90, where it is obviously poetic and symbolic, and on the whole, though the writer has included in his pages such a highly anthropomorphic expression borrowed from his O.T. source as that in 6⁴, it seems most probable that his idea of God was spiritual.

Of God's wrath he speaks in several places (e.g.

$3^{23 \text{ f.}}$, $5^6$, $15^{34}$). He also refers to the love of God (cf. chapter 3 of this work).

Angels play a large part in these pages. They are said to act as God's agents for a variety of purposes (e.g. $3^{15}$, $4^{15, 21}$, $5^6$, $10^{12}$, $18^9$, $19^3$, $32^{21-5}$, $35^{17}$, $41^{24}$), and to preside over all phenomena and over all the spirits of God's creatures in heaven and on earth ($2^2$). This book also contains the earliest known suggestion of the idea that the law was given to Moses by angelic mediation ($1^{27}$, cf. Acts $7^{23}$), and, as we have observed above, the author sometimes declares that God spake to patriarchs by angels, where the O.T. speaks of a direct communication. Moreover, it is his teaching that God has delegated authority over all nations, except Israel, to evil spirits ($15^{31 \text{ f.}}$), He does not, however, teach the doctrine of angelic intercession for men, unless he means this in the words addressed to Levi: "May the Lord of all . . . cause thee and thy seed from among all flesh to approach Him, to serve in His sanctuary, as the angels of the presence, and as the holy ones" ($31^{14}$). But the facts cited show that there is in the book much to make one think that its author conceived of God as remote from man. A consideration of other facts, however, modifies that impression greatly. It is said that the name of God dwells in the Sanctuary. God speaks of "My sanctuary, which I have hallowed for Myself in the midst of the land, that I should set My name upon it, and that it should dwell there" ($1^{10}$). That sanctuary "is the place where it is chosen that His name should dwell" ($32^{10}$). Sometimes, however, the writer describes God Himself as dwelling in Zion. Thus, of the second Temple, God says: "I shall build My sanctuary in their midst, and I shall dwell with them" ($1^{17}$).

Our author appears to regard these two statements as practically having the same meaning, and the thought seems to be, as Dr. G. A. Smith expresses it, that " in the Temple men may call upon Him and may know what He is, as they cannot do anywhere else on earth, or, as one passage explains, the Temple is the place where His eyes and His heart may be constantly (1 Kings 9³), where Israel may be sure of His regard and of His answer to their prayers." * He has other allusions to God's being with man. The Garden of Eden, he says, is God's dwelling (8¹⁹). His view of the ambiguous passage in Genesis 9²⁷ is that " God shall dwell in the dwellings of Shem " (7¹²), unlike the Targum of Onkelos, which paraphrases it : " May He cause His Shechinah to rest in the dwellings of Shem," or that of Jonathan, where the saying is made to refer to Japheth, dwelling in the tents of Shem. † After Gen. 46⁴, the author describes God as saying to Jacob : " I shall go down with thee," i.e. into Egypt (44⁶). He explains the name " Nebaioth " in Gen. 25¹³, by telling how the wife of Ishmael said : " The Lord was nigh to me when I called upon Him " (17¹⁴). In the preceding verse we read that God was with Ishmael, and the same statement is made of Joseph (39², 40⁹), or, as it is put elsewhere : " The Spirit of the Lord was with him " (40⁵). God is also described as saying that, when Israel has had experience of His abiding mercy, " they will recognise that " He has " been truly with them " (1⁶). Similar passages are 27¹⁵—a promise that God will be with Jacob, " for He will not forsake him all his days "—and 39², where it is said of Joseph that " the Lord was with him," and " the Lord made all

* " Jerusalem," vol. ii., p. 311.
† Cited by Charles, " Jubilees," p. 60.

that he did to prosper " (cf. $31^{24}$, $39^{5}$).  In all these passages the doctrine of the God who is not far from Israel is plainly taught again and again.  He is the Helper of men in need, their faithful Friend, who gives prosperity to His servants, and He is all this, not only to the patriarchs, but to Israel, through the ages. Some passages appear to teach predestinarianism.  It is said, for example, that Jacob saw an angel with tablets in his hand, wherein the patriarch read all that would " befall him and his sons throughout all the ages" ($32^{21}$).  Similar doctrine is implied in $2^{20}$, $16^{16}$, $26^{34}$.  But his view of God is also that He is active in the affairs of men through the ages.  He so orders human life that nature smiles on the good. He brings it to pass that the righteous prosper.  He is Himself " the defence of the good " and preserves them from all evil and from every kind of death " ($20^{9}$, $21^{20}$).  God is regarded, moreover, as the active Superintendent of creation.  He is not One who, " having set the engine of the universe going, has retired from it." *  Rather, He " causes the rain and the dew to descend on the earth, and does everything upon the earth " ($12^{4}$).  "If He desires it, He causes it to rain morning and evening, and, if He desires it, He withholds it, and all things are in His hands " ($12^{18}$, cf. $20^{9}$).  It is He who determines the taking place of births ($28^{12, 34}$, after Gen. $29^{31}$, $30^{52}$).

After Exod. $24^{17}$, our author declares that " God spake unto Moses saying, ' Come up unto Me on the mount ' " ($1^{1}$).  Noah, like Moses, is an inspired servant of God, as are also Rebekah and Isaac.  The word of the Lord is put into the mouth of Noah ($8^{20}$). The spirit of prophecy came down into Isaac's mouth ($31^{12}$).  The author is also himself inspired.  That

* Abelson, " Hibbert Journal," January 1912, p. 432.

underlies all he says. His own work is an authoritative supplement to the Pentateuch, which he calls the first law. He makes new laws for Israel, which he promulgates as of divine authority. God was not far from those old servants of His, and He is near to this writer, whose words are His own speech to man.

The heroes of the book also are men who have free access to God in prayer. Abraham prays repeatedly ($11^{17}$, $12^{21}$, $13^{8, 16}$, $22^{7-9, 28-30}$). Noah, Isaac, Jacob, Rebekah, and all Jacob's sons speak to God ($10^3$, $24^{23}$, $25^{12-15}$, $32^7$). Nor is there the slightest hint that angelic mediation is required when men approach God in prayer. On the other hand, God is regarded as distant from the Gentiles. Yet it is to be observed that the spirits who rule the nations are conceived of as strictly subordinate to the Supreme. The powers of Mastema are created to fulfil God's sovereign purposes ($10^5$). When He wills it, they are imprisoned $10^9$, $48^5$). When He ordains it, they are set at liberty to carry out His designs ($48^{16}$, $49^2$). They cherish evil purposes, but are not independent. God hinders them from executing some of their malicious purposes ($48^{2-4}$). God also affects by His sovereign will the policy of Gentile powers, employing them as His instruments, waking up against Israel " the sinners of the Gentiles," and using even their " violence " and " transgression " for His own ends ($23^{23}$).

His delegation of authority to the spirits clearly does not mean that even temporarily He abdicates in their favour. Yet the thought of the writer is that it is to Israel alone that God is near. He only intervenes in the life of the Gentiles when the needs of Israel require it.

THE TESTAMENTS OF THE TWELVE PATRIARCHS

This writer does not make frequent use of great divine titles, but several times he names God " the Most High." He declares that " the works of truth and the works of deceit are written upon the hearts of men, and each one of them the Lord knoweth" (T. Judah 20³, cf. T. Iss. 2³, T. Naph. 2⁵, T. Benj. 6⁶). He teaches that " the great Glory" dwells in the highest heaven, where Levi saw Him on a throne of glory and was addressed by Him (T. Levi 3⁴, 5¹ᶠ·).

But there is a notable absence of any attempt to describe the form or appearance of God, and Levi is only said to have seen Him in a dream (Ibid. 2⁷). It is, however, repeatedly declared in this work that in the last days God will appear on the earth. If we disregard all obviously Christian interpolations, there still remains a number of passages in which this is said. " The Most High shall visit the earth, coming Himself " (T. Asher 7³). " The Lord shall be in the midst of it "—i.e. Jerusalem (T. Dan 5¹³). " Through their tribes [Levi and Judah] shall God appear on earth " (T. Naph. 8³). In T. Sim. 6⁵, T. Levi 2¹¹, 5², there are similar statements, and in T. Zeb. 9⁸ it is said : " Ye shall see Him in Jerusalem." So far as this last passage is concerned, it is to be observed that it occurs after a prophecy of an exile and a restoration, and it is succeeded in the next verse by this statement : " Again, through the wickedness of your works, shall ye provoke Him to anger, and ye shall be cast away by Him unto the time of consummation." This is, then, no notion of a personal coming of God to conclude the course of world history by a visible manifestation of Himself. The thought is obviously that of a new revelation of the power and

4

grace of God to Israel in the giving of a national and religious revival. Charles, however, shows conclusively that this passage belongs to the interpolator, and therefore we cannot use it to illustrate the teaching of the author. But, as we shall show immediately, this writer makes frequent use of very similar language, when it is quite clear that he is teaching God's presence with and in all good men throughout the ages. His style is moulded on the pattern set in such O.T. passages as Zech. 8³ : " I am returned to Zion and will dwell in the midst of Jerusalem." He is prophesying in vivid poetic fashion in a style similar to that of his brother apocalyptist who wrote Enoch 83–90, the glorious new day when God will again favour Israel. In one passage, the doctrine of Omnipresence is stated in express terms : " In all places He is " (T. Jos. 2⁶). This is the reading of A, but B S¹ is similar : " In all places He is at hand." There is, however, another reading : " In all these things does He give protection."

Anthropopathisms are used very freely. God rejoices (T. Levi 18¹³). He is pleased (T. Dan 1³, T. Gad 7⁶). He loves (T. Iss. 1¹, T. Naph. 8⁴, ¹⁰, T. Jos. 1⁴, 9², 10³, 11¹). He is angry (T. Reuben 4⁴, T. Levi 6¹¹). He is provoked (T. Levi 3¹⁰). He hates (T. Naph. 8⁶). Still, He " is not to be put to shame as a man, nor as the son of man is He afraid, nor as one that is earthborn is He weak [or affrighted] (T. Jos. 2⁵).

Angels fill a great space in the work. They are God's agents to instruct, deliver, and guide man (e.g. T. Reuben 3¹⁵, 5³, T. Sim. 2⁸, T. Jud. 3¹⁰, T. Dan 5⁴, T. Asher 6⁶). Moreover, they are mediators. Perhaps this is not taught in T. Levi 5⁶ᶠ·—" I am the angel who intercedeth for the nation of Israel "—for the text of the verses is uncertain, and the true reading may give us the statement that the angel is Israel's patron. But in T. Levi 3⁵ it is said that archangels " minister and make propitiation to the Lord for all the sins of ignorance of the righteous." There is also reference to prayers addressed to angels. Thus, Levi says to an angel: " I pray thee, O lord, tell me thy name, that I may call upon thee in a day of affliction " (T. Levi 5⁵). In T. Dan 6² also one angel is called a mediator, and men are urged to " draw near " to him as well as to God. In one passage there is reference to angels who " bear answers to the angels of the presence of the Lord " (T. Levi 3⁷). Charles would amend the text so as to read " prayers " instead of " answers." But this is uncertain, and A*reads : " They are the messengers (πρέσβεις) of the Godhead," which Charles regards as " apparently a free rendering." * There is no clear allusion to angels as intermediaries between God and praying man, but the two passages which speak of prayer to angels seem to show—if they are his—that the writer was not wholly uninfluenced by the tendency to make God remote. Yet the general drift of his teaching is very strongly in the opposite direction. According to him, God is near to Israel and to all the righteous. In many places he describes men as having immediate access to God in prayer (e.g. T. Reuben 1⁷, T. Naph. 6⁸, T. Jos. 3³, 4⁸, 7⁴, 8¹, T. Gad 5⁹, 7¹). He does not make such assertions as to God's absolute control over the fortunes of nations and individuals as we find in the work of Ben Sira or the Sibyl. Still, he not only teaches that God ordains who shall rule Israel (e.g. T. Reuben 6⁷· ¹¹), but the truth on which he dwells again and again, with a reiteration which shows how greatly he loved it, is that God has the greatest active

* Edition of the Testaments in Greek, in loc.

interest in the righteous, and that, not of Israel alone,
but among all peoples. He delights to trace God's
action in the experiences of Joseph (e.g. T. Reuben
4¹⁰, T. Sim. 2⁸, T. Zeb. 2⁸, T. Dan 1⁹, T. Gad 2⁵,
T. Jos. 1⁵⁻⁷). It is God who gives Joseph favour with
the merchant, and who prospers the merchant in gold
and silver (T. Jos. 11⁶ᶠ·). Nay, more, it is He who
exalts all such men as Joseph (Ibid. 10³, 18¹), and He
ever shields the good (T. Benj. 3⁴).

Again and again he teaches that God is with men.
He visited Joseph when he was sick (T. Jos. 1⁶). He
was with Israel, in light, when they went out of Egypt
(T. Jos. 20²). "If ye follow after chastity and purity,
with patience, and prayer, with fasting in humility
of heart," says Joseph, "the Lord will dwell among
you, because He loveth chastity" (T. Jos. 10², cf.
T. Iss. 7⁷, T. Dan 5¹). Further, we read that God
dwells in a man wherever He finds compassion (T.
Zeb. 8²), and that men are to "cleave unto goodness only, for God hath His habitation therein" (T.
Asher 3¹). This great spiritual teacher does not
speak of God as dwelling in the Temple. His God
"prefers, before all temples, the upright heart and
pure." He dwells in the good man, and "lighteth
up his soul" (T. Benj. 6⁴).

### THE SIBYLLINE ORACLES: BOOK 3⁹⁷⁻⁸²⁹ *

God is the "great God" (97, 162, 194, etc.). He
is immortal, ἀθάνατος (101, 276, etc.), ἄμβροτος (283),
αἰώνιος (309). He is the Most High, the Heavenly
God (286, 519, 719). The prophecies, of course, imply

* Terry's version is usually cited here, but the lines are
given as in Joh. Geffchen's edition of the Greek text—"Die
Oracula Sibyllina" (Leipzig, 1902).

Hi foreknowledge, but omniscience is not expressly taught. He is the Controller of nature, using it when He will to punish sinful men (e.g. 101 f., 338–41, 477–9, 539). Poetic allusions are made to the face of God and to His arm (549, 672), but nothing is said to cast doubt on the Sibyl's belief in His spirituality. God is spoken of as " great, present far and wide . . . a shelter as on all sides around, a wall of blazing fire " (705 f.). Fairweather observes that " there is throughout a studious effort to avoid speaking of the Deity in terms of the life of humanity," * and it must be conceded that such language is sparingly used. Still, the Sibyl speaks of God's love (711), and several times alludes to His anger (e.g. 556, 561, 632, 766). God is called the only Ruler (718). He is the King " who ever rules " (593). His hand is traced in the misfortunes of nations whom He punishes. He appoints Moses to be Israel's leader (252 f.). They are the people whom God " led from Egypt to the Sinai mount " (255 f.). He sends them a king from the East, who " will obey the good decrees of God the mighty " (651, 655 f.).

Angels are not mentioned save in one line of doubtful authority. Terry, commenting on lines 286 f., which he translates—

" And then will God from heaven send a king
To judge each man in blood and light of fire "—

says that the language, " taken apart from the context, naturally suggests a supernatural judge and ruler." But, unlike Ewald, who understands the king to be the Messiah, he considers that " the context here and in the parallel passages points rather to

* " The Background of the Gospels," p. 347.

Cyrus." * The Greek, however, reads Τότε δὴ θεὸς οὐράνιος πέμψει βασιλῆα, and there is thus no idea here of a supernatural person.

God gave His law to Israel, writing it on two flat stones (256 ff.). He gives the holy dream by night (294). The Persian king is guided by His counsels (655 f.). The Sibyl is His inspired servant. "Then a message of the mighty God was set within my breast, and it [or He] bade me proclaim throughout all earth and in royal hearts plant things which are to be, and to my mind this God imparted first" (162–5). This claim is repeated in almost identical terms in lines 297–300, 490 f., and again in substance in 819–21 (cf. 196). The Sibyl prays directly to Him (296). She prophesies a future in which He will dwell in Zion (787), and heathen men will lift up their hearts in prayer to Him (715 f.).

### THE PROEMIUM

God is called by various titles. He is the "Most High" (1⁴), the "Almighty" (Ibid. ⁸), the "Eternal" (αἰώνιος 3¹⁷, ἄμβροτος 1¹¹), the "Incorruptible" (3¹⁷), "The All Supreme" (3³ cf. 1⁷). He "alone is for ever and has been from everlasting, the self-existent, unbegotten One" (1¹⁶ ᶠ), the "All-nourishing Creator" (1⁵), the Sustainer of Life (1⁸). He is "the One who knows, the all-observant Witness of all things" (1³ cf. 1⁸).

Man cannot behold Him. He cannot even endure to see the sun (1⁹⁻¹⁴). Yet God is the Light clear to all (1²⁷ ᶠ).

There is a notable absence of anthropomorphisms, and expressions of an anthropopathic nature are rare,

---

* Terry's version, p. 69.

though in one passage reference is made to God's anger (3$^{19}$).

His habitation is in the sky (1$^{11}$, cf. 3$^{17}$), but "His sweet Spirit " is in all things, and is " Leader of all mortals " (1$^{5\,f.}$). Repeatedly, the writer insists that God reigns. He " alone is the Ruler of the world " (1$^{15}$). He " rules all things throughout all time " (Ibid. $^{17}$). He is the " King who oversees all things " (3$^{42}$). " Hear me," cries the Sibyl, " the King Eternal reigns " (4). He—

> " Sends forth rains and winds,
> Earthquakes and lightnings, famines, pestilence,
> And mournful cares, and storms of ice and snow;
> But why do I speak them one by one ?
> He guides heaven, rules earth, over Hades reigns."

Nothing is said of prayer, but it is taught that men can " lay hold upon the Light " (1$^{27\,f.}$). The only allusion to God's speech with men is in the statement that He enjoins on the Sibyl the duty of speaking in His name (8). She anticipates the day of His coming (8).

## SUMMARY

(1) *Titles.*—These writers express their reverential sense of God's greatness by the titles which they employ when they name Him. The one which occurs most frequently is " the Most High." It is used in every book save Ethiopic Enoch 83–90, whose author speaks, however, of God as " great and mighty in His greatness." Several of these writers describe God as King, attaching predicates of greatness to the title. In Tobit He is the " Great and Everlasting King." In the Additions to Ecclesiasticus He is " King of

all." In Ecclesiasticus and the two sections of Ethiopic Enoch He is " King of kings."

(2) *Everlastingness.*—Everlastingness is sometimes predicated. In Tobit God is called ὁ βασιλεὺς τῶν αἰώνων. In Enoch 1–36 He is God who liveth for ever, and whose throne stands to all generations of the ages. In Enoch 83–90 He is the One who abideth for ever and ever and ever. Ben Sira speaks of Him as from everlasting to everlasting. Certainly, the two Enoch writers appear to be striving to express the idea of an Eternal God, and, though it is obvious that the words used in Tobit and Ben Sira do not necessarily imply that idea, it was doubtless what they meant. But it is only in the third book of the Oracles and the Proemium that this conception finds unequivocal expression. God is called ἀθάνατος and ἄμβροτος as well as αἰώνιος.

(3) *Omniscience.*—The omniscience of God is distinctly taught in Ecclesiasticus, Enoch 1–36, the Testaments, and the Proemium to the Oracles. It is also plain that the authors of Enoch 83–90 and Jubilees taught it, despite passages which at first sight seem to involve a denial of it. In Tobit the doctrine is implied.

(4) *Omnipotence.*—In Ecclesiasticus God is " the Almighty," and the additions to that work emphasise the same truth. Jubilees and the Oracles teach His sovereign control over nature. Enoch 1–36 speaks of His power to convulse nature when He so wills. Enoch 83–90 portrays Him as the mighty Sovereign. While in the Testaments and Tobit omnipotence is not expressly predicated, God is nevertheless regarded byboth writers as One who effects what He wills by the forthputting of His own energy.

(5) *Spirituality.*—Some writers use expressions

which convey the impression that they did not conceive of God as pure Spirit.    In Enoch 1–36 and the
Testaments He is pictured as seated on a throne in
the heavens.    In Enoch 83–90 His appearance is
described.    These three writers, with the author of
Jubilees, speak of Him as coming down to earth.    In
Jubilees and the Testaments it is foretold that in the
last times men will see Him.    In the third book of
the Oracles and the Proemium His coming to earth is
anticipated.    Did these writers hold crude anthropomorphic ideas, or are we to construe their utterance
as the language of poetry ?    The case of Enoch 83–90
is very clear.    We have here, obviously, a highly
dramatic presentation of the story of the Exodus and
a prophecy of the last things in a similar style of
speech.    In the case of the Testaments and Jubilees
it is manifest that, when the writers speak of God as
being with men, they mean that His favour and
gracious help are theirs, and the prophecies of a
divine descent are foretellings of new manifestations
of God's power and grace.    In the Oracles anthropomorphisms are conspicuously absent, and the Sibyl's
announcements of a future divine coming to earth
must be interpreted in the same manner as those in the
apocalyptic books.    If Enoch 1–36 be a homogeneous
work in the main, and if the Ethiopic version be
correct in the passage about the divine invisibility,
it too must be placed in the same category.    On the
whole, it may be concluded with a considerable
degree of confidence that all these writers, with the
doubtful exception of the author of Enoch 1–36, conceived of God as pure Spirit.

(6) *Anthropopathisms.*—These authors did not think
of God as One wholly unlike man.    This is shown by
the use which they make of anthropopathic expres-

sions. These are not much in evidence in Tobit or the Oracles. But the only author who entirely abstains from them is the writer of Enoch 1–36.

(7) *The Divine Remoteness or Nearness.*—Some of these writers seem to set God at a distance from the world and man.

(A) They regard Him as deputing authority to angels or spirits, who act as His viceroys or agents. The doctrine of viceroys was not taught by Ben Sira, though one passage in his work creates at first sight the impression that he did teach it. It makes its first appearance in Enoch 1–36, where certain angels are said to rule the universe, three of them having control over men. In Jubilees, also, it is taught that angels preside over the spirits of all God's creatures. This writer, however, regarded Israel as not being under angelic government, and, seeking to account for the universal wickedness of the Gentiles, he maintained that God had given them over to the government of evil spirits. In Enoch 83–90 the pressure of the problem of Israel's sorrows gives rise in the mind of the author to the doctrine that God, in the days which are to precede the final crisis, allows Israel to be ruled by wicked angels. Two of these writers —the authors of Enoch 1–36 and Jubilees—teach that God uses angelic agents in the affairs of mankind, and this doctrine appears also in the Testaments and Tobit. It is not, however, regarded as God's normal method in Enoch 83–90. There He is represented as exercising an unmediated influence on the fortunes of Israel.

Of these five writers, it is only the author of Enoch 83–90 who teaches that God surrenders the government completely into angelic hands, and this is thought of as temporary and as only affecting Israel.

The writer conceives of God as normally directing the
affairs of Israel, and indeed as governing all things.
In Jubilees the spirits are represented as subject to
the control of God, and He is regarded as sometimes
affecting the policy of Gentile nations.    Within Israel,
according to this writer, He is interested not only in
the affairs of the nation, but also in the fortunes of
the individual, proving Himself the Friend of the good,
and ordering events to the end that they may prosper.
In the Testaments and in Tobit the thought is broader.
God is the helper of all good men.    In the latter
work, a general divine control of all human fortunes
is implied.    While in each of the three last-named
works—Jubilees, Testaments, and Tobit—God is represented as affecting human affairs by means of
angelic spirits, the writers do not suppose that He
can or does only act by such intermediaries.    Each
of them conceives of Him as influencing the life of
man directly.    Enoch 1–36 stands by itself.    In this
book God is the great King and Lord of the world,
its omniscient Master who has dominion over all
things, and from whom angels take orders ere they
act.    But He is distant from all mankind, reigning
in a far-off heaven, and governing this world by angelic
viceroys.    There are no signs of belief in any unmediated action of God affecting the outward fortunes
of men, save at the final judgment of the world.    In
this work alone we have the " false idea of transcendence."

There remain three writers, unmentioned thus far
in this summary, who belong to quite another category.    Ben Sira's doctrine is that of a complete and
direct control of God over all the affairs of mankind.
He regarded God as ordaining all that happens in the
life of all men, whether nations or individuals.    The

scribe, or scribes who wrote in his name, also insisted on the actuality of God's government. If we are to regard the third book of the Oracles and the Proemium as from the same pen, this writer gives us similar doctrine. Neither of these three authors recognises angelic agency in human affairs.

(B) In some of these works it is taught that angels are intermediaries when God would speak to men, and that they intercede for men or present prayers of men to God. That angels act as God's ambassadors is the teaching of all of them except Ben Sira, the scribe or scribes who wrote in his name, and the Sibyl. But in each of the books which contain this doctrine, with the exception of Tobit, there is also assertion of an unmediated speech of God with the great men of past times, and in Tobit God is said to influence the mind of Enemessar. The Testaments have it that God dwells in all the good, lighting up their souls. Jubilees, as we shall see in Chapter III. of this work, teaches that He strengthens praying men to do right. The Sibyl in the Proemium calls Him " the Guide of all mortals."

Ben Sira teaches that there is a constant divine guidance given to men in answer to prayer. Moreover, the basis of the work of each of the apocalyptic writers, and perhaps also that of Ben Sira, is the conviction of an immediate divine inspiration vouchsafed to themselves.

The doctrine of angelic intermediaries between God and praying men appears only in Enoch 1–36 and Tobit. This is not apparently the teaching of the Testaments, though—as in Enoch 1–36—we have the doctrine of prayer to angels, and of their intercession for men. But, unlike Enoch 1–36, the Testaments teach that men have direct access to God Himself in prayer. That is the doctrine of every writer in this period, except the two we have named.

This inquiry leads us to the same result as that obtained in the preceding section. It is in Enoch 1–36 that God is most remote from mankind, though other writers, and notably the author of Tobit, show tendencies in that direction.

## THE FIRST CENTURY B.C.

### I MACCABEES

This author was apparently reluctant to utter the Divine Name. It occurs, according to ℵ V, in $3^{18}$, where those manuscripts read " the God of heaven," but A has " heaven " in this passage. Unfortunately, however, we are without the guidance of the Codex Vaticanus in the books of Maccabees. " Heaven " occurs elsewhere, when the writer means God (e.g. $3^{60}$, $4^{10}$). But sometimes a personal pronoun is used. " He Himself will discomfit them " ($3^{22}$ cf. $2^{61}$, $3^{51-3}$, $7^{37}$). " All the Gentiles shall know," says Judas, " that there is One who redeemeth and saveth Israel " $(4^{11})$.

Of God's power Judas says : " It is an easy thing with Heaven for many to be shut up in the hands of a few, and with Heaven it is all one to save by many or by few " ($3^{18}$). Reference is made to God's knowledge in the prayer of $3^{52}$ : " Thou knowest what things they [the Gentiles] imagine against us." There is sparing use of expressions in which God is likened to man, but there are two allusions in the work to His wrath ($1^{64}$, $3^{8}$).

Fairweather considers that this book shows " the growing tendency of the age to abandon the conception of God, as dwelling among His own people by the Shechinah, in favour of a more transcendental view of God as the God of heaven." * But S. Schechter observes that new epithets of God, such as " Heaven " or " Supreme Being," were accepted by antique piety for the purpose of avoiding the name of God " being uttered in idleness," and he protests against accepting these as indications of the great distance which a Rabbinic Jew is supposed to have felt between himself and his God.† Israel Abrahams also objects to the argument that the term " Heaven " implies the divine remoteness. " This is as false an inference," he says, " as would be a similar conclusion from the opening words of the Lord's prayer." ‡ Unfortunately, owing to the character of 1 Maccabees, our material for determining the theological position of the writer is meagre. His book is a simple chronicle of wars, not interrupted, like the story in 2 Maccabees, by the author's religious reflections. His mental horizon is, moreover, bounded by Israel, and Gentiles only come within his purview when they attack his own nation. Yet we have some data which show how entirely just are the criticisms of Schechter and Abrahams on the view adopted by Fairweather. Almost nothing is said of angels. They are only mentioned in one historic allusion taken from the O.T. ($7^{41}$). God is regarded as active in the affairs of Israel. His wrath is the cause of their troubles ($1^{68}$). He punishes the dying tyrant ($6^{13}$). The leaders hearten Israel to expect God's help by the memory of His early miraculous deeds on behalf of the nation

* I.J.A., January 1907, pp. 4 f. : cf. Cambridge Bible, 1 Maccabees (Introduction).

† J.Q.R., 1894, p. 417.

‡ J.E., art. " Maccabees," p. 243.

($2^{59\ f.}$, $4^{9}$, $7^{41}$). When Israel goes to war He is the great Arbiter of battle. He giveth the victory to whomsoever He will ($3^{22,\ 59\ f.}$, $4^{10}$). He is not regarded as communicating with Israel in the time of the writer, as he did in older days through prophets, but it is expected that He will do so in the future ($4^{46}$, $9^{27}$, $14^{41}$), and He is thought of as immediately accessible to the prayers of Israel ($3^{46}$, $4^{10,\ 30}$, $5^{33}$, $7^{40}$, $11^{71}$). Moreover, Judas and his brethren are regarded as the commissioned servants of God for the deliverance of Israel ($5^{55-62}$).

### ETHIOPIC ENOCH 91-104

This apocalyptist calls God "the Most High" ($98^{11}$, $99^{3,\ 10}$, $100^{4}$), "the Holy and Great One" ($98^{6}$), and "the Great King" ($91^{13}$). God is "He that is great and honoured and mighty in dominion" ($103^{1}$). He knows all the evil actions of sinners. None of their "deeds of oppression are covered or hidden" ($98^{6}$). He inspires Enoch to show men "everything that will befall them for ever" ($91^{1}$).

There are poetic allusions to God's "arising" and "coming forth" ($91^{17}$, $100^{4}$), but there is nothing which implies doubt of His pure spirituality. The author does not profess to have seen God even in vision. Yet God is like man. He is wrathful and indignant ($91^{7}$, $99^{16}$). He is, indeed, so much like man that He rejoices at the destruction of His enemies ($94^{10}$).

God speaks to Enoch by angels ($93^{2}$). Angels are to be His agents to punish sinners and to guard the righteous dead ($100^{4\ f.}$). They mediate between Him and praying men. "Make ready, ye righteous, to raise your prayers as a memorial, and ye will place them as a testimony before the angels, that they may place the sin of the sinners for a memorial before the Most High " (99³). There is thus a tendency here to make God remote. On the other hand, this writer utters the exhortation : " Let not your spirit be troubled on account of the times, for the Holy and Great One has appointed days for all things " (92²). Nature is under His control. He withholds the rain and the dew at His pleasure, and the sea dries up at His reproof (101²ˑ⁷).

The righteous are commanded to fear God " and work no evil in His presence " (101¹). He is the communicating God, who inspires our author and the patriarch in whose name he writes. " The word calls me," says Enoch, " and the Spirit is outpoured upon me " (91¹).

ETHIOPIC ENOCH 37–70

The recurring title of God in this work is the " Lord of Spirits." He is " the Lord of Kings, the Lord of the mighty, the Lord of the rulers, the Lord of glory, and the Lord of Wisdom (before whom) every secret is clear." " His power is from generation to generation, His glory for ever and ever " (63²ˑ⁴). He is the " Head of Days." He " knows what the world is before it is created, and generation unto generation that shall arise " (39¹¹). He knows the secret ways of men (49³ᶠˑ, 61⁹). He dwells in heaven surrounded by an angelic court. Four privileged ones stand " on the four sides of the Lord of Spirits " (40²). Enoch is permitted to behold Him : " I saw One who had a Head of Days, and His head was white like wool " (46¹). " I saw the Head of Days when He had seated Himself on the throne of His glory " (47³). But it is

only in *vision* that Enoch sees God.  It looks otherwise indeed in 39³ : " And in those days a cloud and
a whirlwind carried me off from the earth and set me
down at the end of the heavens."  Charles is naturally led to remark that " this seems to be recounted
as a real translation of Enoch . . . and not as a mere
incident in a dream." *  But it is to be observed
that the title of the book runs thus :  " The vision
which he saw, the second vision of wisdom " (37¹),
and the Ethiopic word which Charles translates " similitudes " is, according to that editor, the equivalent of
παραβολαί.†  Enoch is not described as actually beholding God, and indeed, God is not represented by
this writer as becoming visible to men even in the
final judgment scene.  Messiah alone appears on the
throne, though God is present (62³, ⁵, ⁹).  The idea in
46¹, 47³, obviously borrowed from Dan. 7⁹, is simply
that God is the everlasting King.

The Similitudes do not deal with the course of the
world's history, but only with eschatology.  Consequently, we have little material to determine the ideas
of the writer as to the extent to which normally God
governs this world or intervenes in it.  His mind is
occupied with the great hope of a coming day, when
God will recompense the good and the bad.  But he
seems to recognise God's control in the affairs of
nations generally when he says :  " He [i.e. the Son
of Man] will put down the kings from their thrones
and kingdoms, because they do not extol and praise
Him, nor thankfully acknowledge whence the kingdom
was bestowed upon them " (46⁵).  Charles considers
that " the kings and the mighty " in this work are
" unbelieving native rulers and Sadducees," because
(1) they deny the Lord and His anointed, 48¹⁰, (2)

* Edition of Ethiopic Enoch, p. 115.     † Ibid., p. 111.

5

and a heavenly world—45[1]; (3) they belong to the houses of His congregation, the theocratic community —46[8], and (4) they are an offence thereto on the removal of which the theocratic ideal will be realised. (53[6]).* But as for (1) and (2), this might obviously be said of heathen rulers, and (1) is said of them in the second Psalm. Charles's strongest argument is in (3) and (4), but all that is said in 46[8] is that the kings " will be driven forth from the houses of His congregations," and this need not mean more than that they shall no longer rule over God's chosen people. In 46[7] it is said that " their faith is in the gods which they have made," and this Charles regards as a strong expression for the heathen or Sadduceean attitude of the princes of the Maccabæan house. It seems more probable, however, that it describes *Gentile* monarchs, especially if we bear in mind how general the language is. The rulers spoken of are " all the kings and the mighty and the exalted and those who hold the earth." They " possess the earth." They " rule the earth " (62[3, 6], 63[1, 12], 62[9]). The doctrine seems clearly to be that the rulers of mankind generally are of a divine appointment. We have also the fact that the author regards himself as the recipient of an immediate divine inspiration, and that in an unusually high degree. God has never given such wisdom to men as he has been privileged to receive (37[4]).

Angels appear frequently in these pages. God uses them to punish, to guard, and to help men (55[3], 63[1]; 40[9]). Some have special charge over wounded and diseased men, over the powers, over penitent sinners (40[9]). Angels also intercede with God for men (39[6], 40[6], 47[2]).

A few references to prayers of men occur. The

* Edition of Ethiopic Enoch, p. 113.

cry of the suffering righteous is heard by God ($47^1$). Enoch prays in his dream ($39^{10-13}$). It is foretold that, in the day of distress, the sinful rulers " will implore His angels of punishment . . . to grant them a little respite that they may fall down before the Lord of Spirits and worship and confess their sins before Him," and that this will be followed by an appeal made to God by them ($63^{1-10}$). Charles characterises this last as " an indirect appeal," influenced, no doubt, by the fact that, in large part, it is in the form of a meditation, and God is named in the third person.* But in verse 3 God is addressed directly.

Of the transcendence of God, in the sense of remoteness, Dr. Charles thinks " there is hardly any consciousness in the Similitudes." † This, however, is a matter on which it is difficult to pronounce, because of the absorption of the writer in eschatology. On the one hand, we have apparently a recognition of God's active rule, at least to some extent, over the fortunes of nations, and when prayer is mentioned the supplication is made without the aid of intermediaries. On the other hand, in addition to the doctrine of angels, we have the fact that this writer substitutes for the older ideas of God's unmediated action at the consummation of all things, the notion of judgment by a supernatural Messiah ($62^2$). And, when Charles says that " in the Similitudes earth and heaven are made one community through the Messiah and God and the Son of Man dwells with men," ‡ it is to be observed that this is true, so far as the Messiah is concerned, for it is said that " with that Son of Man they will eat and lie down and rise up for ever ";

* Edition of Ethiopic Enoch, p. 167.
† Ibid., p. 183.
‡ Ibid.

but of God it is simply declared that He " will abide over them " (62¹⁴).

### ETHIOPIC ENOCH 72–82

This " Book of Celestial Physics " contains very little to our purpose. God is called the " Eternal Lord of glory " (75³) and " the Lord of the whole creation of the world " (82⁷). The writer says of the southern quarter of the heavens that " the Most High descends there, and there, in quite a special sense, He who is blessed for ever comes down " (77¹). There is nothing else to notice, except that Uriel, whom God has appointed ruler of the planets (74², 75³, 82⁷), is God's agent for revelation to Enoch (82⁷).

### ETHIOPIC ENOCH—INTERPOLATIONS

God is called the " Most High," " the great and holy One " (10¹¹, 60¹), " the Lord of Spirits " (41⁶ ᶠ·, 43⁴), " the Head of Days " (55¹, 60²). His name is said to be " mighty for ever " (41⁶). Foreknowledge is, of course, implied in the prophecies (e.g. 106 f.). In a " similitude " or vision, Enoch saw God. He " sat on the throne of His glory " (60²). The Spirit translated Enoch into " the heaven of heavens " (71⁵). There, He saw the Head of Days, His head white and pure as wool, and His raiment indescribable " (71¹⁰). But, in one passage, objection is taken to all such representations. " Who is there that can see all the works of heaven ? And how should there be one who would behold the heaven, and who is there that could understand the things of heaven and see a soul or a spirit and tell thereof ? " (93¹¹ ᶠ·). Anger and repentance are predicated of God (18¹⁶, 55¹, 68⁴, 90¹⁵).

There are passages which teach the doctrine of predestination. Thus it is said that the Lord " made a separation between the light and the darkness and divided the spirits of the righteous in the name of His righteousness " (41⁸). Similar doctrine is implied when it is said that, on the heavenly tablets, Enoch read " all the deeds of men and of all the children of flesh that will be upon the earth to the remotest generation " (81²). This idea of a predetermination of all human conduct is, however, quite contradicted by the teaching as to retribution in these interpolations, and it is obviously out of harmony with the expression of thankfulness for God's patience in 81³.

Many allusions are made to angels. There are elemental spirits who are in charge of the thunder, the sea, the frost, the hail, the snow, and the rain (60¹⁵⁻²⁰). Angels are God's agents to communicate with men (10¹, 60⁴⁻²⁵, 80¹). Even Enoch, in his vision of heaven, is addressed by an angel. In 71¹⁴, where we read " And he came and greeted me with his voice," it looks indeed otherwise, for it is God who is spoken of in the preceding verse. But some manuscripts read " that angel " in verse 14, and verse 15 shows that the speaker is not God. Angels made the ark for Noah (67²). Some of them are to be God's agents to punish (66¹). Some arouse nations to war against God's people (56⁵ ᶠ·). But, though God uses angels as His agents, He is not dependent upon them according to the teaching of these fragmentary passages. He speaks to Noah directly (67¹ ᶠ·). He communicates with Enoch by dreams. Almost nothing is said of Him as the prayer-hearing God, but one passage about Noah blessing the Lord implies this doctrine (106¹¹). He intervenes in human affairs to punish (10², 54⁹, 106¹⁸), and uses the great forces of nature for that end (41⁸, 59¹⁻³, 80²⁻⁵).

As we shall show in Chapter III., one of these writers regarded Him as in close contact with the righteous, ministering to them strength of spirit.

### THE PSALMS OF SOLOMON

In these Psalms great titles for God are not employed. In one passage it is said that " He is a great and righteous King " (2$^{36}$), and He is described as " powerful in the greatness of His strength " (Ibid. $^{33}$). Allusion is made to His omniscience : " There shall not be hidden from Thy knowledge any one that doeth evil, and the righteous acts of Thy saints are before Thee. And where shall a man be hidden from Thy knowledge, O Lord ? " (9$^{5 f.}$). "The ways of men are known before Him continually, and He knoweth the secret chambers of the heart before they had their being " (14$^{5}$).

In the usual style of religious poetry, reference is made to the right hand, arm, and ear of God (13$^{1 f.}$, 18$^{3}$), and feelings are predicated of Him akin to those of men. He is provoked to anger (4$^{1, 25}$). He loves (cf. Chapter III. of this work).

There is but slight allusion to the heavenly abode of God. He is described as " King over the heavens " (2$^{34}$), and as " our God dwelling in the highest "(18$^{11}$). While the psalmist teaches that God will use a Messiah sprung from the seed of David to establish the kingdom, he does not say much of angels. Once he says that they give orders to the stars (18$^{14}$). Once he refers to " the holy ones " (17$^{49}$). But he does not speak of angels as being used by God at all in human affairs.

In one passage the author appears to teach determinism and free-will in the same breath. Ryle and

James argue in favour of reading this passage as follows : " Our works are in the (divine) choice and (at the same time) in the power of our own soul to do either righteousness or iniquity in the work of our hands " ($9^7$). They point out that ἐκλογή (" choice ") is always used in N.T., as it is in $18^6$ of this book, of the divine choice, and that $9^7$ is on this view parallel to the saying in Pirke Aboth : " Everything is fore-seen, and free-will is given." But text and meaning in this verse are uncertain, and the Syriac distinctly favours reading it as a simple assertion of free-will : " For we work by free-will and the choice of our own souls to do either good or evil by the work of our own hands." H. M. Hughes considers that support for the view of Ryle and James " is found in a passage which is determinist in tendency," namely, $5^6$ (cited below).* But this passage is not aptly used in this connection, for it clearly refers to outward fortune and not at all to conduct. Moreover, the oft-repeated statements of the writer as to just retribution indicate plainly his belief in man's free-will.

It is clear that the psalmist regarded God as active in the affairs of mankind. As will be seen in our second chapter, he teaches that God punishes Israel, using the Gentiles for the purpose, and that He judgeth kings and rulers " ($2^{34}$).

But besides this, in the manner of Ben Sira, the psalmist avers that God settles what shall be the fortunes of men. " No man taketh spoil from a mighty man, and who shall receive aught of the things that Thou hast made except Thou give it ? Because man and his portion are before Thee in the balance, he addeth not thereto nor increaseth it contrary to Thy judgment, O God " ($5^{4-6}$). And again :

* Op. cit., p. 227.

" Blessed is the man whom God remembereth with a sufficiency convenient " (5¹⁸).

It is taught that in times past God made promises to Israel, and covenanted with the fathers (7⁹, 9¹⁹); but the psalmist makes no claim to be himself a recipient of divine communications. He has, however, a firm belief in God's accessibility to suppliant men. If he is hungry, he will call upon God, and God will feed him (5¹⁰). He says that " the Lord hearkeneth unto the prayer of every one that feareth God " (6⁸, cf. 7⁷, 18³). " The Lord is gracious unto them that call upon Him in patience, to deal according to His mercy with them that are His, that they may stand continually in His presence in strength " (2¹⁰). God's name, he tells us, tabernacles in the midst of Israel (7⁵), and this is evidently the simple equivalent of the idea that He Himself is with them, for in 7¹ he prays : " Remove not Thy habitation from us, O God." This writer's God is, then, One nigh at hand. He determines the outward lot of men. He dwells in the midst of Israel. He is approachable in prayer by all obedient souls, and, as we shall see in Chapter III., the doctrine of the Psalter is that He gives grace to individual men to help them to do right.

## JUDITH

God, in this book, is the " Lord God of heaven " (6¹⁹), " the Most High God " (13¹⁸), and " the Lord Almighty " (8¹¹, 15¹⁰, 16⁶). Fairweather expresses the opinion that to the author God " ranks as the greatest of national deities, who will wreak vengeance on the foes of His people," * and undoubtedly it is true that

* D.B., extra vol., art. " Development of Doctrine in the Apocryphal Period," p. 277.

God is chiefly conceived of as Israel's Almighty
Partisan. But the writer is no henotheist, though he
does again and again claim Jehovah as the God of
Israel. On the contrary, his God is "Lord of the
heavens and of the earth, Creator of the waters, King
of the whole creation" (9¹²). Judith prays that
every nation and tribe of His may know that He is
God (9¹⁴). In the Song of Judith, which may be the
work of a later writer, God is called "the Lord, great
and glorious, marvellous in strength, invincible"
(16¹³). Foreknowledge is His (9⁶).

There is nothing which suggests that God is regarded as other than pure spirit. But He is thought
of as like man. He hates iniquity ; He can be pleased
or provoked to anger (5¹⁷, 15¹⁰, 8¹⁴). Judith, however, who uses this last expression, adds that "God
is not as man, that He should be threatened, neither
as the son of man, that He should be turned by entreaty" (8¹⁶).

Judith says: "Thou wroughtest the things that
were before those things, and those things (i.e. the
vengeance on the Shechemites) and such as ensued
after, and Thou didst devise the things which are now
(i.e. Israel's troubles through the attack of Holofernes)
and the things which are to come" (9⁵). What
happens, at any rate, in the experience of Israel is of
divine ordination, according to our author.

God's abode is heaven (6¹⁸, 11¹⁷), but He is said to
be with His people in this sense, that He shows Himself their ally against Holofernes (13¹¹), or that He
prospers them when they do right (5¹⁷). He goes
before Israel against their foes, and the priests stand
before His face in Jerusalem (8³⁵, 11¹³).

Angels are not once referred to in these pages, and
God is regarded as approachable by the people im-

mediately in prayer ($4^{9,\ 13}$, $6^{18}$, $7^{19}$, $9^1$, $12^8$, $13^{4,\ 7}$). He makes no communication to Israel in the nation's hour of sore need, not even to Judith, though in her deceitful speech to Holofernes she claims to be a recipient of divine revelations ($11^{17}$). But the people show their sense of God's nearness and knowledge when they take Him to witness against the rulers of the city ($7^{28}$).

### 3 ESDRAS

God is entitled " the Most High God " ($6^{31}$, $8^{19,\ 21}$, $9^{46}$). He is " the only Lord " ($8^{25}$), " God of hosts, Almighty " ($9^{46}$). There is no assertion of the doctrine of Omniscience.

The author prefers to avoid the use of even the most innocent anthropomorphisms. Twice, indeed, he copies from his source the phrase " the hand of God " ($8^{47,\ 61}$), but usually he pointedly avoids such expressions. Whereas in Ezra $7^9$ we read that Ezra " came to Jerusalem according to the good hand of his God upon him," our book has this : " He came to Jerusalem according to the prosperous journey which the Lord gave them " ($8^6$). He prefers to say that the power of God was with the returning exiles, instead of speaking, with the original, of the hand of God ($8^{52}$). He does not say that " the eye of their God was upon the elders of the Jews," but that " the Lord visited the captivity " ($6^5$, cf. Ezra $5^5$).

Anthropopathisms, however, are quite freely employed. God has wrath and compassion ($1^{52}$, $8^{21}$, $9^{13}$). He is grieved exceedingly by Israel's sin ($1^{24}$).

God is regarded as active in the affairs of Israel. It is by His fiat that the Chaldeans come up against the people ($1^{52}$). He stirs up the Jews to return to the home-land (2⁸). He influences the minds of foreign kings in their favour (2², 7¹⁵, 8⁸⁰). He gives the exiles a prosperous journey (8⁶). Nay, more, Cyrus is made to acknowledge that the God of Israel has made him " king of the whole world " (2³).

Angels are not mentioned in this work. In the pre-Exilic time God communicates with Israel by messengers (1⁵⁰). He gives wisdom to the youth Zorobabel (4⁵⁹ ᶠ·). He gives command even to a Gentile monarch when Israel's fortunes are involved in his policy (2⁴). His accessibility to suppliant Israelites is clearly taught (e.g. 4⁵⁸ ᶠ·, ⁶², 8⁵⁰, ⁵³, ⁷³ ᶠ·).

He is the " King of heaven," " the Lord of Israel who is in heaven " (4⁵⁸ ᶠ·; 6¹⁵), but He is also in Jeru-salem (2⁵, 8¹³). That city is " His dwelling-place " (1⁵⁰). Our author does not follow Ezra 6¹² in saying that God has caused His name to dwell in Zion, but speaks of " the Lord whose name is there called upon " (6³³). Perhaps this is an explanation of the meaning, in his view, of the old phrase.

## 2 MACCABEES

God is called the " King of kings " (13⁴), " the Al-mighty Lord " (e.g. 3²², ³⁰), " the Sovereign of Spirits " (3²⁴), " the Great Sovereign " (5²⁰), " the Sovereign Lord " (e.g. 6¹⁴), " the King of the world " (7⁹). He is " able at a beck to cast down them that are coming against Israel, and even the whole world " (8¹⁸). He is " the All-seeing Lord " (9⁵), who has " the holy knowledge," and it is manifest to Him how gladly the noble Eleazar suffers for fear of Him (6³⁰, cf. 7⁶, ³⁵).

There is very slight use of anthropomorphisms, but the author speaks of the eyes of God being upon Jerusalem (3³⁹, 5¹⁷), and his description of the divine miraculous intervention by which Heliodorus was alarmed is : " The Almighty Lord appeared " (3¹⁰). He does not speak of an ultimate dwelling of God with men, but foretells only that " the glory of the Lord shall be seen, and the cloud " (2⁸). Of the anger of God he often speaks (e.g. 5¹⁷, 7³³, ³⁸, 8⁵). Repeatedly he alludes to the idea of His being reconciled (e.g. 5²⁰, 8²⁹), Once we have reference to His pity (8³).

Again and again this writer teaches that God is the active Ruler of this world, the constant Supervisor of its affairs. The titles enumerated above lay stress on His sovereignty. The fate of armies in battle is of His determination. To Him Judas commits the decision when he goes to fight Eupator (13¹⁴). " Success," our author says, " cometh not by arms, but . . . according as He [the Lord] shall judge, He gaineth the victory for them that are worthy " (15²¹). He is no fatalist. Prayer and effort must be made. But he firmly holds that God Himself decides the issue. As will be shown in Chapter II., he teaches that God is constantly intervening in miraculous and other ways to punish sinning Israelites and those who oppress the elect people.

Angels are the chosen instruments of God when He would deliver Israel (3²⁴⁻³⁴, 5²⁻⁴, 10²⁹ ᶠ·, 11⁸). They are not, however, intermediaries between God and praying men. Israel's intercessors in the spirit world are dead saints (15¹², ¹⁴). But the people themselves have also direct access to God in prayer (see 1⁶, ⁸, ²⁴, 3¹⁵, ²⁰, 8², ²⁹, 10¹⁶, ²⁶, 11⁶, 13¹⁰).

God is " the Lord, dwelling Himself a Sovereign in heaven " (15⁴, cf. 3¹⁵, ²⁰, ³⁹, 11¹⁰, 15²⁵), but He is also in Israel's midst, " being well pleased that a sanctuary of " His " tabernacling should be set among them " (14³⁵).

### THE ADDITIONS TO DANIEL

In " The Song of the Three Holy Children," God is described as " the only God, and glorious over the whole world " (22). It is said that " He beholdeth the depths " (32). He is like man in that He loves (12). An angel of the Lord delivers Azarias and his fellows from the fire (26), but the three men speak directly to God out of the midst of the flames (1). He punishes the nation for its sins (4–7).

In " The History of Susanna " God is the everlasting God, who knows the secrets, who knows all things before they be (42). Sin is said to be done " in the sight of the Lord " (23). God dwells in heaven (35), and uses angels as His agents for the punishment of sinners (55, 59). But He is also near, hearing prayer and stirring up Daniel to be the spokesman of the injured woman (42–5). The story illustrates how " God saveth them that hope in Him " (60).

### THE EPISTLE OF JEREMY

This epistle, which is a tractate against idolatry, yields little information for our purpose. God is described as the active Ruler of nature (62). He punishes Israel for sin (2). He gives commands to Jeremy (1). He Himself cares for the souls of His people (7).* His angel is said to be with Israel (Ibid.). Israelites are charged to pray (6).

### SUMMARY

(1) *Titles*.—Great divine titles appear in the pages of most of these writers. God is styled the " Most

---

* Perhaps, however, this is meant not of God, but of the angel.

High " in Enoch 91–104, 72–82, and Interpolations, also in Judith and 3 Esdras. In the Similitudes of Enoch He is called the " Lord of Spirits." Titles of royal dignity are very commonly used. They appear in Judith (" King of the whole creation "), 3 Esdras (" the only Lord "), Enoch 91–104 (" the great King "), Enoch 37–70 (" the Lord of kings "), Enoch 37–70, and Interpolations (" the Lord of Spirits "), and 2 Maccabees (" the King of kings "). In the Psalms of Solomon, where there is no tendency to multiply great titles, God is called " King over the heavens." Only in 1 Maccabees is there reluctance to utter the name of God.

(2) *Everlastingness.*—With regard to God's everlastingness, we have only the following facts. In Enoch 37–70 it is said that His glory is for ever and ever, in Enoch 72–82 that He is eternal, in the Enoch Interpolations that His Name is mighty for ever, and in the story of Susanna that He is αἰώνιος. He is the Giver of eternal life according to the psalmist and the author of 2 Maccabees.

(3) *Omniscience.*—The omniscience of God is asserted in the Psalms of Solomon, Enoch 91–104, 37–70, 2 Maccabees, and the Story of Susanna. In 1 Maccabees knowledge of what passes on earth is predicated of Him ; and the other writers, with the exception of the author of 3 Esdras, teach or imply His foreknowledge.

(4) *Omnipotence.*—In Judith, 3 Esdras, and 2 Maccabees God is styled the " Almighty," and that He is omnipotent is unquestionably the thought of the Psalmist. In Enoch 91–104 and Interpolations God is represented as controlling the forces of nature. His might is referred to in the Similitudes of Enoch. Nothing is said of omnipotence in Enoch 72–82, nor

in 1 Maccabees, but in the former God is called " Lord of the whole creation," and in the latter He is said to decide by His fiat the fate of nations in conflict.

(5) *Spirituality.*—In this period the number of writers who attempt to describe God in heaven is small. Such descriptions are only found in the Similitudes and Interpolations of Enoch. The idea of a descent of God to earth only appears in the Additions to the Testaments, and it is clear that this writer's thought is of coming religious and national revival. In the two Enoch writers just mentioned we have the record of *visions*, and their pictures, conjured up by vivid religious imagination, do not enable us to form any idea as to their conceptions of the divine essence. In 2 Maccabees a miraculous intervention of God on behalf of Israel is called an " appearance " of God, and this is a clear illustration of the freedom with which such expressions are used in this literature when nothing of an anthropomorphic nature is intended. In Judith, 1 Maccabees, the Daniel Additions, and the Psalms of Solomon all such expressions are absent, and in 3 Esdras the author pointedly tries to avoid them, altering for his purpose sentences which he copies from the Hebrew text before him.

(6) *Anthropopathisms.*—Anthropopathisms appear in every book except in Enoch 72–82, the Story of Susanna, and perhaps the Epistle of Jeremy.

(7) *The Divine Remoteness or Nearness.*—(A) Much is said of angels by the writers of this period, but there is no doctrine quite like that which appears in some works of the preceding century. The notion that God sets angels or spirits over nations as a punishment for their sin is entirely absent. The doctrine of elemental angels, however, appears in the Enoch

Interpolations, and in Enoch 72–82 Uriel is the ruler of the stars. In the Psalms, also, angels give orders to the stars. The nearest approach to the idea of angelic viceroys over the affairs of men is made in the Similitudes of Enoch ; but in that work the superintending angels are only in charge of departments of service. In this work alone there appears the idea of a supernatural Messiah as the judge of men. There is less said of the activity of angels in the life of man in this world than in the preceding century. Such activity on their part is recognised in 2 Maccabees, the Daniel Additions, and the Enoch Interpolations. But in Enoch 91–104 the angels are not represented as acting thus in the present life, and 1 Maccabees has only a passing allusion to such action as having taken place once, while in Judith and 3 Esdras there is no reference at all to angels. In the Psalms, also, there is no allusion to angels as playing any part in the affairs of men.

Like their predecessors of the second century B.C., these writers believed in an unmediated action of God upon the fortunes of the world and man. That is made clear in the case of each of them, except the author of Enoch 72–82, who, however, is of little importance because his main interest is not theology, and, consequently, his allusions to the subject are only slight and occasional.

There is not much reference in the pages of these writers to the idea of God's active interest in the life of the individual. It appears, however, in the Daniel Additions and in the Psalms of Solomon.

Some of the writers think mainly or exclusively of God as active within Israel. In Judith it is taught that all that happens in the fortunes of the nation is of His will. In the Daniel Additions, 3 Esdras, and

1 Maccabees there is affirmation of a divine activity in the affairs of Israel. The two last, however, look out into the life of the world beyond Israel and see signs of the activity of God there also. In 1 Maccabees God is the Arbiter of battles, at least when Gentiles fight Israel, and He punishes Gentile tyrants. In 3 Esdras it is He who sets up kings. This broad view was apparently that also of the writer of the Similitudes, and in Enoch 91–104 the course of world-history is regarded as of the ordination of God. It is, however, in the Psalms of Solomon, and in 2 Maccabees that we have the clearest statements of the doctrine of God as active Sovereign over the affairs of mankind in general. There is thus no author in this period who sets God at a distance from this world, after the manner of the apocalyptist who wrote Enoch 1–36. Some writer has, however, inserted into the book of Enoch Interpolations which imply a deistic conception, but he stands alone among the writers of this century.

(B) The doctrine of angelic intermediaries between God and men appears again in this period. They are spoken of as ambassadors of God in Enoch 91–104, 72–82, and Interpolations. But there is also in every writer of this period, except Enoch 72–82, the assertion of an unmediated divine speech with man or influence upon man. It is commonly speech with, or influence upon, His chosen servants. A broader idea appears, however, sometimes, as for example in the Similitudes and Interpolations of Enoch, the Psalms of Solomon, 2 Maccabees, and the Song of the Three Children, where God is conceived of as exercising a direct influence on righteous men in general, whom He strengthens for doing right.*

* Cf. Chapter III. of this work.

6

The doctrine of angelic intercessors appears again in Enoch 37–70, and angels are intermediaries when men pray in Enoch 91–104. Elsewhere, the idea is not found, and men have direct access to God in supplication. One book only—Enoch 72–82—does not mention prayer.

### THE FIRST CENTURY A.D.

#### WISDOM

#### *Part* 1

God is " the Power " ($1^3$), " the Most High " ($6^3$), " the Sovereign Lord of all " ($6^7$), " the Almighty " ($7^{25}$). It is said that "He beareth witness of" man's "reins, and is a true observer of his heart, and a hearer of his tongue " ($1^6$). Gregg limits the force of this affirmation by saying that it is " because His deputy (Wisdom) lays them open to His mind." * But, as we shall endeavour to show, it is improbable that this writer thought of Wisdom as a personal deputy.

Anthropomorphisms are not in evidence, with the exception of obviously figurative expressions (e.g. God's hand, $5^{16}$). According to the best manuscripts, the author, after Gen. $1^{26}$, affirms that God made man " an image of His own proper Being " ($2^{23}$); but the variant—" an image of His own everlastingness " may be the true reading, for, although it is not so well supported, it fits the context. Be that, however, as it may, Ps. Solomon clearly conceives of God as not unlike man. God is jealous ($1^{10}$, $5^{17}$), and He loves ($3^9$, $4^{10}$, $7^{28}$, $8^3$). He is even described as searching out things ($4^6$, $6^3$), but this last is obviously a merely rhetorical utterance, since, as we have just seen, God

* Cambridge Bible, "Wisdom," p. xl.

is regarded by the writer as omniscient.  His spiritual
conception of God is seen in the fact that he teaches
the Divine Omnipresence :  " The Spirit of the Lord
hath filled the world " ($1^7$).  The Divine Immortality
is implied in what is said of the " hope full of immortality " which the righteous possess ($3^4$).

The chief difficulty of the book is as to the significance of Wisdom.  Wisdom, in one aspect, is "an
unerring knowledge of the things that are " ($7^{17}$).  In
one passage, at least, Wisdom is clearly an attribute of
Deity :  " He made all  things by His word, and by
His wisdom He formed man " ($9^1$).  But Wisdom is
also personified in this book, as the " artificer of all
things " ($7^{22}$, $8^6$) and the mother of all good things
($7^{12}$).   She is a holy spirit ($1^{4\,f.}$ cf. $7^{22}$), who loves man
($1^6$), orders all things graciously ($8^1$), chooses out God's
works ($8^4$), and sits on His throne ($9^4$).  She is guided
by God ($7^{15}$) and knows Him ($8^4$).  She pervades all
things ($7^{24}$) and passes into holy souls ($7^{27}$).  She is
" a breath of the power of God, a clear effulgence of
the glory of the Almighty . . . an effluence from
everlasting light, an unspotted mirror of the working
of God, and an image of His goodness " ($7^{25}$).  The
representation is not consistent with itself always, for
in $7^{22}$, $8^6$, Wisdom is described as the " artificer of all
things," but in $9^9$ she is simply said to have been
present when God was making the world.  In $6^{22}$
we read of Wisdom coming into being, but perhaps,
as Ewald suggests, we should understand μοι with
πῶς ἐγένετο and read :  " how she began for me." *
To sum up, Wisdom is either agent or spectator of
creation, she shares the government of God, she is an
all-pervading spirit, and she is God's means of grace
and self-revelation to men.

* Cambridge Bible, " Wisdom." p. 62.

It is difficult, perhaps impossible, to say precisely what this language really imports.  It looks as if the author had substituted one august Being for the crowd of angels, who elsewhere are regarded as intermediaries between God and man.  But scholars generally agree that there is no real hypostasis.  Wisdom is vividly personified, but not regarded as a personal agent of God.  Gregg takes the view that " she personifies the train of causal sequences that connect the act of will in the mind of God with the object on which He wills to act." *  Farrar says : " Wisdom is generally used to express the active redeeming principle which is at work in the world, the Divine Providence which protects the righteous because it is trusted in and apprehended by them." †  This last seems to the present writer to be probably the thought of our author.  Davidson says that in O.T. " God's Spirit is merely God in His efficiency, especially as giving life.  The Spirit of God is hardly considered another distinct from Him ; it is God exercising power, communicating Himself, or operating." ‡  It is far from improbable that our author means the same thing by Wisdom.  Of both Wisdom and the Spirit, he says that they fill all things or are in all things ($1^7$, $7^{24}$, $8^1$).  Wisdom is said to be a Spirit ($1^6$), a Holy Spirit ($1^{4\ f.}$).  Moreover, in $9^{17}$ we read : " Whoever gained knowledge of Thy counsel, except Thou gavest wisdom and sendest Thy holy Spirit from on high ? "  Wisdom and the Spirit are here regarded as one and the same.  The lines are clearly in poetic parallelism.  " The Spirit," says H. B. Swete, " is sometimes identified with Wisdom (Wisd. $1^{5\ f.}$, where

* Op. cit., pp. xxxv. f.
† Speaker's Comm., p. 478.
‡ " Theology of O.T.," p. 193.

the linking of the clauses seems to leave no doubt of the author's meaning, cf. $9^{17}$), sometimes regarded as its indwelling power ($7^{22\,\text{f.}}$)." * It seems probable, therefore, that Wisdom is in this book, like our word Providence, a reverential synonym for God, acting on the world and man.

Gregg says : " It is as a transcendent God that the book presents Him. He is, indeed, Creator, Artificer . . . but not directly. His creative action was mediated through Wisdom." † That is, by Gregg's own definition, God set in motion the sequence of causes which at last eventuated in the Creation. But it is far from certain that this is the writer's thought, and no remoteness of God from this world will be implied, if, as the present writer thinks, Wisdom is simply a periphrasis for God in action. Moreover, God hears the prayers of Ps. Solomon ($7^7$, $8^{21}$), He is Himself the Teacher of the author ($7^{15,\,17}$), He is the Friend of the righteous, manifesting Himself to them ($7^{14,\,27}$, $1^2$), and He is regarded as active in human affairs ($3^{5,\,16-19}$, $4^{3-6},\,^{10\,\text{f.}}$). Indeed, He is the actual ruler of mankind, for Wisdom, we read, " reacheth from one end (of the world) to the other with full strength and ordereth all things graciously " ($8^1$).

### Part 2

In $10^1$–$11^1$, which may be by the author of neither of the main parts of this book, nothing is predicated of Wisdom but what might be affirmed of God's Spirit or Providence. The verses celebrate a series of divine interventions on behalf of the forefathers of

* D.B., art. " Holy Spirit," p. 405.
† Op. cit., p. xl.

Israel, and tell how at the Red Sea God's hand fought on their behalf ($10^{20}$).

In $11^2$–$19^{22}$ God is called the "Sovereign Lord" ($11^{26}$, $13^9$). He foreknows the future of men ($19^1$). Stress is laid on the fact that He is the All-powerful ($11^{17}$), whose might none can withstand, before whom the whole world "is as a grain in a balance and as a drop of dew that at morning cometh down upon the earth" ($11^{21\,f.}$). He can make away at once by one stern word with offenders ($12^9$). He has no equal to whom He shall answer for His conduct ($12^{12-14}$). He is perfect in power ($12^{17}$). The power is His whensoever He has the will ($12^{18}$).

In the usual style of religious literature, the writer refers to the hand of God ($11^{17}$, $16^{15}$). There is, however, nothing that suggests doubt of God's spirituality. But He is like man. He is described as "He who is" ($13^1$). This, however, does not mean for the writer that He is the Existent "in the sense that no other quality than pure existence may be attributed to Him." * On the contrary, our author speaks of Him as hating and loving ($12^4$, $11^{24,\,26}$, $16^{26}$).

Wisdom, from $11^2$ onward, sinks into a very subordinate place, never once being personified. Instead of saying, in the manner of the earlier chapters, that Wisdom guides the ship of the mariner, this writer says: "Thy Providence, O Father, guideth it along" ($14^3$). Wisdom is here only a divine attribute ($14^5$). God Himself, and not Wisdom, is Creator or Artificer ($11^{17}$, $13^1$, $14^{11}$, $15^{11}$). In $18^{15}$ the "Word of God" is spoken of as "leaping out of the royal throne, a stern warrior." But there is no reason to regard this as other than rhetorical language, and in $16^{12}$, where we read that it is God's Word "which healeth all things,"

* Gregg, op. cit. in loc.

the thought, as Gregg suggests, is like that in Psalm 107[20], where the idea is simply that men are healed by the expressed will of God.

The writer speaks of " him who was punishing " and calls him " the destroyer " (18[22-25]). It is possible that there is reference here to an angel, but perhaps, as Gregg suggests, the destroyer is the impersonal Word.*

God's interventions in human life are much dwelt upon. His punishments of guilty nations are detailed (12[2-10], 16[1 ff.]). His hand guided the ark (14[6]). In the wilderness He gave Israel the water and the quails (11[4-7], 16[2]). He troubled the ungodly (11[9 f.]). Nor is He a merely intervening God. It is His Providence normally that guides ships across the sea (14[3]). He stands by the side of Israel in every time and place (19[22]). He orders all things (15[1]). His " incorruptible Spirit " is in all things (12[1]). That is, as the context suggests, He is the Preserver of all, the Giver and Sustainer of life (11[25]). No reference is made to divine speech with men, but it is said that He troubled the firstborn of Egypt with dreams (18[19]). Israel, however, calls upon Him in prayer (11[4]), and it is said to be man's duty to speak to God in thanksgiving and pleading (16[28]).

Ps. Solomon speaks of God as creating the world " out of formless matter " (11[17]), and E. J. Hirsch observes that "the uncertainty in the verb ($\kappa\tau i\zeta\omega$) descriptive of God's part in creation suggests that the old Biblical conception of the Creator's functions is in this book attenuated to the bringing into order of formless primeval matter." † But, as Gregg says : " The use of $\kappa\tau i\zeta\epsilon\iota\nu$ here is non-committal ; it leaves

* Op. cit., pp. 178, 180.
† J.E., art. " God," p. 3.

the origin of matter out of sight and deals merely
with the arrangement of matter." *

$$I^{1-15}$$

God is here regarded as like man in that He has
" wrath and indignation " (14). He is approachable
to man (3, 13). He determines how long the Babylonian sovereigns shall live, and favour for Israel in
their sight is His gift (11 f.).

$$I^{15}-3^8$$

God is " the Lord Almighty " ($3^{1, 4}$). He " sits for
ever," while man perishes evermore ($3^3$). He knows
beforehand that Israel will not hearken to His voice
($2^{30}$). In the vivid and natural language of religion,
the penitents pray : " Look down from Thy holy
house and consider us. Incline Thine ear, O Lord,
and hear, open Thine eyes and see " ($2^{16}$). The writer
refers to God's wrath ($2^{13}$).

There is no teaching, express or implied, as to the
divine government of the world at large, but it is
recognised that God brought Israel out of Egypt and
has punished Israel for sin ($1^{19}$, $2^{10}$). He is styled the
" God of Israel " ($2^{11}$, $3^1$), and Fairweather concludes
that " Baruch's idea of God is simply that He is the
Guardian of Israel." † This is, however, too large a
conclusion from the premises. Naturally the suppliants, absorbed in their own troubles, do not turn
aside to give their ideas of the attitude of God to
other races. He is, however, conceived of as near to

---

* Op. cit., p. 110.

† D.B., art. " Development of Doctrine in the Apocryphal
Period," p. 277.

Israel.  He dwells on high in " His holy house" (2¹⁶),
but is accessible to the cry of His people.  To them
He has spoken by the prophets (1²¹, 2²⁸).  He has
put His fear into their hearts (3⁷).

There is no mention of angels.

### 3⁹–4⁴

" He that knoweth all things," says this writer,
" knoweth her (Wisdom).  He found her out with His
understanding. . . . He hath found out all the way
of knowledge " (3³², ³⁶ ᶠ·).  This is part of a highly
rhetorical passage, and obviously involves no denial
of the Divine Omniscience.  God is described as sending forth the light, calling it, and being obeyed (3³³).
Perhaps in 3³⁵ He is represented as the Incomparable
One—" This is our God, and there shall none other
be accounted of in comparison of Him."  But it may
be that we should translate :  " This is our God and
no other [people] shall be accounted as belonging to
Him."  This suits the context at least as well as the
R.V. rendering does.

Anthropomorphisms are absent.  It is said, however, that Israel is God's beloved (3³⁶), and reference
is made to that which pleases Him (4⁴).

In a solitary allusion to the abode of God, the
writer speaks of His house as great, having no end,
high and immeasurable (3²⁴).  Angels do not appear
in these verses, nor is there any reference to prayer,
but God is said to have made revelation to Israel, and
there is recognition of the fact that He punishes the
nation for sin (3³⁶, 4⁴, 3⁹⁻¹³).

### 4⁵–5⁹

A frequent title for God here is " the Everlasting "
(αἰώνιος).  It occurs in 4¹⁰, ¹⁴, ²⁰, ²², ²⁴, ³⁵, 5².  God is

the "Everlasting, your Saviour," "the Holy One"
($4^{22}$). There is no allusion to omniscience. Anthro-
pomorphisms are not used, but the writer speaks of
God's wrath, and Israel is said to have provoked Him
($4^{6,\ 9,\ 25}$, $4^7$). He is described as remembering Israel,
but that is, of course, poetic ($4^{27}$).

Demons are twice spoken of ($4^{7,\ 35}$), but angels are
not mentioned. God is accessible to praying men
($4^{21,\ 27}$). He brought up Israel ($4^8$). He has punished
Israel ($4^{14}$), and will punish Babylon ($4^{34\ f.}$). He uses
that nation when He inflicts penalty on His people
($4^{15}$).

### THE ASSUMPTION OF MOSES

God is to this writer the "Most High," "the eternal
God" ($10^7$), "the Lord of heaven" ($2^4$, $4^4$), "King
on the lofty throne" ($4^2$), "the Lord manifold and
incomprehensible" ($11^{16}$), "who hath foreseen all
things for ever" ($12^{13}$). He is poetically described as
about to "arise from His royal throne" and "go
forth from His holy habitation" ($10^3$). Similarly,
His right hand is spoken of ($12^9$). Otherwise, anthropomorphic expressions are absent from this work.
But God is said to have compassion, to remember,
and to be angry ($4^5$, $8^1$, $10^3$).

The only allusion to angels is in the statement that,
at the establishment of the kingdom, Michael will be
appointed leader and avenger of Israel ($10^2$). But,
inconsistently with this, it is added that the avenging
of Israel will be God's own unmediated act. "The
Most High will arise, the Eternal God alone, to punish
the Gentiles" ($10^7$). The doctrine of the book is that
God governs the world even down to the smallest
details. "All the nations which are in the earth God

hath created as He hath us, and He hath foreseen them
and us from the beginning of the creation of the
earth unto the end of the age, and nothing has been
neglected by Him, even to the least thing, but all
things He hath foreseen and caused all to come
forth" ($12^4$). This is much more than divine foreknowledge. It is God's ordination of events. God
is " the Lord of heaven " indeed ($2^4$, $4^4$), but He is
also the " Lord of the world " ($1^{11}$). He is " Lord of
all, King on the lofty throne, who rules the world "
($4^2$). " The lights of the heaven, the foundation of
the earth, are under the signet-ring of His right hand"
($12^9$).

There is very slight reference to prayer. Daniel,
however, is described as praying for Israel, and Moses
is said to be their intercessor during his life-time, and
afterwards in heaven ($4^1$, $11^{17}$, $12^6$). But 2 Maccabees, which clearly teaches God's approachableness by
praying men on earth, also contains the doctrine of
the intercession of dead saints, so that the doctrine
of the mediatorship of Moses in heaven need not imply
that, to the mind of our author, God was distant from
suppliant souls of men.

### THE APOCALYPSE OF BARUCH

### A¹

The implication of this little apocalypse with its
inspired foretelling of the future is, of course, the foreknowledge of God.

His control of all natural forces is implied in chapter 27. Angels are not once referred to, and the
Messiah is merely a lay figure with no real rôle ($29^3$).
The author regards God as determining the course of
events in the last days. That time, he tells us, is

divided into twelve parts, and " each one of them is reserved for that which is appointed to it " (27¹). The misfortunes that will befall men then are to be of His ordination (27¹⁻¹³). This writer is, however, entirely occupied with the final crisis and the events that are to precede it. Consequently, he gives us no material for determining how far he conceived of God as governing this world or even Israel normally. God is, however, thought of as near to Baruch. He speaks to God, and God speaks to him (28⁶ ᶠ, 27¹, 29¹).

## A²

Like A¹, A² implies the divine foreknowledge. But A² surveys a longer portion of world-history than A¹ does, and he teaches the operation of a divine judgment on nations through the ages (36, 39). God is regarded as fixing the period of Rome's supremacy, for He is represented as saying : " It will come to pass, when the time of his consummation that he should fall has approached, then the time of the principate of My Messiah will be revealed " (39⁷).

As in A¹, God hears Baruch's prayer (38¹), and He speaks to Baruch without any intermediary (39¹). Moreover, A² affirms that God " always enlightens those who are led by understanding " (38¹). As in A¹, angels do not appear, but the Messiah is here the active agent of God (40¹ ᶠ).

## A³

This writer repeatedly calls God " the Mighty One " and the " Most High." He dwells on God's power and wisdom. For Him " nothing is too hard." He does " everything easily by a nod " (54²). Man cannot comprehend His " deep thought of life " (54¹²),

and the world was established " according to the multitude of the intelligence of Him who sent it " (56$^4$).
Man cannot laud Him as is befitting or tell the glory
of His " beauty " (54$^8$). He alone knows " of aforetime the deep things of the world . . . and the end
of the seasons " (54$^1$). " He alone knows what will
befall " (69$^2$). A$^3$ speaks of God's wrath, His long-
suffering, and His love (64$^4$, 59$^6$, 61$^7$).

God dwells in heaven (59$^3$, 64$^4$, 67$^2$). Innumerable
angels stand in His presence and form a hierarchy
(64$^4$, 67$^2$, 56$^{14}$, 59$^3$, 59$^{11}$). One of them destroyed
Sennacherib's host at God's order (63$^{6\ t.}$). God also
employs the Messiah as judge of the nations (72$^2$).
Baruch receives revelation by means of a vision and
through Ramiel. He is " the angel who presides over
true visions," and is sent by God to Baruch (55$^3$).
On the other hand, while the angels are said to be in
God's presence (67$^2$), it is affirmed also that the king
of Babylon boasts over Israel " in the presence of the
Most High " (67$^7$). Baruch prays directly to God
(54$^1$), and God makes revelation not to Baruch only,
but to " those who fear Him " (54$^4$). " Thou re-
vealest," says Baruch, " what is hidden to the pure "
(54$^5$). Moreover, A$^3$ teaches God's control of all
creatures and all events. " The things which befall
in their times Thou bringest about by Thy word "
(54$^1$). " With Thy counsel Thou dost govern all the
creatures which Thy right hand has created " (54$^{13}$).
God is regarded as Sovereign over nature, withholding
rains on account of sin (62$^2$). God is more remote in
A$^3$ than in A$^1$ and in A$^2$, since He does not speak
Himself to Baruch. Yet He is by no means altogether distant, who hears His servant's prayer and
inspires his dream, in whose presence a heathen
king stands as he boasts on earth, who exercises an

effective sovereignty over nature and mankind, and who makes revelation to all the pure in heart.

## B¹

This writer frequently calls God " the Most High " and " the Mighty One." He neither asserts nor implies the doctrine of Omniscience, for the future is looked upon as altogether conditioned by Israel's obedience or disobedience.

No anthropomorphisms are used, but reference is made to God's love and compassion (78³, 81⁴). Except for one passage in which the writer speaks of a merciful purpose of God for Gentiles (1⁴), and an allusion to them as coming to glorify Zion (68⁴), B¹ is entirely absorbed in the present distress of Israel and the prospects of that people. The nations only come within his purview when God uses them to punish Israel (e.g. 78⁵, 79¹ ᶠ·). In that sorrow of Israel which occupies his mind he clearly sees God's hand (1⁴, 77¹⁰, 78⁵).

Angels only appear as God's agents in connection with the fall of the city (6³–8²), and there is no Messiah in this apocalypse. No allusion is made to God's abode, except in an obviously poetic reference to the " throne of the Most High " (46⁴). Baruch has access to Him in prayer, and stands in His presence (3⁴). All the people are exhorted to pray diligently (84¹⁰). Moreover, God speaks to Baruch without intermediary (1¹, 4¹).

## B²

Lofty titles for God occur repeatedly—" the Most High," " the Mighty One," " the Lofty One." He is the Omniscient. He will " examine the secret thoughts and that which is laid up in the secret chambers of all the members of man (83³). The meditation of the reins of sinners will be tried in flame (48³⁹). God explores the limits of the heights and scrutinises the depths of the darkness (48⁵). Man cannot comprehend His intelligence or recount His thoughts (75³). He alone is immortal and past finding out (21¹⁰). " To Thee only," says Baruch, " does this belong, that Thou shouldest do forthwith whatever Thou dost wish " (21⁷). B² uses the analogy of the human personality quite freely. He speaks of God's nod, of His great thought and indignation, of His wrath and His compassions (48¹⁰, 21⁶, 48¹⁴⁻¹⁸).

Angels form a court about God. Armies innumerable stand before Him and minister quietly in their orders at His nod (48¹⁰). Living creatures of great beauty are under His throne (51¹¹). God rules in nature, sending rain in drops by number (21⁸). He ordains the course of things in this world, summoning the advent of the times, arranging the methods of the seasons (48²). He delivered Israel from Egypt (75⁷). He punishes Israel for sin (13⁹). He disciplines the righteous (15⁸). As we shall show in the next chapter, in the midst of all his bitter perplexity over Israel's sorrows, this writer holds firmly by his belief in God's government of Israel.

Baruch stands to pray " in the presence of the mighty One " (21³, 48⁴⁴). God uses no angel as a means of communication, but He is represented as speaking to Baruch from a distance. " I, Baruch, was standing upon Mount Zion, and lo ! a voice came from the height " (13¹). " Lo ! the heavens were opened and I saw, and power was given me, and a voice was heard from on high " (22¹). B² does here seem to represent God as somewhat remote. Was this, however, a device born of his reverence for God ? It seems probable that it was, especially as the writer believed himself to be gifted with an immediate inspiration. The God who hears the cry of His servant and answers, who reads the hearts of men and rules nature and mankind, is in very deed no distant Deity.

## B³

Here, again, God is the "Most High" and "the Mighty One" (vv. 8, 12 ; 2 f.). He is longsuffering (8).

The only other matter calling for attention here is the writer's belief that sinful men need the prayers of the righteous to whom God is accessible. In times past, he says, God heard the intercessory prayers of such men. But he deplores the fact that they are now dead, and, unlike the author of 2 Maccabees, he maintains that those saints do not make intercession for sinners in the heavenly world (2 f.). The brief paragraph gives us no material for determining how far its author thought of God as ruling this world.

## S

In this section God becomes remote even from Israel, whom He entirely forsakes.

It must be remembered that God is thought of as very near to all the authors in these apocalypses, except the despairing writer of the S section (10⁶–12⁴), for the basis of the whole is a belief in His inspiration of their work.

### 4 ESDRAS

*The Salathiel Apocalypse* (S).—S uses frequently the title—" the Most High." God, we read, abides for ever. His chambers are in the air. His throne is inestimable. Before Him hosts of angels stand trembling ($8^{20}$ f.). He dwells above the heavens ($4^{21}$). He is the All-powerful, whose look dries up the depths, who changes His angels to wind and fire by His word. At His indignation the mountains melt away ($8^{22}$ f.). He knows beforehand the ends of the times ($3^{14}$). He is cognisant of the works and feelings of Esdras ($6^{32}$, $10^{39,\ 50}$). In $3^{18}$ f. it is said of God, bringing Israel to Sinai: "Thou bowedst the heavens also, and didst shake (or set fast) the earth and movedst the whole world and madedst the depths to tremble and troubledst the [course of that] age. And Thy glory went through four gates, of fire, and of earthquake, and of wind, and of cold." On this G. H. Box comments: "The writer, in accordance with the developed Jewish conceptions of Jahveh's majesty and transcendence, pictures God as appearing in theophany on earth (at Sinai), in a gradual descent from His throne in the highest of the heavens, through the lower heavens by their successive 'gates.'" * But there seems to be here a pointed avoidance of any anthropomorphic expression. The sentence is in striking contrast to the account in Exodus, where it is said: "The Lord came down upon Mount Sinai" (Exod. $19^{20}$), as well as to such descriptions as we have in Enoch 1–36, 83–90. Reference is made by this writer to God's purpose to visit His creation ($5^{56}$, $6^6$), and to the fact that the saved hasten to behold God's face ($7^{98}$). It is also said: "O Lord, Thou didst show Thyself among us unto our fathers in the wilderness" ($9^{29}$). But the first and last of these are obviously expressions of a poetic character, and the second is well compared by G. H. Box to that in St. Matt. $5^8$—"The pure in heart . . . shall see God." †

* "The Ezra Apocalypse," in loc.        † Ibid.

7

Free use is made of anthropopathisms. God has compassion, long-suffering, and love ($7^{133 \text{ f.}}$, $3^{14}$, $4^{23}$, $5^{40}$, $8^{47}$). He rejoices and can grieve ($7^{60 \text{ f.}}$). He hastens ($4^{34}$). He considers ($6^6$, $9^{20}$).

S denies the idea of any mediatorial agency being used by God, either at creation or in the final judgment ($6^{1-6}$). God, he says, did fashion the earth, and that Himself alone ($3^4$). But apparently, throughout this apocalypse, God is represented as speaking to Esdras by a mediator. It seems otherwise in $8^{37 \text{ ff.}}$. Esdras addresses the Being with whom he is conversing as God ($8^{44 \text{ f.}}$). The speaker is only referred to as " he," and he addresses Esdras as if he were God Himself. But in those passages, where it is clear that he who speaks is an angel, both he and Esdras use the same style of speech (see $5^{40, \ 42}$, $6^{1-6}$ and $5^{41, \ 45, \ 56}$). Of the paragraph $5^{56}$–$6^6$, G. H. Box says : " In this section God is directly addressed, and God is the speaker." * But the same thing may be said of the preceding paragraphs, yet there it is expressly said : " The angel . . . said unto me " ($5^{31}$). $6^1$, just like the other paragraphs, begins : " And he [i.e. the angel] said unto me." Apparently, therefore, throughout S God is represented as using an angel as His messenger.

In $4^{36 \text{ f.}}$ it is said that the great consummation of all things will come when the number of the righteous is fulfilled. God has measured the times and numbered the seasons, and will not stir till the measure is fulfilled. We have here, obviously, the notion of a divine ordering of the general course of world-history. S traces the history of God's active interest in Israel from the times of Abraham till the days of the Exile ($3^{16-27}$). Death comes by God's fiat ($3^7$). He sent

* " The Ezra Apocalypse," p. 63.

the Flood (3$^{9-11}$).   If Babylon is preserved and dominates over Zion, it is by His sovereign will that it is so (3$^{27-30}$).   Amid all the sore perplexity of his mind over Israel's sorrows, the writer holds firmly by his faith in God's active government of the affairs of mankind.

In 10$^{47}$ we have the idea of a dwelling of God in Zion from Solomon's time onwards.   It is to be added that God is thought of as near to Esdras, for the book is a record of his answered prayers, and of course, its basal idea is His nearness to His servant, whom He inspires to write this apocalypse.

Sometimes, in the stress of feeling, the prophet uses great freedom of speech with God.   He declares that God ought to punish Israel with His own hands (5$^{30}$).   He makes daring suggestion in 8$^{42}$ (cf. Chapter II of this work).   In the former case he offers a kind of apology for his speech, and in the latter he receives a sharp rebuke for his impious idea (5$^{34}$, 8$^{47}$).   It seems, therefore, likely that S is here simply uttering the sentiments of his countrymen for the purpose of rebuking all such ideas.   Perhaps, as Mr. Box, commenting on 5$^{38}$, suggests : " The angel has only been introduced to enable the dialogue to be carried on with a freedom which would sometimes prove embarrassing to so pious a writer as this apocalyptist if God were being directly addressed." *

*The Esdras Apocalypse* (E).—Here, again, God is spoken of as " the Most High."   It is said that He " will draw nigh to visit them that dwell upon the earth " (6$^{18}$, cf. 9$^{2}$), and that He will be " revealed upon the seat of judgment " (7$^{33}$).

One of the two Arabic versions has in this last verse the words : " He shall be seen sitting." †

* Op. cit. in loc.          † See Box, op. cit. in loc.

Anthropopathisms are not in evidence, save for one reference to the divine compassion and long-suffering (Ibid.).

Messiah appears in E, but it is not he who will judge mankind. God Himself is the final Judge (7$^{33}$). Of God's normal rule among men nothing is said, for E's whole interest is in eschatological matters. The prophet, who prays directly to God, receives an answer by an angel (4$^{52}$), but in one passage he is said to hear a voice like the sound of many waters (6$^{17}$). Possibly, but not certainly, this is God's own voice.*

*The Vision of the Eagle* (A).—The titles " the Most High " and " the Mighty " are used, but A does not speak of omniscience. Foreknowledge is, however, implied.

A strongly asserts the reality of God's government. He declares that God will say to the eagle, i.e. the Roman Empire : "Art thou not it that remainest of the four beasts whom I made to rule in My world, that the end of My times might come through them ? " (11$^{39}$). Of the last three kings or kingdoms he says that God shall raise them up (12$^{23}$). A writes in a time of cruel oppression, but his strong conviction is that God is the active Overlord of His own world, determining who shall reign in it. God speaks to Esdras apparently by means of an angel (12$^{10}$ ff.), and His final judgment is to be executed by a Messiah (12$^{32}$ f.). But Esdras addresses God directly, and God is in unmediated contact with Esdras, whom He instructs by means of a dream (11$^{1}$ f.).

*The Vision of the Son of Man* (M).—The apocalypse implies that the " Most High " has foreknowledge.

---

* In Ezekiel 1$^{24}$, which is, perhaps, the basis of this, it is the noise of angels' wings that is " like the noise of great waters." Cf. Box, op. cit., p. 73.

If we disregard the passages ascribed to R by Kabisch, there is nothing in M about a general divine government of the world. We have only the statement that God intervened to help the ten exiled tribes (13⁴⁴). It is not God Himself, but His Son who will destroy the sinful nations (13³⁸).

Esdras obtains revelations through a dream, which is interpreted to him apparently by an angel, who sometimes speaks of God in the third person, but sometimes addresses Esdras as if he were God Himself (13³⁷ ᶠ·).

*The Second Esdras Apocalypse* (E²).—There is little here for our purpose. " The Most High " (14⁴²), speaks to Esdras, as to Moses, out of the bush (14¹ ᶠ·). He inspires the prophet to rewrite the Old Testament, and the apocryphal books, in answer to his prayer (14²², ²⁵). He shows Moses the secrets of the times and the ends of the seasons (14⁵). The only anthropopathism is in the statement that Esdras hopes to find favour with God (14²²).

*The Additions of the Editor* (R).—In answer to his prayer, Esdras receives the Word of God, whom he styles " the Most High " and " the Almighty " (13¹², ²³). It comes to him apparently by means of an angel, but God also communicates with him by a dream (10⁵⁸). It is said that God " governeth the times and such things as fall in their seasons " (13⁵⁸). No expression of an anthropopathic character is used except one resembling that noted above in E² (6¹¹).

It looks as if the editor had sought to insist on the fact that God Himself is the Deliverer of His creation, for, according to the Latin version, we have in 13²⁶ the words—" The Most High . . . who, by His own self (*qui per semetipsum*) shall deliver His creature."

But it is possible that this is a reading arising from

a misunderstanding of the original text (cf. Box, op. cit., p. 293).

### 3 MACCABEES *

A great variety of reverential titles for God appears here. In the brief compass of this work we have the following: "The Most High God" ($1^{9, 16}$, $3^{11}$, $4^{16}$, etc.), "the Almighty" ($2^{2, 8}$, etc.), "the Holy God" ($6^{1, 29}$, $7^{10}$), "the Holy King" ($2^{13}$), "the Almighty, heavenly, living God" ($6^{28}$), "the Eternal One"—αἰώνιος ($6^{12}$, $7^{16}$), "the Lord of the whole creation" ($2^{7}$), "the Lord of all power" ($5^{50}$, $7^{9}$), "Protector of the universe" (6), "Lord of the universe" ($6^{5}$), "the glorious God and King of kings" ($5^{35}$), "King most powerful, Most High, Almighty God" ($6^{2}$). He is the all-seeing God, and stands in need of nothing ($2^{21, 9}$).

The writer tells how, in answer to the prayer of the Jews in an hour of trouble that God would deliver them by "a glorious manifestation" ($5^{8, 50}$), and not turn away His face from them ($6^{15}$), two angels descended from heaven for their assistance ($6^{18}$). "The most glorious, almighty, and true God, manifesting His holy countenance, opened the doors of heaven" (Ibid.).

Reference is made to the pity, the hatred, and the love of God ($5^{7}$, $6^{9}$, $2^{10}$).

Angels only appear in this work in the passage just cited. God's habitation, it is said, is the heaven of heavens unapproachable by men ($2^{15}$). Thither men turn their eyes when they pray ($5^{9}$, $6^{17}$). But God has also glorified Zion with His "magnificent presence" ($2^{9}$). He has placed His glory among His people ($2^{16}$). Our author repeatedly affirms God's

* The citations from 3 and 4 Maccabees are given here with the chapters and verses of the LXX.

sovereignty over all His works. He is the only Governor, the Ruler of all creation, who judges those who do anything in insolence and pride ($2^{2\ \text{f.}}$, cf. $5^7$, $6^{2,\ 12}$). This writer dwells on divine interventions to punish or deliver men. But this is not all. God is to him the active Monarch of His universe, whose Providence is invincible ($4^{20}$). Reference is often made to His approachableness in prayer by His troubled people (e.g. $1^{16,\ 24}$, $2^{1}$ ff., $5^{25,\ 50}$, $6^{2,\ 17}$).

### 4 MACCABEES

Great divine titles are not much used in this book. Once God is styled " the only living God " ($5^{24}$), and sometimes the writer uses a periphrasis, e.g. he speaks of a " just and paternal Providence " ($9^{24}$), a " divine and all-wise Providence " ($13^{19}$), and " Divine Justice " ($4^{21}$, $18^{22}$). But usually he simply speaks of " God." God is so great in knowledge that He understands the inward cry of the speechless. " Even though ye take away my tongue," says a martyr, " yet God heareth even the silent" ($10^{18}$). The writer has no word which suggests that God is like man in form, but he speaks of God's sympathy and His wrath ($5^{25}$, $9^{32}$). Once he refers to the divine justice as being provoked ($4^{21}$). The immortality of God is clearly implied, for He is said to give " deathless souls " to the martyrs ($18^{23}$).

There is only one allusion to angels ($4^{10}$). How near God is to man, according to this author, is strikingly shown in the citation made above from $10^{18}$. The phrases cited above concerning Providence show his belief in a divine government. Antiochus, it is said, " has received good things and the kingdom from God " ($12^{11}$). It is shown how God shielded the

Temple by an angelic intervention, and how He punishes sinners (4$^{10, 21}$, 18$^{5, 22}$).

## SLAVONIC ENOCH ; OR, THE BOOK OF THE SECRETS OF ENOCH

In this work God is called " the Lord of lords " (39$^8$).* He is the " Eternal One " (33$^4$), the " Eternal King " (64$^3$), " the Everlasting King " (1$^8$), or, as B reads in this last passage, " the Almighty." "Nothing done is concealed before the Lord " (65$^5$). " The Lord sees everything ; whatever man meditates in his heart, and what counsel he plans, and every thought is continually before the Lord " (66$^3$, cf. 53$^3$). The author professes to give an account of an actual visit to the heavens, where Enoch saw God " from afar, sitting on His lofty throne " (20$^3$). " I have seen the face of the Lord," says Enoch, " as it were iron that is heated in the fire, and when brought out sends forth sparks and burns . . . the eyes of the Lord shining like a ray of the sun and striking with terror human eyes " (39$^{3 f.}$). This is not found in the manuscript B. Again, " I saw the vision of the face of the Lord like iron burnt in the fire and brought forth and emitting sparks and it burns. So I saw the face of the Lord, but the face of the Lord cannot be told. It is wonderful and awful, and very terrible. And who am I that I should tell of the unspeakable being of God and His wonderful face ? " (22$^{1 f.}$). This is according to A, and in Sok we have a similar but slightly different version of the story. " I also saw the Lord face to face. And His face was very glorious, marvellous and terrible, threatening and strange. Who

* The reading in A is : " The heavenly Ruler, the Lord of the living and the dead."

am I to tell of the incomprehensible existence of the Lord, and His face wonderful and not to be spoken of ? " B, however, not only omits these verses, but also significantly adds, after the statement in verse 4— " I fell down "—these words : " and could not see the Lord God." Movement is predicated of God. Before creation He alone " held His course among the invisible things like the sun from the east to the west, and from the west to the east " (24⁴). He came to visit the earth " for the sake of Adam " (58¹). He will come again for a second and last time (32¹, 42⁵). When He comes into Paradise He rests by the tree of life (8³).

The writer appears to be teaching the crudest doctrine of a Deity possessed of bodily form. But there are other facts to be taken into account in the presentation. The right hand of the Lord, it is said, fills the heavens (39⁵). His form is " measureless, and to Him there is no end " (39⁶). Clearly this is symbolic language. It is suggestive, also, that Enoch is said to have seen the angels in heaven as well as God ; yet they are described as " incorporeal hosts " (Introduction). Moreover, God Himself is said to be " inconceivable " (Ibid.) and " invisible " (48⁵). B, however, omits this last and the whole chapter in which it is contained.

God made man, it is said, after His own image and likeness (65²), and our author describes God as devising and feeling in the manner of man. " I planned," says God, " to lay the foundation, and to make the visible creation " (24⁵). His love for Enoch, His anger, and His hatred are referred to (Introduction, 18⁸, 61¹, 63⁴, 66²). But He needs no counsellor and has no inheritor. His " thought is without change " (33⁴).

According to one passage, God predetermines the

conduct of all men. " I have written down," says
Enoch, " all the works of every man before his creation
which is done in the case of all men for ever. And
no man can say or unsay what I have written with
my hand " (53² ᶠ·). This is a clear assertion of a divine
foreordination of every man's conduct, a fore-ordination against which the will of man is powerless. But
B omits important words, and changes the meaning
of the passage : " I have written down all the works
of every man. And no man can destroy what I have
written with my hand." It is certainly difficult to
see how the author can have made such a statement
as that which A gives us, and then have followed it
immediately by the pointless warning : " And now,
my children, pay attention to all the words of your
father, which I say unto you, that ye may not grieve
afterwards " (53⁴). The author's doctrine of recompense and what he says of Adam (30¹⁵) imply his
belief that man has some real though limited freedom.
It looks as though the text has here suffered altera-
tion at the hands of the copyist who wrote A. Charles,
who prefers A to B, admits that A contains interpolations and is very corrupt,* and Tennant argues that,
even if B is a condensation of the original Greek text,
A may be an expansion of it.†

Angels are the messengers of God (1⁸, 21³), His
agents for a variety of purposes (5¹ ᶠ·, 8⁸, 11⁴, 14²), and
His viceroys ruling sun, moon, and stars (4¹, 19²).
They hold in subjection all living things, both in
heaven and earth, having authority over seasons,
rivers, and fruits, and all souls of men, writing down
the works of men (19³⁻⁵). They " superintend the
good or evil condition of the world " (19²).

* Edition of Slav. Enoch, p. xv.
† " The Fall and Original Sin," p. 205.

God is, on the other hand, Himself the Creator of the world. Wisdom is merely an attribute. For though the writer represents God as saying, " I ordered My wisdom to make man " (30⁸), this is but graphic speech, and he adds: " All this . . . He has arranged by His wisdom " (48⁴). " God made man," he says, " with His own hands " (44¹). He tells how God said, " I will bring a deluge upon the earth " (34³), and how He ordained death for Adam's sin (30¹⁶).

Of direct speech of God with man we have only the record that Enoch was twice addressed in heaven by Him (22⁵, 24¹ ff.) and that He spoke to Adam (30¹⁵). The only allusions to prayer are in the two statements that Enoch refused to intercede for the offending angels, and that afterwards he acceded to their request (7⁴, 18⁷). In a notable passage, not found, however, in B, the author teaches the Divine Omnipresence. " If ye look at the heavens, there is the Lord, as the Lord made the heavens. If ye look at the earth, then the Lord is there, since the Lord made firm the earth and established every creature in it. If ye scrutinise the depths of the sea and everything under the earth, there is also the Lord. For the Lord created all things " (66⁴ f.).

### THE APOCALYPSE OF ABRAHAM

The oft-repeated title of God in this book is " He who is before the world." He is the great God (1), the Holy One (10), the Creator of all (7, 10), " the Eternal " (12, 17), " the God of gods " (8), " the Strong Ruler " (13), " the powerful God " (9), " the Mighty Lord " (31). In the Song, which Abraham learns from Javel, He is called the " powerful, holy El, self - become, incorruptible, unspotted, self-existent, unsullied, immortal, self-complete, self-enlightener, motherless, fatherless, unbegotten, the High One . . . holy, very glorious . . . more illuminating than fire, full of light, whose voice is like thunder, whose glance is like lightning, the many-eyed" (17). From His "countenance it becomes day upon the earth," and in "His heavenly dwellings no other light is needed than the unspeakable brightness of His countenance" (Ibid.). The doctrine throughout is that God foreknows all things. In the heavens He is omnipresent. "Observe the expanses which are below the level on which thou art placed," God says, "and see how upon no single expanse is there any other than He whom thou hast sought, and to whom thou hast become dear" (19).

Abraham, brought by Javel into heaven, is thus addressed by the angel: "The One whom thou seest coming straight to us, in many voices of hallowing, that is the One before the world, who has given thee His love; but Himself thou seest not" (16). "And whilst he yet spoke," says Abraham, "see! fire coming towards us round about, and a voice was in the fire, as the voice of many waters, as the voice of the sea in its commotion. And the angel bowed himself with me and worshipped" (17). The author then conceived of God as the Invisible, whose manifestation is fire. He is called in the Song in this chapter "the fiery One." But He loves, He can be provoked, and He has wrath (10, 14, 17, 28, 20, 25, 27).

God is called the "only Ruler" (17). He intervenes to slay Tharah and burn his house (8). He causes Israel to be enslaved or killed by the multitude of the heathen (27). He sends Javel to strengthen Abraham and to speak His message (10). Javel is instructed to be with Abraham and with the race prepared to

spring from him, and he with Michael blesses Abraham
in eternity (10). But Javel is not by any means
always God's instrument. Rather, God speaks to
Abraham Himself. When Abraham says to his
father, " Oh that God would indeed by Himself reveal
Himself to us," the voice of a Strong One speaking in
a fiery cloud-burst falls from heaven. It is God Himself who speaks, saying, " The God of gods thou
seekest . . . I am He " (7, 8). Bonwetsch says:
" An angel brings to Abraham the revelation. He
leads him into the highest heaven, as he also sets
before his eyes the picture of past occurrences and
those still future." * But this is not correct. The
angel *says*, in chapter 12, that he will show Abraham
all things. As a matter of fact, however, it is God
Himself who does it (20, 21). God's great revelation
to Abraham is not made through a mediator. Moreover, when Abraham has once more returned to earth,
he speaks to God in prayer and is answered by God
Himself (30).

God is not remote in this Apocalypse from Abraham. But He dwells in the heavens, and not with
Israel, who have, instead, Javel in their midst perpetually. Still, God is the Judge of Israel, punishing
the sin of the nation within the limits of time, and He
hears the prayers of those who honour Him (17).
Moreover, the course of world-history is ordained by
God's fiat. The æons are prepared and established,
made and renewed, by His word (9).

### THE SIBYLLINE ORACLES, BOOK 4

Divine titles here are the " heavenly God " (e.g.
135) and the " great God " (e.g. 6, 25, 163). God is

* " Die Apoc. Abrahams," p. 55.

the possessor of foreknowledge, striking a whip through the heart of the Sibyl that she may tell of the things past and things to come (18-21). It is not possible to see Him from the earth, nor to measure Him with mortal eyes. He, looking down on all at once, is Himself seen by no one (10-12). He is one who can be wroth (51, 135, 169). Nay, more, it is said that man's sin will cause Him to be " no longer mild, but gnashing with fury, and led to wrath extreme " (160, 162 f.).

He dwells in no earthly temple, but in heaven (8). Thither men are told to stretch their hands. But no mention is made of angels in the book. It was apparently written for the forthsetting of one idea, namely, to warn men that God's interventions to punish nations often take place. The Sibyl's account of world-history, with the rise and fall of empires, is prefaced by the statement that God " Himself, by bringing them to pass, will prove all things " (22 f.). The doctrine clearly is, that God is the active Overlord of nations, raising up and casting down rulers. Nothing is said of divine communications to men, except that He inspires the Sibyl. But Gentile men are urged to lift up their hands in prayer, seeking His pardon (166).

### THE ASCENSION OF ISAIAH

In this work there are no lofty titles for God. He, says the writer, is the Lord " Whose name has not been sent into this world " (1⁷). Foreknowledge is implied in the prophecy of Isaiah (1⁷⁻¹³). The Messiah is described as God's Beloved (1⁷).

Satan is regarded as the monarch of a kingdom of evil, having angels and powers in his service (2²).

Beliar, the " angel of lawlessness," is described as " the ruler of this world " ($2^4$) in a passage quite unique in this literature. But evidence is not wanting that these words do not mean that the world is wholly given over to Beliar. The Messiah, for example, is regarded as possessed of power in human affairs, and as nullifying by his will the purpose of Hezekiah to slay his son ($1^{13}$). Moreover, when Manasseh, under the influence of Beliar, saws Isaiah in sunder ($5^1$), Isaiah says : " To me only hath God mingled the cup " ($5^{13}$). It is thus recognised that what happens on earth, at least in the experience of Isaiah, comes by the will of the Supreme. Of God's nearness to Isaiah this writer several times speaks. The Spirit speaks in him ($1^7$). Isaiah has a vision of the Lord ($3^7$). " His lips spake with the Holy Spirit until He was sawn in twain " ($5^{14}$).

## THE REST OF ESTHER

God is called " Almighty God " ($16^{21}$), the " King Almighty," in whose power the whole world is, whom none can gainsay ($13^9$). He is " the King of the gods and holder of all dominion " ($14^{12}$). He is the Lord of all, and there is no man who can resist Him ($13^{11}$). Artaxerxes calls Him " the Most High and Most Mighty Living God " ($16^{16}$). He knows all things, even the secret feelings of Mardocheus and of Esther ($13^{12}$, $14^{15\ f.}$). He is the " all-seeing God " ($15^2$, cf. $16^4$). The only anthropopathism is in the statement as to the " evil-hating justice of God " ($16^4$).

The only allusion to an angel is in the statement of Esther that the king was as "an angel of God " ($15^{13}$). The Additions seem to have been made for the purpose of asserting the active sovereignty of God, and so supplying what the writer thought to be the deficiency of the canonical book. They celebrate divine deliverances of Israel and God's punishment of the nation's sins (10⁹, 14⁶). They trace the change in the spirit of the king to His operation (15⁸). Artaxerxes is made to acknowledge that God " hath ordered the kingdom both unto us and to our progenitors," and, tracing the punishment of Haman to the decree of God, the king calls Him " God, who ruleth all things " (16¹⁴, ¹⁸). Repeated references are made to the prayers of troubled Israelites to their God (10⁹, 11¹⁰, 13⁸, ¹⁸, 14¹ ᶠ.).

### THE PRAYER OF MANASSES

God is the Lord Most High, the Lord Almighty, whose dwelling is in heaven. He " repents " of bringing evils on men, and is of " great compassion." Even the sinful Manasses may approach Him in prayer without intermediary.

### SUMMARY

(1) *Titles.*—Like their predecessors, the writers of the first century A.D. use great divine titles. The most common is " the Most High." It occurs in Wisdom (Part 1), the Assumption of Moses, the Apocalypse of Baruch (A³, B¹, B², B³), 4 Esdras in all its sections, and the Prayer of Manasses. Similar titles occur in other authors. Thus, in Baruch 4⁵–5⁹ we have : " the Holy One ; in Slavonic Enoch, " the Eternal One " ; in the Oracles, " the great God." Titles of royalty are found in Wisdom (in both parts), the Assumption of Moses, Slavonic Enoch, the Apocalypse of Abraham, and the Esther Additions. But

3 Maccabees alone has the title " King of kings."
The Apocalypse of Abraham uses many names of
greatness for God, as does also 3 Maccabees.   There is
little tendency in this direction in the Book of Baruch,
though in 1¹⁵-3⁸ God is once described as " the Lord
Almighty," and in 4⁵-5⁹ He is usually spoken of as
" the Everlasting."

In the Ascension of Isaiah reverence is shown in
the statement that His Name has not been sent into
the world.

(2) *Everlastingness.*—In the Apocalypse of Abraham God is called the " Immortal " and the " Self-
Existent."   In a doubtful line of the Oracles, He is
named ἀθάνατος.   In Wisdom (Part 1) and 4 Maccabees His everlastingness is distinctly implied.   Slavonic Enoch contains a line in which He is called the
Everlasting King ; but the true reading is uncertain.
He is αἰώνιος in Baruch 4⁵-5⁹, and 3 Maccabees.   In
Baruch 1¹³-3⁸ the enduring One who sits τὸν αἰῶνα is
contrasted with man, who perishes τὸν αἰῶνα, and in
S of 4 Esdras God is addressed as abiding for ever.

(3) *Omniscience.*—The doctrine of Omniscience is
distinctly taught in Wisdom (Part 1) the Assumption
of Moses, Slavonic Enoch, the Esther Additions,
Baruch 3⁹-4⁴, 3 and 4 Maccabees, S of 4 Esdras, and
B² of the Apocalypse of Baruch.   In most of the
books the divine foreknowledge is either asserted or
implied.   Exceptions are B¹ and B³ and Baruch 4⁵-
5⁹, where the future is regarded as conditional, and
the opening verses of the Book of Baruch, which contain no prophecies of the future.

(4) *Omnipotence.*—God is called " the Almighty "
in Wisdom (Part 1), Baruch 1¹⁵-3⁸, R of 4 Esdras,
3 Maccabees, the Esther Additions, and the Prayer of
Manasses.   Wisdom (Part 2), A², A³, and B² of Apoc.

8

Baruch, S of 4 Esdras, the Assumption of Moses, and Slavonic Enoch (in its doctrine of Omnipresence) clearly teach the Divine Almightiness. B¹ and B³ of Apoc. Baruch and A of 4 Esdras call God the " mighty One," and the same title appears in the Apocalypse of Abraham.

(5) *Spirituality.*—In this century there is marked tendency to the disuse of anthropomorphisms. In a considerable number of the books reference is made to the heavenly abode of God, but Slavonic Enoch stands alone in speaking of a coming of God to earth in the last times, and in only two works—the Slavonic Enoch and the Apocalypse of Abraham—do we find attempts to describe His appearance, after the manner of some of the men of the second century B.C. In the case of the latter, however, God is described as One whose essence is fire, and He is said to be invisible. In the case of the former, it is evident that the description is poetic, and—unless B represents the original —this writer also declares the divine invisibility.* Some, e.g. the authors of Wisdom (Part 1 and 2), and Baruch 1¹⁵–3⁸, make such references to the eye, ear, or hand of God as are natural in the speech of religious men at all times, but quite a number of the writers make no use of such expressions. In 3 Maccabees, as in 2 Maccabees, a miraculous intervention is poetically styled an appearance of God, and there is similar language in the Assumption of Moses and in E and S of 4 Esdras.

(6) *Anthropopathisms.*—These are sometimes used sparingly, but they appear in all the writers, save A¹, A² of Apoc. Baruch and A, M of 4 Esdras.

* If, however, B represents the original more accurately than A, the anthropomorphic passages are not from the author of this work, for B omits them.

(7) *The Divine Remoteness or Nearness.*—(A) By a number of these writers God appears to be regarded as distant. The Ascension of Isaiah contains the teaching, unique in this literature, that Beliar is the ruler of this world ; but other expressions make it probable that the writer intends only to assert that Beliar exercises a powerful and baleful influence amongst men. Slavonic Enoch is the only work of this period in which there is a reappearance of the second century B.C. doctrine of angelic viceroys, and its pages contain but slight allusion to any direct activity of God in the life of man. On the other hand, this writer teaches expressly the omnipresence of God. His book contains one passage in which a Deistic view is presented, but it is improbable that this came from his pen. Some scholars regard Wisdom (Part I) as presenting to us the distant Deity ; but, if the view taken of the figure of Wisdom in this thesis be correct, we have in it the doctrine of God as ruling and as present in His world. Five writers of this century teach that God will employ the Messiah as His agent at the great consummation of the world. Of these, E of 4 Esdras is absorbed in eschatology and gives us no material for deciding what were his ideas as to the normal action of God. But the remaining four—A², A³ in Apoc. Baruch and A, M in 4 Esdras—clearly teach a direct action of God upon human life. It is to be added that in E God Himself is to be the ultimate Judge of mankind.

In this century there is a marked decline of the idea that God uses angels as agents in affecting human fortunes. In the Apocalypse of Abraham two angels are Israel's guardians. In Slavonic Enoch, as we have already observed, angels act as viceroys. There are six, or perhaps seven, other writers who refer to the subject of God's employment of angelic agency, i.e. the authors of Apoc. Baruch (A³, B¹, B²), the Assumption of Moses, 3 and 4 Maccabees, and perhaps Wisdom (Part 2). Of these, B² tells of no action of angels in the affairs of man, and the Assumption only prophesies that Michael will avenge Israel, while the rest record each only one case of angelic intervention. The majority of the writers in this century do not refer to the idea. It is conspicuous by its absence from such works as Wisdom (Part 1), Book 4 of the Oracles, and the whole Book of Baruch. Those writers, however, who speak of angelic agents all predicate unmediated action of God in human life.

There is very general recognition in this period of a divine government of the whole world. The Prayer of Manasses, owing to its character, gives us nothing to our purpose. We get little or no information on this subject from 4 Esdras (E, M) or Apoc. Baruch (A¹, B³), because of the absorption of these writers in the last things. The horizon of some writers— Baruch 1¹⁵–3⁸, 3⁹–4⁴, the Ascension of Isaiah—is bounded by Israel, but within that region they recognise the divine activity. But many of the authors look out beyond that frontier. Baruch 4⁵–5⁹ contains the doctrine that God affects at times the policy of Gentile nations. B¹ of Apoc. Baruch teaches that He sometimes acts for their good. In Baruch 1¹⁻¹⁴ it is taught that He decrees how long kings have to live. A considerable number recognise that God ordains the course of events in this world generally. Such are the authors of Apoc. Baruch (A², A³, B²), 4 Esdras (S, A, R), the Oracles, the Apocalypse of Abraham, 3 and 4 Maccabees, Wisdom in both parts, the Esther Additions, and the Assumption of Moses. For these writers, God is not simply the Overlord who intervenes at times in mundane matters : He is the Controller. Slavonic Enoch stands by itself, for its author believed in a general control of God exercised by means of angels.

There is not much said of a divine activity in affecting the fortunes of individuals, but the idea is in evidence in both parts of Wisdom, perhaps also in A³ of Apoc. Baruch, and in the Assumption of Moses, since in this last work divine control of even the smallest matters is asserted.

To sum up, if we except S of Apoc. Baruch, where God becomes at last remote even from Israel, and a passage in Slavonic Enoch which is Deistic, and probably an interpolation, the doctrine of the distant God does not appear in this century, not even in Slavonic Enoch, despite its doctrine of angelic viceroys, since in that work God is the Omnipresent.

(B) In this period there are only eight writers who regard angels as God's ambassadors. These are A³ in Apoc. Baruch, E, S, A, M and R in 4 Esdras, and the writers of Apoc. Abraham and Slavonic Enoch. But the two last record direct speech of God with the fathers, and the others—except E—tell of revelations made to them in visions. Of these writers, therefore, it is only E of 4 Esdras who does not speak of some direct communication of God with men.

There are no references to divine speech with man in S of Apoc. Baruch, 3 and 4 Maccabees, Baruch 1¹⁻¹⁴, Baruch 4⁵–5⁹, the Prayer of Manasses, or the Assumption of Moses. But in Apoc. Baruch A¹, A², B¹, and B² tell of God's unmediated speeches to Baruch; in the Oracles God speaks to the Sibyl, and in the Ascension of Isaiah He speaks to that prophet. In the Esther Additions He is said to influence the mind of a king. In Baruch 1¹⁵–3⁸ 3⁹–4⁴ and B³ of Apoc.

Baruch He is said to have made revelation to Israel.
In Wisdom (Part 1) He is Himself the Teacher of Ps.
Solomon, and in Wisdom (Part 2) He affrights the
Egyptians in dreams.  The great bulk of these writers,
therefore, teach that God does sometimes speak to or
influence the minds of men directly.

Some assert wider doctrine.  In Wisdom (Part 1)
He is said to manifest Himself to all the righteous,
in $A^2$ it is declared that He always enlightens those
who are led by understanding, and the doctrine of
$A^3$ is that He makes revelation to the pure and the
God-fearing.  It is also to be added that the doctrine
of a direct influence of God on the spiritual nature of
man appears, as we shall show in Chapter III., in
Wisdom (Part 1), in Wisdom (chapter 10), in Baruch
$1^{15}$–$3^8$, and apparently in Slavonic Enoch.

In this period the doctrine of angelic mediation between God and praying men is conspicuously absent.
There is one passage in Slavonic Enoch which may
imply angelic intercession, but, if so, it is not from the
pen of the author.  $B^3$ of Apoc. Baruch laments the
sad estate of Israel in that there are no living saints
who can plead effectually on behalf of the nation.  In
the Assumption, Moses is regarded as continuing to
be an intercessor for Israel in heaven, as he was during
his life-time on earth.  But, though there is in these
two writers no assertion of the accessibility of God
to ordinary men, this is not, of course, precluded by
their doctrine of the intercession of saints.  In all
the rest, save the Ascension of Isaiah, M of 4 Esdras,
and Baruch $3^9$–$4^4$, the doctrine of God's approachableness by men on earth is clearly taught.

In a number of the earlier writers there is express
teaching as to the accessibility of God to praying

men in general. Thus, in Enoch 83–90 all Israel approaches Him in prayer; in Enoch 1–36 wronged humanity appeals to Him, though not directly; in the Oracles Gentiles are suppliants at His throne; and in Ecclesiasticus all the troubled have access to Him. In the next age Israel enjoys the privilege according to 1 and 2 Maccabees, Judith, and 3 Esdras, and in Enoch 91–104, 37–70 the righteous have it. In the latter even the wicked kings appeal to God, and the psalmist teaches that He hears the cry of all God-fearing men.

Such accessibility to praying Israel is affirmed again within the last period, in Wisdom (Part 2), Baruch in all its parts save 3⁹–4⁴, and 3 and 4 Maccabees. In Manasses the guilty king is free to pray, and in the Oracles the Gentiles are urged to make supplication. But the rest of the writers in the last century only speak of prayer as offered by saints and prophets. It would be unfair to infer from their silence that they did not believe in God's accessibility to ordinary men; but we miss in their writings any express declaration on the point.

Israel Abrahams observes that "from the Maccabæan period onward, God becomes ever nearer to Israel. If there was a fault at all, it was not that God became too transcendent. The tendency was rather in the direction of over-familiarity than of undue aloofness." * This fault can only be charged against two of our writers—the authors of S in 4 Esdras and B² in Apoc. Baruch. In the case of the former, the too intimate speeches are reprehended afterwards, once by the offender and once by the angel. In the case of the latter, God reproves Baruch. In both cases

* J.E., art. "Maccabees," p. 243.

they arise from strong feeling in the heart of the speaker.

## Conclusions

(1) *Everlastingness.*—A considerable number of the writers emphasise the fact that God endures through age after age, but only in a few of them are words employed which necessarily import the conception of Him as everlasting. Belief in a post-resurrection life of bliss or woe for men was held by a large number of these men, but that life was not conceived of by them all as eternal in the strict sense of the word. It was not, for example, so thought of by the author of Enoch 1–36, and hence there is nothing implied as to God's everlastingness. The first unmistakable assertion of this doctrine appears in an Alexandrian work of the second century B.C.—the third book of the Oracles, and, with one exception, it is only in works which were probably composed in Egypt that the idea is expressed distinctly. It appears in 4 Maccabees, Wisdom (1), and the Apocalypse of Abraham. This last work, like the Proemium to the Oracles and Wisdom (2), speaks of Him as the Self-existent.

(2) *Omniscience.*—A large proportion of the authors in each period, Palestinian and non-Palestinian alike, expressly assert the doctrine of God's Omniscience. Many say or imply that He foreknows the future. There are a few writers, but only a few, in whose works nothing is either said or implied on the subject.

(3) *Omnipotence.*—The great majority of the writers in each of the three centuries make it clear that they believed in the omnipotence of God.

(4) *Spirituality.*—With reference to the use of lan-

guage of a highly anthropomorphic character, examination of the facts leads to the conclusion that the growing tendency was in the direction of its disuse. We may disregard for the moment such references to appearances of God as we find in 2 and 3 Maccabees, and the Additions to the Testaments, for it is quite clear that these writers do but speak of manifestations of God's power or influence. We may also put on one side such allusions to God's arising for judgment or being revealed as we have in the Assumption of Moses or E and S of 4 Esdras, for these are manifestly of a symbolic character. Confining ourselves to writers who give us representations of God as seen and spoken with in heaven, or who picture Him as descending to earth and appearing to men, we observe that these are much more numerous in proportion to the total number of writers in the second century B.C. than they are subsequently. We have only three such writers in the first century B.C., and there are two only in the following century. Only in Slavonic Enoch, among the non-Palestinian writers, does language occur which might be capable of being understood as a denial of pure spirituality.

Nevertheless, it would be a mistake to conclude that the avoidance of such language indicates a change in the conception of the nature of Deity. We are warned against too readily taking allusions to the appearance of God as being other than poetic, by the free use of language of this kind in 2 and 3 Maccabees and the Testaments Additions, where there can be no mistake as to its real significance. Such speech is obviously rhetorical in the vivid descriptions of Enoch 83–90. Moreover, in Slavonic Enoch, where God is said to have been seen, and in the Apocalypse of Abraham, where He is represented as talking with a man in heaven, it is expressly affirmed that He is the invisible One. Perhaps also the author of Enoch 1–36 held the same doctrine. Such visions of God as are described in the Testaments, the Enoch Similitudes, and the Enoch Interpolations do not furnish us with material from which we can judge the nature of the conception of God held by their authors. And we have seen that, in the case of Jubilees and the Testaments, the vivid language obviously imports no anthropomorphic ideas. On the whole, we may fairly conclude that there is no evidence whatever of denial of the spirituality of God in this literature. Language capable of being misconstrued tends to disappear, but there is no antagonism of thought between those who use anthropomorphic expressions and those who avoid them.

(5) *Anthropopathisms.*—Anthropopathic expressions are sparingly used by some writers, and do not appear at all in a few of the books. By the majority of the authors they are used quite freely in each century, nor is there any difference in this respect between Palestinian and non-Palestinian writings.

(6) *The Divine Remoteness or Nearness.*—The doctrine of angels as viceroys of God in the government of this world is in evidence in three works of the second century B.C. Each of these is of Palestinian origin. Beyond the bare statement of the idea that angels are so employed, there is, however, no agreement whatever between them. Each writer elaborates conceptions which are peculiar to himself. In the next century there is nothing quite like the teaching of these three. Enoch 72–82 and the Enoch Interpolations contain, like Jubilees in the preceding century, the idea of angels or spirits who rule the forces of nature. In the Psalms of Solomon, too, God is said

to rule the stars through angels. Angels superintend some human affairs according to the Similitudes. But the doctrine of angelic viceroys over the world or over nations was not taught by any of our writers in the last pre-Christian century. Nor does it appear in this literature in any work of the first century A.D. save for Slavonic Enoch. But for this one work the idea is peculiarly Palestinian, and it appears in no other work after the close of the second century B.C.

The doctrine of God's normal use of angels in affecting the fortunes of men is much less in evidence in the two later centuries than in the earliest of the three. Some writers of the second century B.C. do not teach the doctrine, but in four works of that period it appears. In the following century the idea. of any frequent employment of angels only appears in three works, and the same decline is observable in the first Christian century. It is mainly in Palestinian works that the notion of a frequent action on their part appears, though the idea of some intervention of angels is found in a few of the writings which emanate from Egypt.

The same tendency is seen to have been in operation if we consider the teaching of these writers as to God's use of angels as His ambassadors, or as intermediaries when men pray. In the earliest of our three centuries the doctrine of angelic ambassadors is found in every writer, except Ben Sira and the Sibyl. In the next century, save for Enoch 91–104, 72–82, and the Enoch Interpolations, it disappears. In the first century A.D. we find it only in the Apocalypse of Abraham, Slavonic Enoch, 4 Esdras (all sections), and A³ of Apoc. Baruch.

The notion of angelic intercessors or intermediaries. between God and praying men was one held by only a small number of writers from the beginning. Enoch 1–36, Tobit, and the Testaments have it in the second century B.C. In the next century it is in evidence again in Enoch 91–104, 37–70. In the last period it is entirely wanting, save for a dubious passage of Slavonic Enoch, whose author, however, categorically contradicts the idea. The great bulk of the authors show no sign of acquaintance with the conception, and it is purely a Palestinian idea. So is also the notion of angelic ambassadors, save for the fact that it appears in Slavonic Enoch.

But in each century the clear doctrine of the majority of the authors, whatever their angelology, is that of a God who is in unmediated contact with His creation. He is not conceived of as dependent on the angelic servants whom He sometimes elects to employ. The authors are, indeed, of very varying ideas as to the *extent* to which God influences mundane affairs, but almost all assert, in some way or other, the doctrine of a direct contact. Two writers have made interpolations—one in the Ethiopic and one in the Slavonic Enoch—in which a doctrine of predestinarianism is taught, and it is a fore-ordination so complete as to suggest the idea of One who has set a machine going and then retired from it. Three other writers—the authors of Enoch 1–36, 72–82, and Slavonic Enoch—appear to set God at a distance from the world. Apart from these, every writer, except those who are wholly absorbed in matters eschatological, affirms a direct influence of God on human fortunes. Since it only makes brief and incidental allusion to theological questions, Enoch 72–82 is negligible, and in the Slavonic Enoch God is certainly not remote—despite the angelology of the writer—for He is omnipresent. It is, therefore, only in Enoch 1–36 and in the two predestinarian passages that we have the idea of the distant God.

These results are confirmed by a consideration of the teaching as to God's speech with man and man's approach to God in prayer. In the two earlier centuries every writer—save the author of Enoch 72–82 —teaches that Gods speaks to or influences man without mediation, and the same doctrine appears in the majority of the works of the last period. Those writers of the first century A.D. whose books do not contain this doctrine, nevertheless, declare God's nearness to man, for they teach His immediate accessibility to suppliants. This last is a doctrine appearing in most of the books of each age. There are, indeed, a few who are silent on that subject, or who regard angels as intermediaries between God and praying men, but with the exception of the writer of Enoch 72– 82 each of these teaches God's direct speech or influence. That God is in immediate contact with man is the teaching, moreover, of those writers referred to above as absorbed in eschatology, for they speak of Him as the Hearer of prayer or as the communicating God. It is important also to observe that even in Enoch 1–36 God is represented as exercising an unmediated influence on the mind of Enoch. Normally, God is remote from man in that book, yet is it clear that the writer regarded Him as One who can and does come into an immediate contact with chosen men at times. The facts compel us, therefore, to dissent from Fairweather when he says that in apocalyptic literature God is "thought of as occupying an inaccessible throne." * Such an affirmation, in our judgment, may only be made of Enoch 1–36, S of Apoc. Baruch, and the two interpolators referred

* " The Background of the Gospels," p. 280.

to above. Of the rest of our authors, apocalyptic and apocryphal, it may be said truly that to them God was nigh at hand and not far off.

As to the *extent* of God's active interest in and control over the fortunes of men, there are a limited number of writers who do not speak of any action of His save in the affairs of the chosen people. In Judith, the doctrine is that of a complete divine control over all events in the life of Israel. In Baruch $1^{15}$–$3^8$, $3^9$–$4^4$, the Ascension of Isaiah, and the Daniel Additions, such high doctrine does not appear, unless it is implied in the case of the Ascension in what is said of the fate of Isaiah. But God is regarded in these works as actively concerned in Israel's affairs. It must not be affirmed that they conceived of God as inactive beyond the borders of Israel. We can only say that they make no reference to the subject. But the majority of the writers, while recognising God's special interest in Israel, look out into the life of the world beyond the confines of their own race, and in varying degrees they discern a divine activity. They fall into three distinct categories.

(1) There are those who hold the doctrine of a delegated sovereignty, as we have seen, but in each case (save Enoch 83–90, where the delegation is temporary and only affects Israel), God is regarded as controlling subordinate powers. This is expressly stated in Enoch 1–36 and Jubilees, and it is surely implied in Slavonic Enoch by the writer's doctrine of Omnipresence.

(2) There are those who see God intervening in the life of Gentile nations. Some only discern Him as the punishing Judge of men. That is the vision in M of 4 Esdras, Baruch $4^5$–$5^9$, 1 Maccabees, and the Enoch Interpolations. Some see One who acts for

the good of the peoples.    Such are B¹ in Apoc. Baruch, and the scribe who has apparently inserted generous utterances into B² of that work.*

(3) But most of our authors go very much further. They see God ordaining the general course of events in the world, determining who shall reign, and how long their power shall continue.    The writers of Enoch 83–90, 91–104, 37–70, S, A, R, in 4 Esdras, B² and A² in Apoc. Baruch, the fourth book of the Oracles, the Apocalypse of Abraham, 3 Esdras, 4 Maccabees, the Esther Additions, probably also Baruch 1¹⁻¹⁴, take this view.    In a considerable number of works, however, the doctrine is that of a very complete divine control over all events.    Writers of this class are the authors of the Ecclesiasticus Additions, the third Book of the Oracles, Tobit, the Psalms of Solomon, 2 and 3 Maccabees, A³ in Apoc. Baruch, Wisdom (Parts 1 and 2), the Assumption of Moses, with Ben Sira, who most of them all insists on the doctrine of the absolute and active sovereignty of God over all human affairs.    Jubilees and the Testaments we have not included among the foregoing because there are not in them such assertions of God's entire control, but both of these represent Him as ordering life generally with a view to the prosperity of the righteous.

Of the idea of an active interest of God in the affairs of the individual in this world, there is little or no trace in many of the writers.    Their absorbing interest is the nation or the world and their future.    But the idea appears in such works as Jubilees, the Testaments, Tobit, B², A³ of Apoc. Baruch, the Daniel Additions, Wisdom in both parts, as well as in Ecclesiasticus, and the Psalms of Solomon, where the fortunes

* Cf. Chapter II. of this Thesis.

of the individual in this life are conceived of as entirely under the direction of the Supreme. It is implied also in the Assumption of Moses, whose teaching is that God ordains even the smallest things in this world, and in the Additions to the work of Ben Sira, which appear to have been written to emphasise this doctrine.

On a survey, therefore, of the whole literature it must be concluded that, though some writers do not assert so much, the majority do distinctly teach the doctrine of a God who is not simply an occasionally intervening Sovereign, but the active Governor of the world, while some go beyond this and assert God's control of the fortunes of the individual. The belief in God's government was not destroyed by the events of A.D. 70, save for S in Apoc. Baruch. It appears in each century and in writers both of the homeland and the Dispersion.

If inquiry be made for passages in which there is express declaration of the doctrine of Omnipresence —passages similar to 1 Kings 8$^{27}$, Jer. 23$^{24}$, Isaiah 66$^{1}$, and Psalm 139$^{7-10}$, the answer must be that, as in O.T., they are rare. Passages of this character are to be found in Enoch 83–90, the Testaments (a dubious reading), the third Book of the Oracles and Proemium, Wisdom in both parts, and Slavonic Enoch. Similar passages are to be found in such works as the Psalms of Solomon and A$^{3}$ of Apoc. Baruch, where men are said to stand in God's presence while they are on this earth. In the Apocalypse of Abraham God is said to be present everywhere in the heavens, and the old Latin version of Ecclesiasticus gives us an assertion of His presence in all things. But J. E. Hirsch says that in Palestinian apocryphal literature " God is omnipresent. Though He is on high, He takes heed of man's ways. Mountains and the ocean are in His power." * Kautzch considers that " the strongest evidence of the firmness of the belief " of the prophets in omnipresence is " the conviction that Jahweh hears, and for the most part also answers the prayers of His people." † Dr. W. N. Clarke, as we have observed already at the beginning of this chapter, takes much the same view of the notion of omnipresence, defining it as God's freedom " from all limitations of space in His activities." If, then, omnipresence be understood in this sense, it may be affirmed that the doctrine was held by the writers of this literature. Reference to the summaries and conclusions in this work as to omnipotence and omniscience will show that a large proportion of them clearly express their belief in God as the Almighty and the All-knowing. But, apart from this, as we have shown in the last paragraph, nearly every writer makes it clear that he believed in the God who is able by the mere forthputting of His will to affect man and the world. They differ as to the *extent* to which God acts upon men and their fortunes. They do not differ as to the fact that He can and does so act. Even Enoch 1–36 teaches this.

* J.E., art. " God," p. 2 b.
† D.B., art. " Religion of Israel," p. 684.

# CHAPTER II

## THE JUSTICE OF GOD

It is intended in this chapter to set forth the doctrine of God which is involved in the ideas of the writers of this literature as to (*a*) His attitude to Israel and the Gentiles ; (*b*) the allotment of prosperity and adversity under His government, and (*c*) the divine permission of moral evil in the universe. We shall confine ourselves here, as far as is possible, to the question : How far is God conceived of as just ? It will be convenient to reserve, as far as we can, to a later chapter the inquiry : Is He represented as the gracious and loving God ? This latter question will indeed necessarily be answered to some extent in the present chapter. But, for a full statement of the case, it will be necessary to consider other facts which do not come under our purview in this part of the work.

## THE SECOND CENTURY B.C.

### ECCLESIASTICUS

*Israel and the Gentiles.*—Ben Sira clearly recognises and greatly glories in the favoured position of Israel. As G. A. Smith truly observes : " Ben Sira, for all his foreign culture, is proud of the story of his little people, and carried away with the glory of their worship. It surprises one to see his prudence change to passion when he turns to these subjects ; to find a man so travelled, so aware of the world, and liberal in his views, as in his tastes, celebrate like any Deuteronomist the divine story of Israel and the splendours of the national ritual." * That people, he declares, is permanently God's chosen. He " will not blot out the prosperity of His elect, and the seed of him that loved Him He will not annihilate " ($47^{22}$). " The days of Israel are innumerable " ($37^{25}$).

But Wisdom, he says, had formerly obtained a possession in every nation and had sought rest with these. She had asked the question—" In whose inheritance shall I lodge ? " ($24^{6 \, f.}$), and she had found her abiding place in Israel (Ibid. 8–12). " We can scarcely doubt," says Edersheim, " that the question here propounded by Wisdom expresses what was afterwards formulated by the Rabbis in the legend that the law had been offered to and refused by every nation before it was accepted by Israel at Mount Sinai." † That God did not originally confine wisdom to Israel is taught, when Ben Sira says that He " poured her out upon all His works, with all flesh, according to His gift, and He supplied her abundantly to them that love Him " ($1^{9 \, f.}$). The insertion in the R.V. of the words " She is " before " with all flesh " is misleading. Ben Sira is asserting that Wisdom was God's gift to all men originally, though now she is Israel's unique possession. In harmony with this, he cites the Abrahamic promise that Israel should be a blessing to all the nations ($44^{21}$), and declares that " the mercy of a man is upon his neighbour, but the mercy of the Lord is upon all flesh " ($18^{13}$). He sees

* " Jerusalem," vol. ii., p. 421.
† Speaker's Comm., p. 127.

in anticipation the widening out of the channel of Wisdom into a river and then into a sea. She will no longer water an orchard only. She is to be no more Jewish only, but universal. She will yet light up instruction as the dawn ($24^{30-33}$).

He also has the following prayer for the " strange nations " : " Let them know Thee as we have also known Thee, that there is no other God, but only Thou O God " ($36^5$), and he adds, according to the Hebrew, " Let all the ends of the earth know that Thou art our God for ever (?) " ($36^{17c}$). The Greek, however, gives a somewhat broader idea. " All they that are on the earth shall know that Thou art the Lord, the God of the ages " ($36^{17}$). One of the most striking passages in the book on this subject is $10^{22}$. In the Greek we have : " The rich man and the honourable and the poor, their glorying is the fear of the Lord." But the Hebrew gives us a much finer idea. " A stranger and a foreigner, an alien and a poor man, their glorying is the fear of the Lord." The Syro-Hexaplar is very similar. " Stranger and alien, foreigner and pauper, their glory is the fear of the Lord."

The Prologue must also be cited in this connection. " It is necessary," says Ben Sira, " not only that the readers themselves become intelligent, but also that to them which are without the lovers of learning be able to be useful, both speaking and writing." As H. J. A. Hart observes : " It is natural to suppose that the phrase ' them which are without ' refers to persons outside Palestine, and, to the mind of the grandfather, who recognised this duty, denoted Gentiles." * The lovers of learning " have clearly the function of missionaries in respect of the Gentiles." †

* " Ecclus. in Greek," p. 244 f.        † Ibid. p. 238.

C. H. Toy remarks that Ben Sira is so much absorbed in desire for Israel's prosperity "that he does not think of a conversion of foreign nations to the worship of Yahwe." * And Canon Dobson finds in the book only one passage (36¹⁻¹⁷) which " postulates any relations at all between the God of Israel and the rest of mankind." Ben Sira, he says, " recognised the sovereignty of Jehovah over the whole earth—he could hardly avoid that—but the conception did not suggest to his mind much hope and still less any duty on his own part for the outside peoples—the issues of belief towards humanity at large were not within his purview." † But surely in view of the facts which we have noted above, H. J. A. Hart is right when he says : " Jesus Ben Sira and his fellow sages inherited the prophecy that Israel should be the light of the Gentiles and strove to effect its fulfilment. They had a care for those without, whether they were Jews who needed confirmation, proselytes who needed instruction, or pagans who needed conversion." ‡

It is clear, then, that Ben Sira worshipped no merely national Deity, but the God who has mercy on all men and is willing to bestow wisdom on all who seek it.

*The Problem of Prosperity and Adversity.*—The sorrows of men, according to Ben Sira, are very often to be explained as God's penalty for sin. God overthrows kings and peoples for evil-doing (10¹³ ᶠ.). History and experience demonstrate the fact that punishment is largely in operation—so largely, indeed, that it is a wonder if one stiff-necked person should escape

* E.B., art. " Ecclus.," 1176.
† I.J.A., " The Missionary Outlook in the Apocrypha," January 1909, p. 8.
‡ Op. cit., p. 245.

it (16[11], cf. 7[8]). Calamities are created for the wicked (40[10]). They come indeed on all mankind, but seven times more on sinners than on other men (40[8]). It is certain that the ungodly will not go to Hades unpunished (9[12]). This truth finds striking expression in one passage of the Hebrew text: "Surely upon me He will not set His heart; and my ways who will consider? If I have sinned, no eye shall see me; or if I have dealt falsely in any secret place (?) who shall know? Work of right who shall declare unto Him? and what is there of hope that I should be righteous (?)? They that want understanding will think such things; and a perverse man (?) will imagine this" (16[20-3]).

In this judgment of man, God acts according to the law of solidarity. The ungodly are punished in their children (23[24 f.], 40[15 f.], 41[6]), and conversely the good deeds of parents benefit their children (44[10-13]). This happens not by the nature of things, but because God wills it. We all die on account of Eve (25[24]). Solomon's sin brings wrath on his seed (47[20]). But the children of the godly "are within the covenants. Their seed standeth fast and their children for their sakes" (44[11 f.]).

Ben Sira is alive, however, to the fact that there is a problem for faith in human sorrows. So shrewd a man could not fail to be face to face with this. In the Hebrew, for example, we have this exhortation: "Do not (envy) at the ungodly man who is prosperous. Remember till death he shall not go unpunished" (9[12]). Though the Greek gives us a different idea in this passage, both versions have a similar thought in verse 11: "Envy not the glory of a sinner, for thou knowest not what shall be his overthrow." The ways of God are likened to "a

tempest which no man shall see." " Yea," says Ben
Sira, " the more part of His works are hidden " (16³¹).
Still, events, he holds, will surely vindicate all that
God does. All His works are " exceeding good."
" None can say what is this, or wherefore is that ? "
(39¹⁶, ²¹). They " shall all be well approved of in
their season " (39³⁴). Man should submit himself to
God's decrees. Death is His will, and we ought to
bow to it uncomplainingly (41⁴). Besides, God will
prove Himself the Helper of the humble (35¹⁴). All
history shows that trust in God is vindicated by human
experience (2¹⁰). If men come forward to serve Him,
says Ben Sira, they must expect to experience πειρασμόν,
and the context shows that he means that they will
be tried by adversity (2¹). But this comes of God's
goodness. " Gold is tried in the fire and acceptable
men in the furnace of affliction " (2⁵). " The mercy
of the Lord is on all flesh, reproving, and chastening,
and teaching, and bringing back as a shepherd doth
his flock. He hath mercy on them that accept
chastening " (18¹³ ᶠ).*

The views which he thus expresses are such as he
was determined to hold, and from which he would
not allow himself to swerve. " Therefore," he says,
" from the beginning I was resolved, and I thought
this and I left it in writing. All the works of the
Lord are good " (39³²).

As R. G. Moulton says : " He has reached the very
brink of the Rubicon of doubt, which nevertheless he
has firmly resolved not to cross." †

---

* Edersheim, commenting on the passage, " A wise man
will not hate the law" (33²) conjectures that the original
was מוסר. But we must not now use that verse in this connection, since we know that the original is תורה.

† I.J.A., January 1907, p. 14.

*Moral Evil.*—The most important passage here is 15¹¹⁻¹⁷. The Hebrew gives us the following :

11. " Say not ' My transgression was of God,'
    For that which He hateth He made not,
12. Lest thou say : ' He it was that made me to stumble,'
    For there is no need of men of violence.
13. Wickedness and an abomination the Lord hateth ;
    And will not let it befall them that fear Him.
14. For (?) God created man from the beginning
    And put him into the hand of him that would spoil him
    And gave him into the hand of his inclination.
15. If thou choose, thou mayst keep the commandment ;
    And it is understanding to do His will.
15¹. If thou trust him, thou shalt even live.
16. Fire and water are poured out before thee :
    Upon whichsoever thou choosest stretch forth thy hands.
17. Death and life are before a man :
    That which he shall choose shall be given him."

According to the Greek version we have the following :

11. " Say not thou, ' It is through the Lord that I fell away,'
    For thou shalt not do the things that He hateth.
12. Say not thou, ' It is He that hath caused me to err,'
    For He hath no need of a sinful man.
13. The Lord hateth every abomination
    And they that fear Him love it not.

14. He Himself made man from the beginning
    And left him in the hand of his own counsel.
15. If thou wilt, thou shalt keep the commandments
    And to perform faithfulness is of (thine own)
    good pleasure.
16. He hath set fire and water before thee :
    Thou shalt stretch forth thy hand unto which-
    soever thou wilt ;
17. Before man is life and death,
    And whichsoever he liketh it shall be given
    him."

Attention is called by Dr. C. Taylor to a conjectural
emendation of verse 14b in the Hebrew text, suggested
by Professor Bevan on the ground that " the sense demands an assertion of man's free-will." * But in a note
on this line Schechter and Taylor say : " In the Rabbinic literature the evil Yetzer is called, among other
names, צר and שונא as well as מלאך המות. In Sirach
(below, l. 4), we find the חתף in apposition to צר ." †
There seems, therefore, to be no need to amend the
חותפו in line 14b, for the new line is a mere doublet of
14c. As Tennant suggests, it may be that the new line
was omitted by scribes who viewed it with disfavour
" as suggesting too much intention on the part of God
that man should fall into sin." ‡ If it is Ben Sira's,
he makes God the author of the possibility and likeli-
hood of sin, for, as Tennant says : " The Yetzer is a
disposition implanted in man by God from which
evidently there proceeds the solicitation to sin. It
is therefore spoken of as man's spoiler." §

* J.Q.R., vol. xv., p. 625.
† " Wisdom of Ben Sira," p. 51.
‡ Tennant, op. cit., p. 114, n. 2.
§ Op. cit., p. 115.

There are other passages in which possibly Ben Sira gives us the same teaching. In $21^{11}$ the Syriac has : " He that keepeth the law constrains or oppresses his Yetzer," and Edersheim thinks that the Greek should be similarly rendered on the ground that ἐννόημα can hardly mean " understanding " of the law.*

In $37^3$ the Syriac reads : " Enemy and evil, to what end were they created ? " But the Greek has : " O wicked imagination, whence camest thou rolling in ? " Possibly the original here was Yetzer.

But, in the light of the immediately preceding context, it is probable that Fritzsche is right in his suggestion that this verse is only " an apostrophe of the horrible idea of the friend becoming unfaithful." †

Tennant and Cheyne express the opinion that in $21^{27}$—" When the ungodly curseth Satan he curseth his own soul "—Satan is perhaps identified with the evil impulse.‡ C. H. Toy objects to this on the ground that it would be " a conception foreign to the whole pre-Christian time as well as to N.T." § In view, however, of Ben Sira's general attitude to the idea of angels or spirits, the idea that he rationalised Satan into the Yetzer seems very likely to be correct. It must be admitted, however, that the only positive piece of evidence for the existence of the doctrine of the Yetzer within the work is $15^{14}$ of the Hebrew text.

There is a passage in which Ben Sira seems to speak of sin as almost inevitable to man by reason of the frailty of the nature which God has given him, but the meaning of this passage is doubtful ($17^{29}$ ff.).

* Speaker's Comm. in loc.  † Ibid.
‡ Tennant, op. cit., p. 115.  E.B., art. " Ecclesiasticus," 1175.
§ E.B., art. " Ecclus.," 1175.

## ADDITIONS TO ECCLESIASTICUS

There are two important dicta preserved in the manuscript 248. "The beginning of reception ($\pi\rho\grave{o}\ \lambda\acute{\eta}\xi\epsilon\omega s$) is the fear of the Lord, and the beginning of rejection ($\grave{\epsilon}\kappa\beta o\lambda\acute{\eta}$) is the hardening of pride" (10²¹). "The fear of the Lord is the beginning of reception ($\pi\rho o\sigma\lambda\acute{\eta}\psi\epsilon\omega s$) and wisdom from Him winneth love" (19¹⁸). This last is also in the manuscript 70, while 10²¹ is substantially supported by 106, 241, and the Syro-Hexaplar. As Hart points out, $\pi\rho\acute{o}\sigma\lambda\eta\psi\iota s$ and $\grave{a}\pi o\beta o\lambda\acute{\eta}$ are technical theological terms (cf. Romans 11¹⁵),* and probably the verses are the insertion into the text of some large-hearted Jew, who desired to emphasise the fact that God's mercy and favour know no racial limitations, but are bestowed solely on ethical grounds. The MS. 248 also contains this statement: "Every man from his youth up (is given) to evil. Neither could they make to themselves fleshly hearts from stony. . . . But Israel is the Lord's portion, whom, being His firstborn, He nourisheth with discipline, and giving him the light of His love, He doth not forsake Him" (17¹⁵⁻¹⁸). The manuscripts 70 and 106 also contain this statement, but substitute for "every man" the words "their ways." Israel is thus regarded as permanently God's people, and apparently his sorrows are looked upon as God's gracious discipline of His own.

### TOBIT

*Israel and the Gentiles.*—This writer did not endorse the idea of an original willingness of God to give light to all the nations. The ignorance of the Gentiles is of His decree. "Every nation hath not counsel, but

* Op. cit., p. 302.

the Lord Himself giveth all good things, and He humbleth whom He will as He will " ($4^{19}$). Israel is His people abidingly, if they be faithful. He is their " Father for ever " ($13^4$). He will gather them out of all the nations among whom they are scattered. But it is plainly taught that this is conditional. If they turn to Him with their whole heart and soul to do truth before Him, then He will turn to them and not hide His face from them ($13^{5f.}$). Confident that Israel will do this, Tobit prophesies that Jerusalem shall be exalted for ever ($13^{18}$). The conception is clearly based on faith in God as true to His promises. " The house of God," says Tobit, " shall be built up in it for ever . . . even as the prophets spake concerning it " ($14^5$).

But the author is far from being narrow in his conception of God's attitude to the Gentiles. Tobit declares that he will give God thanks and " show His strength and His majesty to a nation of sinners," and then, apparently turning to the Gentiles, he says : " Turn, ye sinners, and do righteousness before Him. Who can tell if He will accept you and have mercy upon you ? " ($13^6$). Possibly, however, as Fuller suggests, he is here addressing Jews.* Be that as it may, his broad-mindedness is clearly seen in the following two passages. " Many nations shall come from far to the name of the Lord God, with gifts in their hands, even gifts to the King of Heaven " ($13^{11}$). " And all the nations shall turn to fear the Lord God truly and shall bury their idols, and all the nations shall bless the Lord " ($14^6$).

*The Problem of Prosperity and Adversity.*—There is no problem for faith to this writer. As we have observed in Chapter I., his creed is that it is God's

* Speaker's Comm. in loc.

rule to prosper the good ($4^6$). The living and dead
of the nation are a unity when God punishes sin. The
sins of the fathers are visited upon their children.
"They disobeyed Thy commandments, and Thou
gavest us for a spoil and for captivity and for death"
($3^4$). In this God is righteous and true, for the generation on which the penalty falls has imitated the evil
ways of its forbears ($3^5$). It is recognised that trouble
comes to the righteous. It comes to Tobit and to
Sarah. The action of a demon is its cause in Sarah's
case ($3^{7\,f.}$). It is God's own act in the case of Tobit
($11^{14\,f.}$). It was probably quite sufficiently accounted
for to the mind of the writer by that sense of personal
demerit before God which is manifest, despite all
Tobit's self-complacency (e.g. $3^3$). Since the author
expected that after the Exile there would be a great
turning of Israel to God, it is possible that he thought
of the punishment of the nation as intended by God
to be disciplinary.

*Moral Evil.*—Nothing is said in this book as to the
origin of sin.

## ETHIOPIC ENOCH, 1–36

*Israel and the Gentiles.*—In an article on the "Historic Succession of the Books of Enoch," L. S. A.
Wells writes concerning this author: "It cannot be
said that a world judgment or a world ideal has any
real place in his scheme. . . . The real ultimate issue
of this world's history is determined not by moral
but by racial considerations." * But, in the judgment
of the present writer, a far truer statement of the
case is made by G. H. Box, who, writing on "Some
Characteristics of the Apocalyptic Literature," says :

* I.J.A., October 1910, p. 74.

" The exalted religious scheme which dominates these books tended to overcome national and particularistic limitations." * This writer teaches indeed that the chosen race is " the best part of mankind " ($20^5$), and that the joys of the coming theocratic kingdom will be for the " elect " ($1^8$, $5^{7 \text{ f.}}$, $25^5$). But he also represents God as saying : " All the children of men shall become righteous, and all nations shall offer Me adoration and praise, and all shall worship Me " ($10^{21}$). Moreover, we have not only this statement, but apparently also in chapter 22 the doctrine of a resurrection which will be of all mankind, save one class. Of that one class he affirms that they will not be slain on the day of judgment nor raised out of Sheol ($22^{13}$). This, taken along with his statement that " all the souls of the children of men " are assembled in the hollow places till the day of their judgment ($22^{3 \text{ f.}}$), and that judgment will be at the last " upon everything and upon all the righteous " ($1^7$), seems to point to the conclusion that all men, save the one class, are to be raised. Charles, however, is of opinion that this resurrection is of Israel only. He thinks that the entire section 1–36 would lead us to infer this. " Otherwise," he says, " this declaration of a general resurrection is solitary and unique in pre-Christian-Jewish Apocrypha." † But, as a matter of fact, a universal resurrection is clearly taught in $51^1$ of the Similitudes of Enoch. Charles argues that it is not so, but he admits that the words seem to point that way.‡ And, again, the doctrine is taught in " the Testaments of the Twelve Patriarchs." " Then also all men shall rise, some unto glory and some unto shame " (T.

* I.J.A., April 1908, p. 7.
† Edition of Ethiopic Enoch, p. 96.
‡ Ibid., p. 139.

Benj. 10$^8$). In that passage, indeed, there is another reading, but Charles regards it as corrupt.

It is possible also to come to an opposite conclusion from that of Charles on the ground of the general tone of the work. For it is clear from the universalistic passage in 10$^{21}$, and from the fact that in 22$^{3\ f.}$ the writer deals with the fate of all souls of the dead, that here is no narrow and nationalistic conception of God.

*The Problem of Prosperity and Adversity.*—Under the government of God's angel viceroys it happens, according to our author, that the righteous sometimes suffer a violent and undeserved death, while sinners die unpunished and are honourably buried (22$^{7,\ 10}$). He says that, in the ages which preceded the Flood, angels came down to earth and wrought oppression (7$^{3-5}$). Then " the earth complained of the unrighteous ones " (7$^6$), and four great angels " looked down from heaven and saw the great quantity of blood that had been shed upon the earth, and all the wrong that had been wrought upon the earth " (9$^1$). To them, souls of men prayed : " Procure us justice with the Most High " (9$^3$). The angels, perplexed at what they saw, remonstrated daringly with God. " Thou knowest this thing and everything affecting them and yet Thou didst not speak to us " (9$^{11}$). It seems clear that the apocalyptist was concerned to offer some explanation of the injustices which are permitted under the divine government. His doctrine for the comfort of his co-religionists is that God is the God of compensation. He who punished of old the sinning stars and the hosts of Azazel will punish all sinners (1$^{1,\ 9}$, 5$^5$, 10$^{4\ ff.}$, 21$^6$). Already, in Sheol, He makes a difference between the righteous and the wicked, as also between men punished in this life

and men who escaped the due reward of their works
while on earth ($22^{9\,ff.}$). Moreover, He has a goal in
view. Earth will be purified and made peaceful, and
men will live in it to a patriarchal age, possessing all
sensuous good ($5^{7-9}$, $10^{16-22}$, $25^{4-6}$). L. S. A. Wells
says that the teaching of this book is " that the
martyrs are indeed to be raised, but the other righteous
of old days who happened to die in bed are left to
sleep, comfortably it is true, yet to sleep after all." *
But nothing of this kind is said or implied. If we
may safely draw any inference at all from the writer's
scanty statements it is that, while he knew nothing of
an eternal life in heaven, he did contemplate a resurrection of all the righteous dead to a long life in the
kingdom of God on earth. His God is apparently
One who gives compensation to all men of past ages
who have served Him. In one passage he teaches
that sorrows of men in all ages are to be accounted for
by the action of malign spirits, who will disturb the
lives of men and be a cause of trouble until the consummation of all things ($15^{10}-16^1$). But he has nothing to say as to any divine reason for the permission
of this.

The only allusion to the idea of solidarity in penalties
appears in the statement that Abel in Sheol " keeps
on complaining " of Cain " till his seed is destroyed
from the face of the earth " ($22^7$).

*Moral Evil.*—Mankind was corrupted in the age
before the Flood by Azazel, according to this author.
" The whole earth has been defiled through the teaching of Azazel : to him ascribe all the sin " ($10^8$). It
is not, however, taught that God permits demons constantly to assail man's virtue. Tennant is of the

* I.J.A., art. " Historic Succession of the Books of Enoch,"
October 1910, pp. 74 f.

contrary opinion. "The fall of the watchers," he says, "is said in one passage to have been the cause of the existence of the postdiluvian demons on earth, and is connected therefore with present sin as well as with that which provoked the deluge." * He expresses his disagreement with the opinion of Lods, who maintains that the author does not seek in the story of the fall of the angels an explanation of sin on the earth, but tells the tale out of interest in these superior beings, and because it furnishes a striking example of the irresistible justice of God.† The truth is that the author *does* find in the fall of the angels the beginning of sin on the earth, but that he does not represent mankind as exposed constantly to the assaults of tempting spirits. They are a constant cause of trouble indeed. "The spirits of the giants will devour, oppress, destroy, attack, do battle, and cause destruction on the earth, and work affliction " (15¹¹). "They will destroy until the day of the great consummation" (16¹). It is not said that they will solicit men to sin. The language is in most striking contrast to that of the Book of Jubilees, where the demons are expressly described as seducers of mankind continually by the sovereign appointment of God.

### ETHIOPIC ENOCH 83–90

*Israel and the Gentiles.*—Israel, according to the teaching of this section, is in perpetuity God's chosen people. Their oppressors are destined to be at last destroyed by their sword (90¹⁹). Then the surviving Gentiles will submit to them. " I saw all the sheep

* Op. cit., p. 186.
† Tennant, op. cit., p. 185 and note 2.

which had been left, and all the beasts on the earth, and all the birds of the heaven, falling down and doing homage to those sheep and making petition to and obeying them in every word " ($90^{30}$). But the Israel which is thus favoured is a people purged of its unworthy members ($90^{26}$) and become regenerate. Apparently also, the submissive Gentiles do not simply yield to superior arms, but are converted. " Those sheep were all white, and their wool was abundant and clean ; and all that had been destroyed and dispersed, and all the beasts of the field, and all the birds of the heaven assembled in that house, and the Lord of the sheep rejoiced with great joy because they were all good and had returned to His house " ($90^{32\,f.}$). In this passage the " dispersed " are obviously Israelites of the Exile, and the " destroyed " are Israel's dead. Charles regards the verse as meaning that " all the righteous dead will be raised to take part in the kingdom." * The language, however, seems to suggest that all Israelites are to enjoy this privilege except perhaps the " blinded sheep " whose casting into the fire is narrated in the immediately preceding context ($90^{26}$). But, since a clear distinction is made in the judgment of faithful and apostate Israelites living in the last times, and only the faithful survive the great ordeal, it is probable that Charles is right and that the language used in $90^{33}$ is lacking in precision.

*The Problem of Prosperity and Adversity.*—The writer narrates instances of God's punitive justice in the past (88, $89^{1-8}$, $89^{54\,f.}$). He regards Israel in his own time as paying the penalty of transgression. But that penalty is out of all proportion to its offences to his mind, and he accounts for it by his theory that it is

* Edition of Ethiopic Enoch, p. 223.

not God, but the angel rulers, who thus treat Israel unjustly. God has given them power over the nation in consequence of its sin (89⁵⁹). They inflict excessive punishment (Ibid. ⁶⁵). But God knows (Ibid. ⁷⁰), and will in the end punish them for it (90²²⁻²⁵). He will give due recompense to all, faithful and sinners alike, in due time. The writer does not raise the question why God tolerates the unjust action of the angels. But, since the upshot of Israel's troubles is a large conversion, it is possible that he regarded them as having a divine disciplinary purpose.

*Moral Evil.*—It was the sin of the fallen angels that corrupted the earth in antediluvian times, according to this writer; but he does not attempt to account for the presence of sin in the world after the Flood.

### JUBILEES

*Israel and the Gentiles.*—In a variety of passages, this writer teaches that there will be no blessed future for the races that were in conflict with Israel in his own day. None of those who spring from Canaan " will be saved in the day of judgment " (22²¹). Neither Esau nor his seed " is to be saved, but destroyed from the earth " (35¹⁴). Not one of the race of the Philistines " will be saved on the day of the wrath of judgment. . . . Though he descend into Sheol, there also will his condemnation be great, and there also he will have no peace. . . . Into eternal malediction will he depart. And thus is it written and engraved concerning him on the heavenly tablets " (24³⁰⁻³). " As for all the worshippers of idols and the profane, there will be no hope for them in the land of the living. . . . They will descend into Sheol and into the place of condemnation will they go " (22²²). The author never

hints at the possibility of repentance on the part of
these. He calmly announces that whole nations are
to be consigned to hopeless condemnation, and looks
forward to the time when the righteous " will rejoice
for ever and ever and will see all their judgments and
their curses on their enemies " ($23^{30f.}$). Even the
blessing pronounced by Isaac on Esau is turned by
him into a curse, for he adds to it these words : " Thou
wilt sin a complete sin unto death, and thy seed will
be rooted out from under heaven " ($26^{34}$; cf. Gen. $27^{39}$).
Looking into the future, he anticipates the day when
Israel will become the dominant race. He records
the promise to Jacob (after Gen. $35^{10f.}$) and adds :
" They [Israel] will judge everywhere wherever the
foot of the sons of men has trodden. And I shall give
to thy seed all the earth which is under heaven and
they will judge all the nations according to their
desires, and after that they will get possession of the
whole earth and inherit it for ever " ($32^{18f.}$). Abraham also is described as praying thus : " May nations
serve thee, and all the nations bow themselves before
thy seed " ($22^{11}$). In fact, no writer in this literature
furnishes a better illustration of Sanday's dictum :
" However much it [Judaism] might avoid the con-
ceiving of God in the likeness of man generally, it had
not the same hesitation to conceive of Him as made
in the likeness of the ideal Jew." * For it is clear that
this Jew regarded his God as sharing his own racial
antipathies, despite the fact that he names Him as
" God of the spirits of all flesh " ($10^3$).

On the other hand, it is to be observed that he
cites repeatedly the promises made to the patriarchs
concerning Israel's destiny to be a blessing to the
nations. This idea occurs even when he is not simply

* D.B., art. " God," p. 207.

transferring O.T. words to his pages (e.g. 19$^{17}$, 21$^{25}$). This is the more significant, since it was his habit to omit or alter anything in the Scriptures which offended his susceptibilities. Apparently he conceived of a future kingdom of God which would include penitent Gentiles, who would be blessed by becoming subject to the chosen race.

There are, moreover, passages in which this Jew attempts, as it seems designedly, to offer explanation and vindication of the divine particularism. In a notable passage he declares that "there are many nations and many peoples, and all are His, and over all hath He placed spirits in authority to lead them astray from Him. But over Israel He did not appoint any angel or spirit, for He alone is their ruler" (15$^{31 f.}$). Concerning this passage Charles says: "I think we may assume that the statement in our text is made on the same principle as many in the Scriptures (cf. Isa. 6$^9$, Matt. 13$^{14}$, Mark 4$^{12}$, etc.), in which the ultimate result of an action or a series of actions is declared to have been the immediate object of them." * But so to explain the passage is to overlook the significance of similar statements elsewhere in these pages. The author has included in his work a fragment from a lost apocalypse of Noah, and in it we are told that God, at Noah's desire, gave orders to bind all the evil spirits, the sons of the watchers (10$^{5-7}$). Then "the chief of the spirits, Mastema, came and said: 'Lord Creator, let some of them remain before me, and let them hearken to my voice and do all that I shall say unto them, for, if some of them are not left to me, I shall not be able to execute the power of my will on the sons of men, for these are for corruption and leading astray before my judg-

* Edition of Jubilees, p. 112.

ment, for great is the wickedness of the sons of men ' "
($10^{7 a.}$). Charles considers that, while in this passage
the spirits are demons, in $15^{31 f.}$ they are angels.*
But they are not described in $15^{31}$ as angels, but as
" spirits in authority," and in the context the spirits
are expressly distinguished from angels. " He will
require them at the hand of all His angels and His
spirits " ($15^{32}$). It seems probable, therefore, that
the two passages refer to the same evil spirits, who
are the sons of the watchers ($10^{5}$). Now, according
to $10^{7 a.}$, God consents that the spirits of Mastema
shall remain for the express purpose of corrupting
the Gentiles, and Mastema prevails by the plea that
they are very sinful. We have a similar statement
of the functions of those spirits in $48^{17}$, where it is said
that Mastema hardened the hearts of the Egyptians
and " made them stubborn, and the device was de-
vised by the Lord our God that He might smite the
Egyptians and cast them into the sea." It seems,
therefore, clear that the spirits who ruled mankind,
according to the teaching of our author, were possessed of that power in consequence of the transgressions of men. They were sinful, and their punishment,
judicially ordained of God, is that they are made more
sinful, through the divinely ordained action of seducing
spirits.

There are also passages whose implication is that
God chose Israel for the merits of the nation's forbears. He chose the seed of Jacob from amongst all
that He saw at the time of the creation ($2^{20}$). The
choice was based on His foreknowledge of the character
of Israel. He did not choose Ishmael or Esau, for
He knew them ($15^{30}$). The destined heir of the promises is recognised by Abraham by his good conduct

* Edition of Jubilees, p. 112.

(19$^{16}$). Our author thus justifies the ways of God in the election of Israel and the exclusion of the Gentiles. God gave to each the reward of his conduct.

This writer, however, very clearly teaches that Israel's highly privileged position can only be maintained by the nation's loyalty to God. Abraham warns Isaac that for a sin unto death, if they do it, his name and his seed "will perish from the whole earth" (21$^{22}$). Isaac commands his sons to do right "that the Lord may bring on you all that the Lord said that He would do to Abraham and his seed" (36$^{9}$). Israel is "not to eat blood, so that their names and their seed may be before the Lord God continually" (6$^{13}$). God's choice of Israel to be permanently His own people is, in fact, dependent on the continued fulfilment of certain conditions on the part of the nation. Accordingly, Abraham hopes and prays that the people may be eternally God's own, and expresses his fear that all Israel's sons by fornication may be destroyed by the sword, and become accursed as Sodom and all the remnant as the sons of Gomorrah (20$^{6}$). Moreover, immediately after the splendid promise of Israel's permanent position in 15$^{32}$, comes the awful announcement by the angel that Israel "will not keep true to this ordinance [circumcision] for in the flesh of their uncircumcision they will omit this circumcision of their sons, and all of them, sons of Beliar, will leave their sons uncircumcised as they were born" (15$^{33}$). This Jew, writing in an age of that widespread neglect of the legal cultus which he regards as apostasy from God, feels impelled to warn his compatriots in the most solemn terms that God's covenant may be annulled by their transgression. He also feels called to warn Israelites that individuals may forfeit their privileges. A child of Abraham may be recorded on the heavenly tablets as an adversary, and be destroyed out of the book of life (30²²). On the other hand, the deep and strong conviction of the writer, often expressed in these pages, is that God will not " cast off His people whom He foreknew " (Rom. 11²). He will " preserve them and bless them that they may be His and that He may be theirs from henceforth for ever " (15³²). " To Jacob and his seed it was granted that they should be the blessed and holy ones of the first testimony and law " (2²⁴). Abraham says to Jacob : " Thy seed and thy name will stand throughout all generations " (22²⁴), and God Himself says : " I shall cleanse them so that they shall not turn away from Me from that day unto eternity " (1²³).

In summing up briefly our results, it may be said that the doctrine of God in His relations to Israel and the world, while undoubtedly containing unworthy elements, is by no means altogether of an unworthy character. God's choice of Israel and His rejection of the Gentiles did not arise in arbitrary fashion. He had regard to the known character of nations. Israel also can only maintain its privileged position by continued faithfulness. God does not make them His elect in any unworthy manner. On the other hand, our author is deeply convinced that His patient love to Israel will be finally victorious over all that people's evil tendencies. First impressions of the thinking of the author are seriously modified on a full consideration of all the data which he supplies.

Nevertheless, the great blot upon his book remains. He could not conceive of any grace from God for the majority of the Gentile world. He owns repeatedly that Israel is sinful even as the Gentiles, and that despite all light and privilege. Yet Israel is not

punished in the same severe fashion as the nations,
and the penalty which comes on the Gentile world
is not that which follows inevitably from their fault.
It is not that deterioration of character which comes
about through the nature of things, by which it
happens to all mankind that " the reward of a sin is
a sin." It comes rather by an arbitrary fiat of the
Supreme, who hands them all over to the dominion
of evil spirits that they may be led astray from Him.

 *The Problem of Prosperity and Adversity.*—The writer
offers many illustrations of the doctrine that there
are numerous sorrows of men which are the consequences of a divine judgment on sin. The Flood and
the destruction of Sodom were the acts of God ($4^{24}$,
$20^5$). It was the Lord who delivered the Shechemites
" into the hand of the sons of Jacob that they might
exterminate them with the sword and execute judgment upon them " ($30^6$). He brings all sorts of
calamities on " an evil generation which transgresses
on the earth " ($23^{13\,f.}$). He will deliver Israel into
the hand of the Gentiles, if they sin, and will root them
out of the land ($1^{13}$, $21^{22}$). The death of Cain, by the
falling of his house, was no accident. It was a
" righteous judgment " on him and took place according to that *lex talionis*, which is " ordained on the
heavenly tablets " ($4^{32}$), as an abiding and divinely
sanctioned principle for human jurisprudence. In
one passage the writer's fierce nationalism leads him
to ascribe gross injustice to God, who, he says, " took
vengeance on a million of the Egyptians, and one
thousand strong and energetic men were destroyed
on account of one suckling of the children of Thy
people which they had thrown into the river " ($48^{14}$).

God acts upon the principle of solidarity in His
judgment. It is laid down that " the whole nation

will be judged for all the uncleanness and profanation " of one sinner (30¹⁵). Our author thus gives a
much wider application to the principle which is
enunciated in Leviticus 20⁵, for there it applies only
to the family of the offender, but here to all the nation.
In this book the principle thus broadly understood
is often insisted upon. Lot and his descendants are
to be blotted out for his fault. It is " commanded
and engraven on the heavenly tablets " (16⁹). The
family of Ham and Canaan suffer in the same way
(22²¹). Isaac's fault may entail a similar fate on Israel
(21²²). Should brother devise evil against brother,
" he will be rooted out of the land of the living and
his seed shall be destroyed from under heaven " (36⁹).
Even the perfect Abraham grew old prematurely
because of the general wickedness (23¹⁰). Moreover,
it is laid down that God will act on this principle in
the final judgment. The unfortunate child whose
parents have not circumcised him on the eighth day
is involved in the meshes of this net (15¹⁴). He " belongs not to the children of the covenant which the
Lord made with Abraham, but to the children of
destruction . . . to be destroyed and slain from the
earth " (15²⁶). Poor innocent wight ! " He has broken
the covenant of the Lord " (15²⁶). Here, in his zeal for
the due observance of the sacred rite, the author goes
beyond the statement in the Massoretic text of
Gen. 17¹⁴, once again attributing serious injustice to
God.* He manifests a defective sense of the rights of
the individual, teaching that God judges families and
nations as entities without just regard to units. On
the other hand, he teaches that men benefit by the

---

* The words " on the eighth day," which are not in the
Hebrew, are found, as Charles notes, in Sam. and LXX, though
not in Syr. and Vulgate. Cf. Edition of Jubilees, p. 108.

righteousness of forbears. The sons of Noah, he says, escaped the Flood through his merits ($5^{19}$). Abraham's seed is blessed by the angels throughout all the generations of the earth because he celebrated aright the feast of tabernacles ($16^{28}$). The seed of Levi obtained the priesthood through his good conduct in the matter of the revenge for the wrong done to Dinah ($30^{18}$). The angels remember his righteousness, and it will come to him and his descendants after him ($30^{29}$). With further reference to what has been said above as to this writer's defective sense of what is due to the individual, it is to be observed that he does show some sense of what is due to the righteous dead. It is impossible to say whether he thought, like the author of Enoch 83–90, that they would be raised to participate in the joys of the earthly kingdom. There is ambiguity in the solitary statement which he makes on this matter: "At that time the Lord will heal His servants, and they will rise up and see great peace and drive out their adversaries" ($23^{30}$). Probably these words only refer to the triumph of living Israel. The words which follow seem to imply this. But clearly he held the doctrine of a blessed life for the righteous in the spirit world. "Their bones will rest in the earth and their spirits will have much joy" ($23^{31}$).

Our author teaches that material prosperity is normally conditioned by righteousness. In a time of widespread corruption, Mastema is permitted to punish man, sending "ravens and birds to destroy the seed which was sown in the land in order to destroy the land and rob the children of men of their labours" ($11^{11f.}$). Abraham is described as saying: "Serve ye the Most High God . . . that He may have pleasure in you, and grant you His mercy, and send rain upon you morning and evening, and bless all your works . . . and bless thy bread and thy water, and bless the fruit of thy womb and the fruit of thy land and the herds of thy cattle and the flocks of thy sheep " ($20^9$).

As we have observed in Chapter I., it is said that God is " the defence of the good " ($21^{20}$), and Isaac is charged by Abraham to observe certain laws that he may be " preserved from all evil " and that God may save him " from every kind of death " (Ibid.).

This writer is not, however, oblivious of the fact that trouble comes to good men, though he nowhere gives the faintest indication that he found in such cases any problem for faith. He notes the fact that Abraham had trials, and of this he has his own explanation. It was God who tried Abraham and knew thereby his faithfulness ($17^{17}$). Mastema desired that he should be tried, and the result was that " the prince of the Mastema was put to shame " ($17^{16}$, $18^{12}$). " Now I have shown that thou fearest the Lord," says the angel ($18^{11}$). " I have shown to all," says God, " that thou art faithful unto Me " ($18^{16}$).

The teaching, doubtless, based on the story in the first chapter of the book of Job, is that good men may suffer in order that it may be shown to supernatural beings that God has loyal servants amongst men. The same idea recurs when we are told that the angels subsequently tested Abraham to see if he were patient ($19^3$). It is also taught by an example, that the righteous may have trouble from Mastema. Charles contends indeed that it is not so. The demons, he says, " cannot touch the righteous " ($10^6$) ; every breach of the law, however, exposes men to their malignant influence " ($48^2$).* But, of the two

* Edition of Jubilees, p. 80.

passages cited, 10⁶ is only a prayer that they may not rule the sons of the righteous, and 48²ᶠ· is the curious passage in which the writer ascribes to Mastema what in Exodus is said to have been done by God (Exod. 4²⁴). Mastema is here said to have sought with all his power to kill Moses when he was returning into Egypt and to have been prevented by angelic interposition. In 10¹⁰⁻¹³, the story is told of the mission of angels to teach the sons of Noah the use of certain medicines by which the evil spirits would be hindered from hurting them. "For He knew that they would not walk in righteousness." Evidently our author teaches that unrighteousness exposes men to the arts of Mastema. He also tells, in a tale about Abraham, how the righteous counterwork his malicious designs (11¹⁹ᶠ·). Still, it is clear that Moses, though not killed by Mastema, was greatly troubled by him, and it is not the teaching of Jubilees that Mastema "cannot touch the righteous." Its doctrine is much the same in this respect as that of Enoch 1–36.

The idea of a merciful divine discipline of Israel by means of national sufferings is clearly implied in 1¹²⁻¹⁵. God will hide His face from them and deliver them to captivity among the Gentiles (1¹²ᶠ·). "And after this, they will turn to Me from amongst the Gentiles . . . and they will seek Me so that I shall be found of them, when they seek Me with all their heart and with all their soul " (1¹⁵).

*Moral Evil.*—The entrance of sin into the world is described after the manner of Genesis (3¹⁷⁻²⁶). The story of the sin of the watchers in causing the primitive corruption of the way of all flesh is told, and the writer says that God sent these on the earth (5¹ᶠ·). As we have already seen, he teaches that the Gentiles are given over by God to evil spirits. Sin after the

Flood is ascribed to their influence ($7^{27}$, $10^1$, $11^{4\,f.}$, $12^{20}$).
But, in his account of the sin of the watchers, this
writer says they came to earth " that they should
instruct the children of men that they should do
judgment and uprightness on the earth " ($4^{15}$).  In
this, as in his teaching as to evil spirits generally, this
writer is unique among the authors of this literature,
and evidently he cherished an apologetic design.  He
was concerned to show, in the one case, how a beneficent design of God was frustrated, and in the other
case he desired to vindicate the justice of God.  In
one passage he seems to teach that God determines
conduct, for he represents Isaac as telling Esau that
he will " sin a complete sin unto death " ($26^{34}$).  But
this is utterly opposed to the general tenor of his
thinking, since he warns men against sin and insists
on the possibility of repentance (e.g. $41^{25}$), and affirms
that the retributions of God await transgressors.


### THE TESTAMENTS OF THE TWELVE PATRIARCHS

*Israel and the Gentiles.*—In the work of this large-
hearted writer we have the noblest teaching as to the
attitude of God to Israel and the Gentiles.  Israel is
abidingly His people.  Only once is its position
spoken of as conditional.  " If ye, my children, walk
in holiness according to the commandments of the
Lord, ye shall again dwell securely with me and all
Israel shall be gathered unto the Lord " (T. Benj. $10^{11}$).
But usually the future is regarded as certain.  Levi
will " sacrifice for all Israel until the consummation
of the times " (T. Reub. $6^8$).  The coming Priest-King
" shall give the majesty of the Lord to the sons of
God for ever " (T. Levi $18^8$).  When the salvation of
God comes, " no longer shall Jerusalem endure desola-

tion, nor Israel be led captive " (T. Dan 5¹³). If, however, this writer looks so confidently on the future of the nation, it is because he believes in the ultimate triumph of righteousness among them. Sin will come to an end (T. Levi 18⁹). God "will pour out the spirit of grace upon you," he says, "and ye shall be unto Him sons in truth, and ye shall walk in His commandments first and last " (T. Jud. 24³). That does not mean the ultimate salvation of every Israelite. " I shall rise in the midst of you," says Zebulun, " and I shall rejoice in the midst of my tribe, as many as shall keep the law of the Lord " (T. Zeb. 10²). Dan warns his sons to refrain from lying and anger, or they will perish (T. Dan 2¹; cf. 6¹⁰). " The Lord shall judge Israel first for their unrighteousness . . . and He shall convict Israel through the chosen ones of the Gentiles " (T. Benj. 10⁸, ¹⁰).

Like Ben Sira, our author held that God originally gave light to all men. The Gentiles "went astray and forsook the Lord and changed their order and worshipped stocks and stones, spirits of deceit " (T. Naph. 3³). In a number of passages in the work the Gentiles are named before Israel, and these are almost certainly interpolations of a Christian origin. If, with Charles, we disregard these, there still remain many sentences which show that this Jew of the second century B.C. held the most catholic ideas of God's justice and mercy for all mankind.

He looks for a Priest in whose days " the Gentiles shall be multiplied in knowledge upon the earth and enlightened through the grace of the Lord " (T. Levi 18⁹). " All the peoples shall glorify the Lord for ever " (T. Jud. 25⁵). " His name shall be in every place of Israel and among the Gentiles " (T. Dan 6⁷). " He shall save Israel and all the Gentiles " (T.

Asher 7³). "The twelve tribes shall be gathered together and all the Gentiles" (T. Benj. 9²). "The Lord shall reveal His salvation to all the Gentiles" (T. Benj. 10⁵). Perhaps the passage in T. Levi 4⁴— "The Lord will visit all the Gentiles in His tender mercy"—should not be cited here, because, as Charles suggests, the plural may have been substituted for the singular by a Christian hand.* Nor perhaps should we make use of T. Naph. 8³, where it is said that God will "appear on earth to save the race of Israel and to gather together the righteous from amongst the Gentiles," for that might obviously refer only to the Israel of the Dispersion. But the writer's doctrine is most clearly stated in the other passages cited above, and in T. Naph. 8⁴ he teaches that through a righteous Israel "God shall be glorified among the Gentiles." There are two other important passages in which it is taught that Israel's destiny is to be God's agent to convert the Gentiles: "If ye be darkened through transgressions, what therefore will all the Gentiles do, living in blindness? Yea, ye shall bring a curse upon our race, because the light of the law, which was given to lighten every man, this ye desire to destroy" (T. Levi 14⁴). "From your root shall arise a stem, and from it shall grow a rod of righteousness to the Gentiles, to judge and save all that call upon the Lord" (T. Jud. 24⁵). These two passages, however, are part of the work of the later writer who inserted into the text of the Testaments his attack on the Maccabæan house. They are, therefore, interesting and important evidence of the existence of these broad views in a later time, probably between 70 and 40 B.C.

*The Problem of Prosperity and Adversity.*—According

* "Greek Versions of the Testaments," p. 36.

to this writer, punishment for sin falls on the nation
(T. Levi 10[4], 15[1], 16[5]; T. Jud. 23[3]; T. Iss. 6[8]; T.
Asher 7[6]), and the interpolator has the same teaching
(T. Zeb. 9[6]; T. Naph. 4[2, 5]). Individuals get a just
retribution in physical penalties (T. Reub. 1[7]; T.
Sim. 2[12]; T. Gad 5[9-11]), and in their state of mind,
troubled or peaceful, in the article of death (T.
Asher 6[4-6]). The principle of solidarity in punishments and rewards is acted upon by God. The sons
of Zebulun escaped prevalent sickness because of his
compassion, while the sons of his brother suffered for
the sin against Joseph (T. Zeb. 5[3f.]). In two passages
of the interpolator a wider application of this principle
is asserted. He says that if Levi's sons should not
receive mercy through Abraham, Isaac, and Jacob,
not one of them would be left upon the earth (T. Levi
15[4]), and he utters the prophecy: "The Lord will
gather you together in faith, through His tender
mercy, and for the sake of Abraham, Isaac, and
Jacob" (T. Asher 7[7]).

God's rule in the government of the world is stated
thus: "Even as a man doeth to his neighbour, even
so also the Lord will do to him." This is illustrated
by the fact that Zebulun's kindness to his neighbour
was rewarded with an abundance of fish (T. Zeb. 5[3], 6[6]).
Still, the writer is alive to the fact that good men
have troubles. He often refers to the story of the
wrongs of righteous Joseph. He speaks of men who
died in grief, and were poor for the Lord's sake, and
for His sake were put to death (T. Jud. 25[4]). He says
that craft has increased on the earth, and the wickedness of man has prospered (T. Iss. 1[11]). But he
betrays no feeling of perplexity, though now and then
he manifests his consciousness of the fact that some
things in the present order call for explanation. Six

suggestions are offered by him: (1) God is the faithful Friend of the good, who sometimes departs from men for a space to try them (T. Jos. 2⁴⁻⁶). (2) Righteous men may suffer for the good of their fellows, like Joseph, of whom his father says : " In thee shall be fulfilled the prophecy of heaven that a blameless one shall be delivered up for lawless men and a sinless shall die for ungodly men " (T. Benj. 3⁸). (3) God gives a man what He knows is best for him, so that " if a man liveth in chastity, and desireth also glory, and the Most High knoweth that it is expedient for him, He bestoweth this also upon him " (T. Jos. 9³). (4) A tried man must patiently trust. " Though a man become rich by evil means, even as Esau the brother of my father, be not jealous, but wait for the end of the Lord " (T. Gad 7⁴). (5) The satisfying good of life is wisdom. " Get wisdom in the fear of God with diligence. For though there be a leading away into captivity, and cities and lands be destroyed, and gold and silver and every possession perish, the wisdom of the wise naught can take away, save the blindness of ungodliness and the callousness [that comes] of sin." (T. Levi 13⁶). (6) The justice of God, largely operative in the present time, is destined to receive a complete manifestation. Justice will be done to the righteous dead, who will awake to life (T. Jud. 25¹· ⁴; T. Sim. 6⁷; T. Levi 13⁵ etc.), and sinners will get due punishment (T. Levi 3ˢ·ᵗ, 4¹; T. Zeb. 10³). " All men shall rise, some unto glory and some unto shame " (T. Benj. 10⁸). It must be added that, according to this book, human sorrows sometimes come from the action of evil spirits ; but these cannot injure the good. " Fear the Lord and love your neighbour, and, even though the spirits of Beliar claim you to afflict you with every evil, yet shall they not have dominion over you, even as they had not over Joseph your brother. How many men wished to slay him, and God shielded him! For he that feareth God and loveth his neighbour cannot be smitten by the spirits of Beliar, being shielded by the fear of God " (T. Benj. 3$^{3\,4.}$).

*Moral Evil.*—The teaching is that God allows evil spirits to tempt men. Sometimes in this book, malign spirits are simply personifications of evil influences (e.g. T. Jud. 16$^1$, 20$^1$). This, however, is not always the case. It is clear that the writer believed in the activities of one who is the " Devil," or Satan, or " the Prince of Deceit " (T. Naph. 8$^{4.\ 6}$; T. Gad 4$^7$; T. Dan 6$^1$; T. Sim. 2$^7$). A spirit of Beliar stirred Dan against Joseph (T. Dan 1$^7$). The temptress of Joseph was troubled by the spirit of Beliar (T. Jos. 7$^4$). Perhaps, also, the doctrine appears in T. Zeb. 9$^7$: " The spirits of deceit deceive men in all their deeds "; but there is a various reading here: " They are deceived through their own wicked deeds." No man, however, need be led astray by the spirits. If one be a good man, they are powerless (T. Benj. 6$^1$; T. Iss. 4$^4$). Concerning the origin of evil, the author teaches a unique doctrine. It was the women who tempted the watchers (T. Reub. 5). Sin also arises, he says, from man's God-given nature. It is due to his limitations. He is flesh, and is deceived (T. Zeb. 9$^7$). He sins because he has no perception of the things which angels see (T. Levi 3$^{9\,4.}$). The body is a cause of sin, and God knows how far it will persist in goodness and when it begins in evil (T. Naph. 2$^4$). The existence of the Yetzer Hara in man is a peril. " Two ways hath God given to the sons of men, and two inclinations " (T. Asher 1$^3$). Still, God has made man able to win the victory. Man may annul his liberty by habitual

sin and become the devil's " own peculiar instrument "
(T. Naph. 8⁶); but, if he takes pleasure in the good,
he overthrows the evil and uproots the sin (T. Asher 1⁷).
He may even destroy " the [evil] inclination " by good
works (T. Asher 3²). It is for a man to choose for
himself the light or the darkness, the law of God or
the works of Beliar (T. Levi 19¹).

A passage from the pen of the Jewish interpolator
gives evidence of the existence of the doctrine of evil
spirits as tempters in the next century: " Your prince
is Satan, and all the spirits of wickedness and pride
will conspire to attend constantly on the sons of
Levi to cause them to sin before the Lord " (T. Dan 5⁶).

## THE SIBYLLINE ORACLES, BOOK 3⁹⁷⁻⁸²⁹

*Israel and the Gentiles.*—The Sibyl affirms that to
Israel alone—

" The mighty God His gracious counsel gave,
And faith and noblest thought within their hearts " (584 f.).

They are a royal tribe whose race will be unfailing.
In coming times " this race shall bear rule and begin
to build God's temple anew " (288–90). " The nation
of the mighty God " will once again be strong, and
will be " guides of life to all men " (194 f.). Notwithstanding what is said in 584 f., it seems to be
implied that some light was given to all mankind upon
conduct, for the Sibyl in one passage speaks of various
nations as—

" Transgressing the immortal God's pure law,
Which they were under " (599 f.).*

Charles rightly says that, directly or indirectly, the

* There are various readings. Ὅνπερ is read followed by
ἔδωκεν or ὑπῆσαν or ἔλυσαν in the different MSS.

aim of these Oracles " was the propagation of Judaism among the Gentiles." * The Sibyl makes appeal to Greece to put no more her trust in idols, but to " honour the All-Father's name and let it not escape " her (545–50). " Wretched Hellas," she cries, " stop thy arrogance and be wise ; and entreat the Immortal One magnanimous " (732 f.). God is called " the Immortal Sire of all men " (604), " Father of all gods and men " (278). It is foretold that, in coming days, Egyptians " before the mighty God " shall bend the knee and He shall " bestow great joy on men " (616–19). The Sibyl anticipates a time when Asia and Europe shall be blest with freedom from plague, poverty, and moral evil, " for from the starry heaven shall all good order come upon mankind " (367 ff.). The day will come when " all the islands and the cities " will call upon God and go to the temple in procession, abandoning idolatry (715–20).

> " Out of every land unto the house
> Of the great God shall they bring frankincense
> And gifts " (772 f.).

*The Problem of Prosperity and Adversity.*—The main burden of the book is God's punitive justice. It is because God punishes sin that nations experience famine, plagues, and war (e.g. 317, 332, 538 ff., 601–6). The sufferings and downfall of nations throughout the world come from this cause, and the Sibyl dwells on this fact again and again throughout the Oracles. But penalty is not thought of as merely of a retributive character. Rather, God disciplines the nations with a view to a righteous humanity in the future. He troubles Egypt, but the result will be that Egypt will bend the knee to Him (616 f.). He manifests anger

* E.B., art. " Apocalyptic Literature," 245.

against Greece, but the effect will be that "all souls of men" will begin to seek His help "with mighty groaning, lifting up their hands to the broad heaven" (556-61). It is recognised that an evil fate sometimes overtakes the righteous (312), but there is no sign of perplexity as to this in the mind of the Sibyl. The only reference to the life beyond is in the promise in 770 f., that God will open to the pious "portals of the blessed and all joy and mind immortal and eternal bliss."

THE PROEMIUM

*Israel and the Gentiles.*—The Sibyl appeals to idolaters to cease offering sacrifices to demons and to wander no more in the darkness: "Come, do not always chase darkness and gloom" ($1^{25-9}$). She exhorts them to bend the neck to the only One, and reproaches them for not coming to a sound mind and knowing God ($3^{41 f.}$). She admonishes them of the ill fate reserved for idolaters in the life to come and of the blessedness of the pious ($3^{43-8}$). The implication of these Oracles clearly is that God is willing to receive Gentile men if they turn unto Him.

*The Problem of Prosperity and Adversity.*—God is described as—

> "Dealing out
> Unto all mortals in a common light
> The judgment" ($1^{18}$).

and as—

> "Bringing unto the good, good recompense
> Much more abundant, but awakening wrath
> And anger for the evil and unjust,
> And war and pestilence and tearful woes" ($3^{18-20}$)

(cf. $3^{8 ff.}$). That judgment of God will be in evidence

also in the future, when the disobedient will " be with torches burned the livelong day through an eternal age," while the pious shall " inherit life " and dwell for ever in the " fertile field of Paradise " (3⁴⁸⁻⁹).

## SUMMARY

(1) *The Justice of God in His Attitude to Israel and the Gentiles.*—(A) That Israel is destined to be for ever the chosen people of God is a doctrine confidently proclaimed in the Oracles, Enoch 1–36, 83–90, and Ecclesiasticus. In Tobit, Jubilees, and the Testaments there are prophetic passages in which the same affirmation is strongly made in unqualified fashion. Yet each of these three contains passages in which the future of Israel is spoken of as conditional, and the writers solemnly insist on the necessity of a right attitude on the part of the people Godward. The author of Jubilees was haunted by the gravest apprehensions as to the possibility of the nation's forfeiting its high estate by disloyalty, and serious fears of the same fate for Israelites find expression in the Testaments. What these writers devoutly hoped for was a future in which the whole people would be loyal to God, and that was the confidence which strongly animated the author of Tobit. Their great hope was that God's continued grace would triumph over all the perversity of His people. This, too, was the confidence of the Sibyl, the author of Enoch 83–90, and the writer or writers of the Additions to Ben Sira.

In Enoch 1–36 Israel is the " elect " who are to enjoy the privileges of the kingdom at last ; but here it is made plain that only the righteous will be citizens in that ideal community. Ben Sira denies altogether the idea that Israel will ever be cast away by God ;

but the relationship which He sustains to Israel is conceived of as being of an ethical character, and Ben Sira is far from thinking of Israel as destined to enjoy exclusive privilege.

Five of these writers speak of a post-resurrection life, and in them all, except Enoch 83–90, the express teaching is that the fate of the individual Israelite is determined by his conduct. The author of Enoch 83–90 would probably have subscribed to the same doctrine.

(B) The conception of God as having purposes of mercy for all nations is very general among these authors. The one work in which a most narrow view of God is taken is the book of Jubilees, and perhaps its author, who clearly did not dream of any mercy from God for the vast majority of the Gentile world, conceived of a future in which the last survivors of the nations would be blessed by becoming subject to Israel. The idea that light was originally offered to all mankind appears in the Testaments and Ecclesiasticus. The Sibyl also has a passage whose implication is that the Gentiles have some light on duty. Even in Jubilees there is an attempt to explain and vindicate the divine attitude to the Gentiles by the theory that it was the penal consequence of their sin. On this matter the Enoch writers are silent, and the author of Tobit contents himself with the statement that God gives counsel to whom He pleases. The tendency, on the whole, therefore, was to oppose the idea that God had arbitrarily rejected the nations, refusing to give them light.

It is very manifest that Ben Sira held the most catholic ideas of God's justice and mercy to all mankind. The same must be said of the author or authors of the additions to his work. In Enoch 1–36, Tobit, the Oracles, and, above all, in the work of that great-hearted Jew who wrote the Testaments, the express teaching is that there will be a general acceptance by God at the last of converted nations. The same confident assurance characterised the writer of Enoch 83–90, for, though he regarded the Gentiles as destined to occupy a subordinate place in the kingdom of God, he nevertheless included them among the converted over whom in the last times God would rejoice.

(2) *The Justice of God in the Allotment of Prosperity and Adversity.*—(A) There is very frequent allusion to a divine justice which is manifestly operative in human fortune within the limits of the present life. Ben Sira regarded it as so completely in operation that it was a wonder if any sinner should escape paying penalties. In Tobit, the Testaments, and Jubilees the teaching is that, as a general rule, God awards fortune to men in strict proportion to their deserts. The Sibyl traces the operation of His justice in the sorrows of nations. Of these five writers, however, only the last-named gives no sign of acquaintance with hard facts that do not appear to harmonise with the doctrine of a divine regnant justice. Ben Sira had to resolve, in view of the facts of human life, that he *would* think that all that is good which God ordains. In other books it is not unrecognised by the writers that merit and fortune are not always equal in this world, though neither of them seems to have found in the facts of life any baffling problem.

Turning from these to the Enoch writers, we find ourselves in a very different atmosphere. The first of them encourages his readers by the memory of one signal act of God's punitive righteousness, but describes a world in which the grossest wrongs are allowed to be perpetrated. The second, while he recognises

that in the past God's justice has been notably seen
in punishments and deliverances, looks round on a
world in which God allows His people to suffer far
more than they deserve, while He stands aloof and
does not interfere on their behalf. These two, unlike
the rest, felt deeply the need of a theodicy.

(B) Nearly all the writers affirm the doctrine of the
solidarity of men in the judgments of God on conduct.
Ben Sira alone asserts this of the entire race, teaching
that Adam's sin is the cause of death to all. He and
the author of Jubilees say that the sins of the fathers
are visited on the children. This is also the doctrine
in Enoch 1–36 and Tobit, where, however, the teaching is that remote descendants suffer for the sin of
an ancestor. In one book only—Jubilees—is it maintained that a whole nation suffers for the sin of a
part. Some of the writers teach that children derive
benefits from the righteousness of parents. This is
the doctrine of Ecclesiasticus, Jubilees, and the
Testaments. They do not in any way imply that this
solidarity of men in God's judgments arises from the
nature of things. They did not think of good or
evil conduct as having inevitable consequences, which
would, of necessity, involve others beside the doers.
Rather, they regarded it as happening by the will of
the Supreme. In one passage of the Testaments
there is apparently evidence of the existence of a
finer view. The suffering of Joseph is regarded as a
means of benefit to a whole people, and the author—
inspired perhaps by the vision of the Suffering Servant
of the Lord in Isaiah 53—seems to have discerned
that, in the slow outworking of the purposes of the
Infinite Wisdom, the pain of one righteous man may
be made a means of the highest good to all his race.
In Tobit, also, the solidarity of the living and the dead

in penalties is justified by the fact that the living are sinners even as the fathers were.

(C) The supreme consolation for the sorrows of the present, to the majority of these men, was the assured belief in the God of compensations. They held that His justice would be completely vindicated in the future by due awards. This was not the faith of Ben Sira or the author of Tobit. They believed that the justice of God is fully manifested here and now. The rest of our authors were not of that mind. In Enoch 1–36, whose author, unlike Ben Sira, held that much sin goes unpunished in this world, it is maintained that at death God makes distinction in Hades between man and man according to desert. In that teaching this work is unique; but in Jubilees, the Testaments, Enoch 1–36, 83–90, and the Oracles, the doctrine is that there will be a future in which God will judge the dead, whether they be righteous or sinners. In Jubilees, however, the idea of God as doing ultimate justice to the individual is marred by the writer's doctrine that, even in the final settlement of their destiny, men will suffer from the operation of the principle of solidarity.

(D) The idea that God mercifully inflicts chastisement on men for their good occurs sometimes. It gets its noblest expression in Ecclesiasticus. No writer in his own time, or in the subsequent periods, is quite the peer of Ben Sira in this respect. He teaches that God acts in this way toward all mankind. The doctrine of the Testaments is that God tries good men, giving them such prosperity as is expedient for them. The implied teaching in Tobit, Jubilees, and Enoch 83–90 is that He disciplines Israel by chastisement. The Sibyl teaches by implication that He designs thus to correct the Gentiles.

(E) We find also in these works the doctrine that evil angels or spirits cause trouble to mankind. Enoch 1–36, Jubilees, Tobit, and the Testaments contain this idea, and in Enoch 83–90 evil angels trouble Israel. But in the last named this source of trouble is of a temporary character, while in the others it appears to be normally in operation. In Enoch 1–36 it is expressly said that such spirits will trouble mankind until the end. There is an important difference between the Testaments and Enoch 83–90 on the one hand, and Enoch 1–36, Jubilees, and Tobit on the other. In the former, it is sin which makes men the victims of the evil powers. They who thus suffer are men whom God punishes. In the latter it is not so. In Enoch 83–90 the design is to lay the blame for Israel's excessive suffering upon the evil angels rather than on God.

(F) A unique suggestion appears in Jubilees, where it is taught that a good man may be allowed by God to suffer for instruction to beings in the unseen world.

(3) *The Justice of God in the Permission of Moral Evil.*—(A) God is sometimes regarded as the author of the possibility of moral evil, in virtue of the nature which He has given to mankind. The Testaments teach that sin arises from the Yetzer Hara, implanted in men from the creation. Apparently, Ben Sira also held this doctrine. That man is exposed to peril by his physical constitution and his limitations of perception is the teaching in the Testaments. In a dubious passage of Ben Sira the frailty of man is regarded as a cause of sin. But these two writers insist that God has so made man that he is able to win moral victory.

(B) In a passage of Ecclesiasticus God is apparently regarded as determining what man shall be and do, but this is a verse of dubious authority. One sentence in Jubilees is of similar import. Each of these writers, however, emphasises man's moral freedom and responsibility.

(C) In Enoch 1–36, 83–90, and Jubilees the doctrine is that evil spirits introduced sin into the world. The Enoch writers, however, do not teach that such spirits constantly assail men, but that doctrine appears in Jubilees and the Testaments. These two writers offer explanations. According to Jubilees, a beneficent purpose of God in sending the spirits to earth was frustrated by their conduct, and only those men who have sinned are exposed to demonic assaults. In the Testaments it is said that the initiative in evil came from the women, and that good men are immune from the attacks of the tempting spirits.

## THE FIRST CENTURY B.C.

### I MACCABEES

*Israel and the Gentiles.*—Judas expresses the hope that all the Gentiles may know that " there is One who redeemeth and saveth Israel " (4¹¹); but the book gives us no information as to the author's ideas about God's attitude to the Gentiles. He did not, however, think of God as simply the great Partisan of his race. Rather, the hope of victory is based on the justice of Israel's cause (3²⁰ᶠ·).

*The Problem of Prosperity and Adversity.*—The speeches of Judas give no hint of a belief that Israel is suffering for sin. The penitential note is entirely wanting. But the author twice recognises the operation of a punitive justice (1⁶⁸, 6¹³). Mattathias and Judas are pictured as heartening the people by the memory of God's miraculous interventions in the past, and assuring them that He will not fail to give strength and victory ($2^{49-61}$, $4^9$, $7^{41}$; $2^{61}$, $3^{18-22}$). But Judas sometimes speaks in a less confident tone. He counsels his men to gird themselves for battle, saying : " It is better for us to die than to look on the evils of our nation and the holy place. Nevertheless, as may be the will in heaven, so shall He do " ($3^{59 f.}$). And again : " Let us cry unto Heaven, if He will have us " ($4^{10}$). Judas is thus represented as one who has learned by the hard logic of facts that the God who determines the fate of battles ($3^{18 f.}$) may will the triumph of the tyrant.

### ETHIOPIC ENOCH, 91–104

*Israel and the Gentiles.*—" In the third week, at its close," says this writer, " a man will be chosen as the plant of righteous judgment, and after him will come for evermore the plant of righteousness " ($93^5$). " In the fifth week, at its close, will the house of glory and dominion be built for ever " (Ibid. $^7$). Israel is " the eternal plant of righteousness " (Ibid. $^{10}$). But ruin awaits the faithless Israelite. " Woe to them . . . who transgress the eternal law and transform themselves into what they were not [i.e. into sinners]: they shall be trodden underfoot upon the earth " ($99^2$). " Woe to them who reject the measure and the eternal heritage of their fathers, and whose souls follow after idols, for they will have no rest " ($99^{14}$).

In one place the writer affirms the coming universal rejection of the Gentiles. When the idol temples are burned in the day of God's judgment, the heathen " will be cast into the judgment of fire and will perish in wrath and in grievous eternal judgment " ($91^9$).

But, in the same chapter, there is a prophecy of the domination of the earth by the righteous in the eighth week of the world's history, and of a judgment of the sword to be executed by them. Then, in the ninth week, according to our author, " the righteous judgment will be revealed to the whole world, and all the works of the godless will vanish from the whole earth, and the world will be written down for destruction, and all mankind will look to the path of uprightness " (Ibid. ¹²⁻¹⁴). Charles remarks that the "reprobation of the heathen " in verse 9 " does not appear to agree with the teaching of verse 14, where the conversion of the heathen is expected." He would account for the apparent contradiction by the fact that verse 14 " belongs to the Apocalypse of Weeks, which has all the appearance of an earlier fragment incorporated in his work by the original author of 91–104." * It seems clear that this is correct, for in 91⁵⁻⁹ the apocalyptist's idea is that the condition of the world will gradually become worse until the end of all things, and the future of the heathen is hopeless.

*The Problem of Prosperity and Adversity.*—The Flood and the Israelitish exile were God's punitive acts (93⁴, ⁸). That punitive justice is seen when a woman dies without children " on account of the works of her hands," and when rain is withheld because of sin (98⁵, 101²). Nevertheless, the author is keenly alive to the fact that desert and fortune are by no means equal in this world. The riches of the wicked make them appear like the righteous, he says, while their hearts convict them that they are sinners (96⁴). Righteous men die in grief and do not fare as their goodness deserves. Sinners can ask in scorn what advantage the righteous have over themselves (102⁵⁻⁷).

* Edition of Ethiopic Enoch, p. 267.

But evil men die in prosperity, with no experience of
troubles. The facts tempt men to say : " Blessed are
they, the sinners " ($103^{5\,f.}$). The righteous, on the
other hand, are worn out with trouble, appealing to
rulers in vain for justice ($103^{9-15}$). Our author, however, offers no explanation of all this. His only
comfort for the righteous is that God's justice will be
manifested in the future. It will be seen in the coming
days when the righteous will dominate the earth
($91^{13}$, $95^7$, $96^1$, $98^{12}$), and still more strikingly in the
great day when the wicked will be cast into a hell of
blazing fire and when the righteous will obtain all
manner of joyous compensations ($94^9$, $97^{1,\,5}$, $99^{11\,f.,\,16}$,
$100^{7,\,9}$, $103^{7\,f.}$, $92^{3\,f.}$, $96^{3,\,8}$, $104^2$). The sinners only
*seem* to escape penalty. Their deeds are constantly
noted in heaven ($98^7$).

*Moral Evil.*—In its origin sin is man's own doing.
In one place mention is made indeed in this apocalypse of " those who brought down sin " ($100^4$), and
Charles considers that the reference can only be to
the fallen angels.* But some MSS. read " who aided
sin," and if this be correct our apocalypse contains
perhaps no allusion to those angels. $98^4$ seems to be
an emphatic denial of that story: " I have sworn
unto you, ye sinners, as a mountain does not become
a slave and will not, nor a hill the handmaid of a
woman, even so sin has not been sent on the earth,
but man himself has created it." It is taught that
there is such a thing as judicial hardness. " In the
sixth week all those who live in it will be blinded,
and the hearts of all of them will be given over to a
wicked forgetfulness of wisdom " ($93^8$). " They will
become godless by reason of the foolishness of their
hearts, and their eyes will be blinded through the

* Edition of Ethiopic Enoch, p. 287.

fear of their hearts, and through visions in their dreams. Through these they will become godless and fearful, because they work all their works in a lie and they worship a stone" (99⁸ᶠ·). The author thus teaches a doctrine very similar to that of St. Paul in Romans 1²⁴⁻³².

ETHIOPIC ENOCH 37–70

*Israel and the Gentiles.*—Israel is permanently God's elect, to whom the Messiah hidden in His presence is revealed, i.e. through the spirit of prophecy in the O.T. (48⁶, 62⁷). God will in the end " transform the earth and make it a blessing." He will cause His elect ones to dwell in it (45⁵). There are several indications of a broad view in this writer which incline one to dissent from the judgment of Charles that " annihilation appears to await the Gentile in this book." * It is taught that Wisdom offered herself to the children of men and was rejected (42¹ᶠ·). The author thus takes up the same position in that matter as Ben Sira does. The Messiah, he says, is to be " the light of the Gentiles, and all who dwell on earth will fall down and bow the knee before him, and will bless and laud and celebrate with song the Lord of Spirits " (48⁴ᶠ·). For that end God has chosen the Messiah (48⁶). Moreover, we have this highly significant passage : " In those days will the earth also give back those who are treasured up within it, and Sheol also will give back that which it has received, and hell will give back that which it owes " (51¹). It is precarious to argue, with Charles, that this verse only teaches the resurrection of all

* " Eschatology," p. 240 ; cf. E.B., art. " Eschatology," 1366.

12

Israel, on the ground that "the whole history of Jewish thought points in an opposite direction" and "that no Jewish book except 4 Ezra teaches indubitably the doctrine of a general resurrection." * For, apart from the fact that—as we have seen above —this doctrine is clearly taught in the Testaments, it may be reasonably argued that possibly our author held a unique view. Charles himself illustrates the peril of his own argument when, on the same page, he says that Talmudic theology had for its accepted doctrine the resurrection of righteous Israelites only, but "individual voices were not wanting who asserted the resurrection of pious Gentiles."

It is also to be observed that the activities of the two angels, who respectively intercede for men and hinder the Satans, are not represented as being on Israel's behalf alone, but for those "who dwell on the earth" (40⁶ᶠ·). "They interceded and prayed for the children of men" (39⁵).

*The Problem of Prosperity and Adversity.*—By the plan of the work, reference to historical retributions is excluded. The author only deals with his own and the last times. Under the present government of God rulers are permitted to abuse their power. They shed the blood of the righteous (47¹ᶠ·). This God will presently punish in the most drastic manner (e.g. 62¹⁰ᶠ·, 63¹⁻¹²). Then also He will punish all classes of sinners, as well as the kings against whom this writer's invective is chiefly directed (38¹⁻³, 41², 45², ⁵ᶠ·, 51⁵, 53⁸, 62⁸). When that times comes the humiliation of the righteous will be ended. Even on earth righteousness will be established, and eventually the reward of the righteous will be the life eternal (38¹, 45², ⁵ᶠ·, 53⁸; 37⁴, 58³).

* Edition of Ethiopic Enoch, p. 139.

*Moral Evil.*—Brief allusions are made to Azazel and his hosts " leading astray those who dwell on the earth " in the old time and " seducing the children of men into committing sin " (54$^6$, 64$^{1L}$). But the author does not teach that evil angels are allowed constantly to assail the virtue of men.

### ETHIOPIC ENOCH : INTERPOLATIONS

*Israel and the Gentiles.*—There is one very important passage. " On the day of affliction, evil will gather over the sinners, but the righteous will be victorious in the name of the Lord of Spirits : and He will cause the Gentiles [lit., the others] to witness [this judgment] that they may repent and forego the works of their hands. They will have no honour through the name of the Lord of Spirits, yet through His name will they be saved, and the Lord of Spirits will have compassion, for His compassion is great " (50$^{2L}$). The doctrine of Israel's permanence as God's people, holy and righteous, is taught in 65$^{12}$ (cf. 67$^2$).

*The Problem of Prosperity and Adversity.*—The continued action of nature in ripening harvests is regarded as contingent on man's good conduct (80$^{2L}$). Death was no original part of the divine order (69$^{11}$). There is scant allusion to sufferings of the righteous, but in one place it is said that righteous men " will die on account of the deeds of men, and be gathered together on account of the doings of the godless " (81$^9$), and in another we have the statement that God hath assigned to the faithful who have been trodden underfoot of wicked men " their recompense " (108$^{10}$). The apportionment of fortune to men is no perplexity. It is explained sufficiently by the doctrine of the compensating God, who will reward the righteous and punish the wicked in the great Day (19$^1$).

*Moral Evil.*—In chapter 69 there is an account of angels who introduced evil knowledge to men, and in one passage of these *disjecta membra* it is said by Uriel that the fallen angels who have defiled mankind " will lead them astray into sacrificing to demons as gods " (19¹). As we have noticed in Chapter I., the idea of a divine determination of human conduct appears in the Interpolations, but it is not consistent with the general position of the writers.

### THE PSALMS OF SOLOMON

*Israel and the Gentiles.*—The psalmist is deeply impressed with Israel's sinfulness: " Their transgressions were greater than those of the heathen that were before them " (1⁸). He offers supplications that God will not " overlook and neglect " Israel nor remove His mercy from them (8³⁶, 9¹⁶). But he is confident that God will not do this. " Thou wilt have pity for evermore on the house of Israel, and wilt not cast them off ; and, as for us, we are beneath Thy yoke for evermore." " Thou didst set Thy name upon us, O Lord, and Thou wilt not desist for ever " (9¹⁸).* In Psalm 11 the coming restoration of Israel is celebrated and in the last psalms the reign of Messiah is foretold. Then all Israelites will be the sons of God, who is their God for evermore (17³⁰, 17¹, ⁵¹).

This does not, however, mean that every Israelite will be saved. Sanday and Headlam, citing from Pesikta 38a the dictum that " no Israelite can go into Gehenna," and from Sanhedrin 1 the statement that " all Israelites have their portion in the world to come," add that " this belief was shared by St. Paul's

---

* Perhaps we should read, " Thou wilt abide among us for ever," substituting συ for ού. See Ryle and James in loc.

contemporaries," and, commenting on Ps. Sol. 12⁷ᵇ,
they say : " While Israel is always to enjoy the
divine mercy, sinners [i.e. Gentiles] are to be destroyed
before the face of the Lord " *   Now 12⁷ᵇ reads :
" The salvation of the Lord be upon Israel His servant
for ever and let the sinners be destroyed from before
the face of the Lord together : and let the saints of
the Lord inherit the promises of the Lord." But it
is to be observed that the sinners who are denounced
in the Psalms are Jews. They are those who live in
hypocrisy with the saints and who usurped the throne
of David (4⁷⁻⁹, 17⁵⁻⁸).   It is of an ecclesia in ecclesia
that this book predicates a permanent position as
God's chosen.   It is the saints of the Lord who shall
live in the law for ever.   It is their planting that is
rooted for ever.   It is they who shall not be " plucked
up all the days of heaven " (14²ᵇ).

In 7¹⁻³ the nations are apparently spoken of as
having been cast off by God. " Remove not Thy
habitation from us, O God, lest they fall upon us
that hate us without a cause. Nay, as for those
whom Thou hast cast off, O God, let not their foot
tread the inheritance of Thy sanctuary. Do Thou
chasten us in Thy good pleasure, but give us not
over to the Gentiles." Ryle and James incline to the
view that it is the Sadducees who are here described
as cast off.† But the last sentence surely makes
it probable that the singer is speaking of the Gentiles.
He celebrates, however, God's kindness and justice
to all peoples (5¹⁷, 9⁴, 18³). Yet he draws a great
distinction between His attitude to Israel and to the
Gentiles. His mercy is on all the earth in kindness—
χρηστότης—(5¹⁷). His judgments are on all the earth

* " Commentary on Romans," p. 249.
† Edition of the Psalms, p. 70.

with mercy, and His love—ἀγάπη—is toward the seed
of Abraham (18³ ᵗ·). He judges all the earth in
righteousness (8²⁹). He judges Israel with chastening
—παιδεία (8³²). Messiah, it is said, will destroy the
ungodly nations by the word of his mouth, but the
psalmist also looks for a general subjugation of the
Gentiles to him. " He shall possess the nations of
the heathen to serve him beneath his yoke " (17²⁷, ³²).
Drummond regards this verse as indicating a mere
desire to enhance the splendour of Messiah's reign.*
But in the Syriac version, as Rendel Harris translates
it, we have this reading of 17³² : " And he shall possess
a people from among the Gentiles, and they shall
serve him under his yoke." And, where in the same
verse the Greek has : " He [Messiah] shall glorify the
Lord in a place to be seen of the whole earth," the
Syriac gives us this : " And they [the Gentiles] shall
praise the Lord openly over all the earth." If, then,
the Syriac be correct, it would seem that the psalmist
foretold no mere dominance of Messiah, but widespread conversions amongst the heathen. It must be
allowed, however, that the prediction of the removal
from Israel's midst of all aliens in Messiah's day (17³¹)
makes it doubtful whether this broad sentiment came
from the pen of the original author.

*The Problem of Prosperity and Adversity.*—The
psalmist firmly believed in the operation here and
now of a divine justice. When Pompey troubles
Jerusalem it is God who decrees war. He brings the
mighty striker from the ends of the earth (8¹⁶ ᵗ·). If
the mistaken rulers of the city welcome Pompey, it
is because God " hath mingled for them a spirit of
error " (8¹⁵). This is punishment. " The sons of
Jerusalem defiled the holy things of the Lord and

* " The Jewish Messiah," p. 330.

polluted the gifts of God with iniquities. "For this
cause said He, ' Cast ye them afar off from Me ' "
(2³ᴸ).* When Pompey is slain, it is punishment.
" God set him at nought in dishonour " (2³³). Possibly this clause, ambiguous in the original, should be
translated : " For he [Pompey] set Him [God] at
nought in dishonour." But, in either case, the teaching is the same. The experience of Pompey and Israel
illustrates the dictum that God's judgments are upon
all the earth (18³). In that judgment there is discrimination. The singer's experience has taught him
that, when calamities are abroad, God is mindful of
His own. He celebrates the fact that, in a time of
great distress, the Lord's arm saved the righteous
from the sword, from famine, and from the plague
that vexed sinners (13²). In 17⁸ he seems to teach
that there is such discrimination when judgment
comes on sinners. God is mindful of their merits and
demerits. Writing of the men who usurped the
throne of David, and whom God cast down, he says :
" According to their sins didst Thou recompense them,
O God ; yea, it befell them according to their works.
According to their works, God had compassion on
them ; He sought out their seed diligently and forsook them not—οὐκ ἀφῆκεν αὐτούς (17¹⁰ᴸ). Ryle
and James point out that this might be understood
ironically, especially as ἐξερευνάω, the word rendered
" sought out " in the last clause, is generally employed
in a hostile sense. But they prefer to take it literally,
" on the ground that the tone of irony does not appear
to correspond with the general style of our psalmist,
and that the transition from denunciation to the
declaration of mercy is explained by Pompey's treat-

* Ἀυτά refers to δῶρα, but perhaps as Geiger thinks, it is a
mistranslation for αὐτούς. Cf. Ryle and James in loc.

ment of Hyrcanus the Second, who was left in occupation of the High Priesthood." * Probably, however, these editors would now change their interpretation of this passage in view of the fact that the Syriac version, which had not been discovered when their edition was published, blots out the idea of the compassion of God toward the usurpers. This verse, in Rendel Harris's version of the Syriac, runs as follows : " According to their sins Thou wilt reward them, O God ; and it shall befall them according to their works, and Thou wilt not have mercy upon them, O God. Command their seed, and do not leave a single one of them." Perhaps the Greek text of this verse, whose mixed tenses, aorist and future, make its translation so difficult, should here be rendered by futures only. It may be that the Hebrew original has been misunderstood by the translator and perhaps in verse 11a a negative has been left out. This would bring the whole passage into harmony with the statement in verse 8b : " Thou wilt cast them down and wilt remove their seed from the earth." The Syriac in that verse agrees with the Greek. We should then understand the οὐκ ἀφῆκεν αὐτούς, as the editors suggest, as meaning : " He letteth none of them go." †

The idea of the solidarity of families in God's judgment appears in $15^{13}$ as well as in $17^{10 \iota}$. " Their iniquities shall pursue them as far as Hades beneath, and their inheritance shall not be found of their children."

But our psalmist is very alive to the fact that righteous men suffer. He has learned that outward prosperity is no sure index of righteousness in him who enjoys it ($1^3$). On this subject he teaches noble doctrine. The word " chastening " is of very fre-

* Op. cit., p. 132.  † Ibid. p. 132.

quent occurrence in his pages. " Blessed is the man," says he, " whom the Lord remembereth with reproving, and he is fenced about [or turned aside] from the way of evil by affliction that he may be cleansed from sin lest he abound therein " ($10^{1 L}$). "For my sin Thou dost chasten me to the end I may be restored " ($16^{11}$). " Thy chastening is upon us as upon a firstborn son, only begotten, to convert the soul that is obedient from simpleness and from sins of ignorance " ($18^{4 L}$). This great truth had been learned by our psalmist in a sharp personal trial. His soul " slumbered and fell away from the Lord." He was " hard unto the gates of Hades in the company of the sinner " ($16^{1 L}$). But God, he says, " pricked me as a man pricketh his horse, that I might watch unto Him " ($16^{4}$). So God helped him unto salvation (Ibid. [5]). Perhaps the same thought is suggested in the difficult passages—ἐν περιστολῇ παιδεύεται δίκαιος ($13^{7}$). The verb περιστέλλω is used in $16^{10}$ of this Psalter : " My tongue and my lips do Thou guard about," and the view of the editors is that the righteous is, in $13^{7}$, said to be chastened " with regard," that is, "with the view of correcting him and preventing him from erring so that the enemies of the Lord might blaspheme." *  In $9^{15}$ we have a singular statement out of harmony with all the passages we have cited : " The righteous Thou wilt bless and wilt not correct them for the sins they have committed, and Thy kindness is toward them that sin if they repent." The editors point out that the sense required here is : " Thou wilt not exact the full penalty," and that the word εὐθύνω is used in that sense in 3 Macc. $2^{17}$. In the Syriac, however, we have simply this : " For the righteous Thou dost bless and dost not reprove them for any of their sins :

* Op. cit., p. 109.

for Thy grace is on those that have sinned, when
they have repented." This suits the whole context,
and, if it be correct, the singer is simply affirming the
completeness of God's pardoning grace toward repentant men. His ideas on the subject, however,
were most narrow as compared with those of Ben
Sira, or with those expressed in the broader passages
of the second part of the book of Wisdom. He did
not dream of a divine correction designed to benefit
men who stood outside the circle of the saints. It is
the righteous whom God chastens.

The Psalms also contain the teaching that the
sufferings of the righteous constitute an atonement.
" The Lord will spare His servants, and will blot out
their transgression with His chastening " (13⁹).

The psalmist looks for the establishment of righteousness in the earth, and the destruction of the ungodly
nations (17²⁷ ᶠ·). But, beyond this, he awaits the
day when the faithful " shall rise again into life
eternal " (3¹⁶). Justice will thus be done to dead
saints, and the sinners will be " taken away into destruction " (13¹⁰).

*Moral Evil.*—The psalmist does not discuss the
origin of sin, and, as we have seen in Chapter I., did
not hold the idea of a divine determination of man's
conduct. But that God's penalty on sin is that
deterioration of character which issues in more sin
appears plainly to be the teaching in 2¹³ ¹⁵. For he
says that " God set forth the sons of Jerusalem that
they should be as harlots in her midst," and that " the
daughters of Jerusalem were polluted according to "
God's " judgment, because they had defiled themselves in unclean intercourse."

## JUDITH

*Israel and the Gentiles.*—Achior the Ammonite is described as believing in God exceedingly and becoming "joined unto the house of Israel" as a result of the nation's deliverance from Holofernes ($14^{10}$). Judith not only utters the expectation that God will work great things by her, "whereat all the earth shall be astonished" ($11^{16}$), but also prays : "Make every nation and tribe of Thine to know that Thou art God, the God of all power and might, and that there is none other that protecteth the race of Israel but Thou" ($9^{14}$). "It is desired," says H. M. Hughes, "that God may be made known to them, only that they may know that there is none other that protecteth the race of Israel but Thou." * But it is to be remarked that Judith calls all the nations "Thine" and desires that they may "know that Thou art God." No doubt C. J. Ball's caution is to be borne in mind : "Volkmar lays too much stress upon the proselytising of an individual, and that under altogether peculiar circumstances." † But, taking the prayer of Judith and the story of the reception of Achior together, it seems that the author manifests a spirit by no means wholly uncatholic, and Canon Dobson has some justification for regarding Judith's prayer as an indication of a "preparatio evangelica." ‡

The song at the end of the book, which is possibly the work of another writer, breathes a different spirit. It expresses what André calls "la haine sauvage des Israélites contre les païens." § God is there regarded

* Op. cit., p. 84.
† Speaker's Comm., p. 347.
‡ I.J.A., January 1909, art. "The Missionary Outlook in the Apocryphia," p. 9.
§ "Les apocryphes de L'Ancien Testament," p. 155.

as the great Partisan of Israel. " Woe to the nations that rise up against my race. The Lord Almighty will take vengeance of them in the day of judgment, to put fire and worms in their flesh ; and they shall weep and feel their pain for ever " (16$^{17}$).

*The Problem of Prosperity and Adversity.*—Once, in this book, confession is made that God is punishing the people for their own sins and those of their fathers (7$^{28}$). The principle of solidarity in penalties is also recognised in the prayer of Judith, where the revengeful act of Simeon and Levi is described as God's own punishment (9$^{3}$). Gaster says of this author : " He manifests his strong belief that God is sure to grant His aid to those who have not sinned. He takes the greatest care to emphasise the ruin that is sure to follow upon any meddling with the tithes or other sacred things ; he abhors all ceremonial defilement, and dwells upon the efficacy of prayer ; the prayer of the righteous and pure widow is sure to be heard, and her intercession saves the Jewish race." * André sums up similarly the teaching of the book : " Aussi longtemps qu'il ne commet pas de péché contre Dieu, Israël est heureux car Dieu est avec lui ; mais des qu'il dévie de la règle tracée toutes sortes de malheurs fondent sur lui." † Now there are several passages in the book in which this view is most distinctly enunciated. Achior in his speech declares, in the manner of the book of Judges, that Israel's historic experience has been that God prospered them when they were righteous and brought them into adversity as soon as they sinned. Accordingly, he advises the tyrant not to attack Israel unless it be ascertained that they are now offending (5$^{17-21}$). Judith expresses the same belief in her words to Holofernes : " Our

* E.B., art. " Judith," 2644.    † Op. cit., " Judith."

race shall not be punished, neither shall the sword prevail against them, except they sin against their God " ($11^{9\,f.}$). The Vulgate omits $4^{13}$ and substitutes for it the statement that the High-priest said to all Israel : " Know ye that the Lord will hearken unto your prayers, if ye steadfastly continue in fastings and prayers in the sight of the Lord." To this, according to the Vulgate, the High-priest added that, as Amalek was overthrown by the prayers of Moses, " so shall all the enemies of Israel be if ye persevere in this work that ye have begun." * But in her speech in chapter 8 the heroine suggests the possibility that the nation, despite present fidelity, may not be delivered in the hour of its dire straits. Judith's own generation is indeed quite free from the taint of idolatry; yet she thinks that, nevertheless, God may not deliver them. She does not share the confidence of Ozias, who declares that God will be sure to answer her prayers, since she is a godly woman ($8^{31}$). He is not one, she says, who can be turned aside from His own purposes by entreaty (Ibid. $^{16}$). After the fashion of Judas in 1 Maccabees, she urges that Israel should call on God for help, and declares that He will hear them " if it please Him " (Ibid. $^{17}$). Israel's freedom from idolatry creates hope within her heart that He will not despise the people. Besides, it seems almost unthinkable that all Judæa should be brought low and the sanctuary spoiled ($8^{20\,f.}$). Still, in $8^{21-3}$, she distinctly contemplates this as a possibility. Is it that experience of what really happens to the righteous in this world has taught the author that even a people loyal to God may pass through the most troublous experiences ? Did he put this speech on the lips of

* C. J. Ball thinks that the idioms here point to a Chaldee original (Speaker's Comm., in loc.).

his faultless heroine to controvert accepted ideas on the subject ? That is one's first impression, but in verses 21 f. Judith declares that, should the dreaded calamity befall Israel, her people would be punished among the Gentiles for the profanation of the Temple. They will be the guilty authors of that great calamity. It seems clear, therefore, that the fears of Judith arise from the question in her mind whether Israel is now so thoroughly faithful that they may rightly be confident of divine help. She is not impugning the doctrine that He would be sure to deliver a righteous nation.

Moreover, she is sure that, if He punishes, His penalties are no mere acts of retribution. They are corrective in their design. The ways of God are, she says, mysterious, and man, who cannot comprehend his fellow, certainly cannot "search out God" and "know His mind and comprehend His purpose" (Ibid. ¹⁴). But this much is quite clear to her. Israel's true temper is thankful submission to Him who tries them (Ibid. ²⁵), and "the Lord doth scourge them that come near unto Him to admonish them (Ibid. ²⁷).

### 3 ESDRAS

*Israel and the Gentiles.*—This writer gives us very scanty material for forming an idea of his conceptions as to God's attitude to the nations. He says that God is true in that a root has been left to Israel and the nation has not been destroyed (8⁸⁸ᶠ·). While it is said that God gave commands to Cyrus where Israel's interests were at stake, the writer declines to say, as the chronicler does, that God warned Josiah by the Egyptian king Neco (2 Chron. 35²²). He substitutes for this the statement that the warning came by Jeremiah (1²⁸). God is repeatedly called " our God " and " the God of Israel."

*The Problem of Prosperity and Adversity.*—We have only to note the recognition in this book of the fact that the Exile was due to God's wrath (6¹⁵) and the statement that Israelites suffer for their own sins and those of their fathers (8⁷⁷).

### 2 MACCABEES

*Israel and the Gentiles.*—God is here described as the Sovereign Lord of all, but He is regarded by the author as one who cares only for Israel. The writer describes Jonathan as praying that the heathen may know that the Lord is the God of Israel (1²⁷), but no idea is further from his mind than that God can be any other than the great Patron and Partisan of His own nation. " He that hath His dwelling in heaven, Himself hath His eyes upon that place [Jerusalem], and helpeth it, and them that come to hurt it He smiteth and destroyeth " (3³⁹). That sentence, indeed, like the prayer in 10²⁶ that God would be " an enemy to their enemies and an adversary to their adversaries," might easily have been uttered in a time of oppression by an Israelite of a catholic spirit. But our author was no such man. His doctrine is that " in the case of the other nations the Sovereign Lord doth with long-suffering forbear until that He punish them when they have attained unto the full measure of sins ; but not so judgeth He as touching us, that He may not take vengeance on us afterward when we be come to the height of our sins. Wherefore He never withdraweth His mercy from us ; but, though He chasteneth with calamity, yet doth He not forsake His own people " (6¹⁴⁻¹⁶). Israel is thus thought

of as God's own people for ever, but the rest of mankind are looked upon as outside the pale. Probably
he regarded them as doomed to destruction, for André
has only too much justification for saying that, if the
author had believed in a future of torment for them,
" il n'aurait pas manqué de le dire à satiété, trop
heureux d'avoir de quoi augmenter les tourments des
ennemis nationaux." * Sacrifice is offered by the
High-priest to save the life of the Gentile Heliodorus,
but the author quite characteristically explains that
he was moved to do this simply by fears for Israel's
safety ($3^{32}$).

*The Problem of Prosperity and Adversity.*—Wrong-
doers are punished in this story with poetic justice.
When the priests of Nanæa's temple slay Antiochus
our author makes the devout comment : " Blessed be
our God in all things, who gave (for a prey) them
that had committed impiety " ($1^{17}$). When Androni-
cus is killed for the murder of Onias, it is the act of
God, " the Lord rendering to him the punishment he
had deserved " ($4^{38}$). The mortal illness of the tyrant
comes upon him because " the all-seeing God smote
him with a fatal and invisible stroke " ($9^{5}$). The
cruel fate of Menelaus befalls him because " the King
of kings stirred up the passion of Antiochus against
the wicked wretch," and it fell out so " right justly "
($13^{4, 7}$).

Once in this book it is taught that the seed of a
sinner is involved in the penalty of his sin. This is
when the martyr says to the king : " Hold thou on
thy way and behold His sovereign majesty how it
will torture thee and thy seed " ($7^{17}$). The author
expresses the hope that all Israel will benefit by the
fidelity of the martyrs ($7^{38}$). Israel itself, suffering at

* Op. cit., p. 101.

the hand of Antiochus, is regarded as paying the penalty of sins ($7^{18, \; 33}$). But, in this case, the race is being chastened, and Israelites have not only the prospect of a glorious national future, but also, if they be faithful, the hope of the life eternal ($6^{12, \; 16}$; $2^{7 f.}$; $7^{9-11, \; 14, \; 29}$).

### THE ADDITIONS TO DANIEL

*Israel and the Gentiles.*—In the Song Israel is not conceived of as necessarily the people of God abidingly. Rather, Azariah prays : "Deliver us not up utterly, for Thy name's sake, neither disannul Thou Thy covenant : and cause not Thy mercy to depart from us (v. 11). There is only one reference to the Gentiles, and that is in the wish that the oppressors of Israel may have their strength broken and may know that Jehovah is the only God, and glorious over the whole world (20–22).

*The Problem of Prosperity and Adversity.*—The Song celebrates the fact that, in His punishment of Israel, God has acted "according to truth and justice" (5), and tells how God delivered the three children (26 f., 66). In the Story of Susanna, the design appears to be to illustrate the truth that God punishes sinners and saves those who hope in Him (60).

### THE EPISTLE OF JEREMY

There is nothing here to our point except the statement that sin was the cause of the Exile (ver. 11).

### SUMMARY

(1) *The Justice of God in His Attitude to Israel and the Gentiles.*—(A) Writers who look forward with

13

assurance to the future of Israel as God's people in this world are the authors of Enoch 91–104, the Enoch Similitudes, and Interpolations, but each of these anticipates that only righteous Israelites will share the future joys of the elect. In 2 Maccabees the author expresses the strongest possible confidence on this subject, and he does not fear for a moment that Israel can ever be rejected. Yet he does not conceive of the relationship in an altogether unethical manner, for God is represented as correcting Israel. In 3 Esdras, also, the doctrine of permanence is implied when it is said that God's truth has been manifested in that the nation is not destroyed; but here also God is Judge, chastising the people for their sin. In the Song of the Three Children the suppliant expresses his fear that God may disannul His covenant with Israel. In the Psalms of Solomon the singer speaks confidently of Israel's future, looking for the time when the nation will be purged and regenerate, but sometimes fears born of Israel's sin are expressed. Of these writers, four teach the doctrine of a life after death—the authors of Enoch 91–104, 37–70, Interpolations, and the Psalms of Solomon—and in each the destiny of the individual Israelite turns on conduct. 2 Maccabees also teaches a life beyond for the faithful Israelite, but adds the singular doctrine that the faithless may be transferred to the company of the blessed by sacrifices offered on their behalf (cf. Chapter III. of this work).

(B) There are three writers of this century who give expression to the narrowest ideas of God in His relation to the Gentiles. One of these is the author of the Song of Judith. The second is the writer of Enoch 91–104, where the idea is that all the heathen are to be reprobated. The third is the bitter patriot who wrote 2 Maccabees. His God, made in his own image, is One who accords endless mercy to Israel, but gives none to the great world of nations. No writer of the previous century conceived of God in so mean a fashion, for even in Jubilees there is consciousness of the need of explaining and vindicating the divine particularism as being justice; but in this book God is represented as One who favours one small tribe while He damns the mass of mankind of His own arbitrary will without the least compunction.

The other writers are of a finer spirit. Some, indeed, give but slight indications of holding a broad idea of God's character. 1 Maccabees contains no sign that its author supposed that God had any interest in the nations, but this is the less important because the book is a mere chronicle of wars. In the Song we have simply the wish expressed that the nations may know that Jehovah is the one God. Judith contains the utterance of a similar wish, and a proselyte in that work is thought of as acceptable to God. The hope of a future in which there will be a general conversion of heathen men appears in the Similitudes of Enoch, in the Interpolations, and in a passage of Enoch 91–104, where, however, it is probable that we have an addition to the original work. The Enoch Similitudes—unique in this among the books of the century—contain the idea of a primitive rejection of wisdom by the nations. The general doctrine of the Psalms of Solomon is that of a divine mercy for all mankind, and, if the Syriac version represents the original, the psalmist looked for widespread conversions among the Gentiles.

It is the opinion of Dr. Charles that the favourable views of the Judaism of the second century B.C. as to the future of the Gentiles all but wholly disappeared in this age.\* The facts which we have cited lead us, however, to dissent from this view. Some of the books furnish us with clear evidence of declension in the idea of God in the Judaism of this century as compared with that which preceded it. The declension, however, was very far from being universal. The three Enoch writers and the psalmist witness to the existence of the broader doctrine in this age, and further evidence is supplied by the Additions made to the Testaments by a Jew who held that Israel was meant to be God's agent for the enlightenment of all peoples. If we include the book of Wisdom amongst works written in this century, as perhaps we should, the evidence for the continued existence of the broader view within this age is still stronger.

(2) *The Justice of God in the Allotment of Prosperity and Adversity.*—(A) No writer of this period, save the author of the Enoch Similitudes, fails to give some recognition to the fact of a punitive justice within the present order. God's deliverances of His people are celebrated in 1 and 2 Maccabees, the Psalms, and the Daniel Additions. But these authors differ from their predecessors in not insisting on the doctrine that God normally proportions prosperity to desert in this world. The nearest approach to this is made in a passage in the Enoch Interpolations, where harvests are said to be contingent on man's conduct. The psalmist, and the authors of 1 Maccabees, the Enoch Similitudes, and Interpolations recognise the fact that good men have sorrows. In Enoch 91–104 the apocalyptic writer looks round on a world in which most emphatically justice is done to neither

* " Jewish and Christian Eschatology," p. 240 f. ; cf. E.B., art. " Eschatology," 1366.

sinners nor saints. There is not, however, one among them for whom the facts of life raised a perplexing problem of faith, though some of them realised the need of explanation and attempted to furnish it for their readers.

(B) The doctrine of solidarity in penalties appears in three works. According to the Psalms, Judith, and 3 Esdras, the children suffer for the sins of parents. According to Judith, a whole tribe suffers for the sin of a part. But the doctrine of solidarity in benefits under God's judgment only appears in the Additions to the Testaments and 2 Maccabees. In the first named the teaching is that remote descendants benefit by the merits of ancestors.

(C) The doctrine of future compensations for the righteous and the wicked is strongly insisted upon in Enoch 91-104, 37-70 and Interpolations, as well as in the Psalms and 2 Maccabees. Probably these last two held that the destiny of the wicked was annihilation. Several books, however—1 Maccabees, Judith, 3 Esdras, the Epistle of Jeremy, and the Daniel Additions—contain no hint of a future judgment of God. It is a moot point whether a final judgment is or is not foretold in the Song of Judith.

(D) The psalmist teaches that God's purpose in the sorrows of saints is the purifying of their character. In the Additions to the Testaments it is implied that God mercifully chastises Israel. In 2 Maccabees and Judith it is expressly said that God has this purpose in the sorrows of His own people. Each of the four is narrow as compared with Ben Sira, who maintained that God acts thus to all men. The other writers of the century do not even imply such an idea. Even in Enoch 91-104, where the righteous are seen by the author in the most distressing circumstances, it does not occur. His one comfort for tried men is future compensation. It would seem that the idea of a merciful divine discipline was not in all his thoughts, or he, whose purpose was consolation, had surely made it a prominent thought.

(E) The idea that angels or spirits are a cause of trouble to men does not appear in this century.

(F) The Psalms contain the unique suggestion that suffering constitutes an atonement for a man's own sin.

(3) *The Justice of God in the Permission of Moral Evil.*—(A) The idea that sin has its origin in man's God-given original constitution does not appear in this century.

(B) The idea of God as settling what man shall be in character occurs in a passage which some one inserted in the Book of Enoch. Otherwise, it is not in evidence, and it is entirely opposed to the doctrine of the writers.

(C) That evil spirits brought sin into this world is the teaching of Enoch 37–70, and perhaps of one passage in Enoch 91–104, but this latter writer seems to deny it in another place. In the Interpolations the idolatry of mankind is traced to seducing spirits, and in the Testaments Additions it is announced that they will assail the virtue of the sons of Levi. Nowhere else does the idea appear that these spirits are normally the active spiritual foes of the human race.

(D) The idea of a deterioration of character in men through their own sin appears in Enoch 91–104, and in the Psalms, and this is conceived of as a divinely appointed punishment.

## THE FIRST CENTURY A.D.

### WISDOM

#### Part 1

*Israel and the Gentiles.*—The larger thought of God seems to be implied in the words addressed to the judges of the earth, who are exhorted to seek the Lord and assured that He is manifested to those who do not distrust Him (1¹ ᶠ·). Canon Dobson regards the address to the kings, "the judges of the ends of the earth," in 6¹⁻²¹ as a generous missionary sermon designed to win over the Gentiles to God.* Farrar, however, thinks that "the writer can hardly have expected that his book would really fall into the hands of heathen rulers," and he considers that the appeal to the kings "belongs only to the rhetorical force of the book and to his assumption of the person of Solomon." † Still, whatever may have been the design of the address, it must be admitted that the teaching of these sections is much like that in the words of St. Peter : "God is no respecter of persons : but in every nation he that feareth Him and worketh righteousness is acceptable to Him" (Acts 10³⁴ ᶠ·). If we cannot safely affirm that Ps. Solomon contemplated any missionary endeavour, we may nevertheless maintain that his idea of God is not that of a merely nationalistic Deity. God is one who taketh thought alike for all (6⁷), and of Wisdom, His image (7²⁶), it is said that she is "a spirit that loveth man" (1⁶, 7²³).‡

* I.J.A., January 1909.
† Speaker's Comm., p. 454.
‡ Farrar thinks that φιλάνθρωπον, though sometimes only meaning "gentle," retains here its true sense : "loving mankind" (op. cit., p. 426).

Farrar thinks that " the Messianic hope " in this work " has come to mean nothing but the dominance of Israel and the universal worship of Jehovah." *
He cites in support $3^8$, $5^{16}$, $8^{14}$. But $3^8$ appears to be a description of the honours of the righteous in the unseen world, and Farrar admits that its true interpretation is doubtful †; $5^{16}$ appears to refer also to the future life; $8^{14}$ will not bear this weight of meaning, since it is simply Solomon's anticipation of his coming success. In fact, nothing definite can be extracted from our book as to the ultimate destinies of Israel or a conversion of the Gentiles.

*The Problem of Prosperity and Adversity.*—Ps. Solomon subscribes to the doctrine of an operative divine judgment on sinners in this world, and teaches that God proceeds on the principle of solidarity when He punishes ($3^{16-19}$, $4^{3-6}$). Even in " the day of decision " the children of adulterers will find no consolation ($3^{18}$). Evil-doing makes a land desolate and overthrows thrones ($5^{23}$). But our author's thought is chiefly centred on the punishment which comes on sinners in the unseen world. Justice will pass by no man that uttereth unrighteous things ($1^8$). The wicked " shall become a dishonoured carcase and a reproach among the dead for ever "—they will lie waste in anguish—in distress of spirit they will groan ($4^{18}$–$5^3$). It is also with the sure hope of coming compensations that our author seeks to comfort the troubled saints. The mockers' taunt appears to be justified. " If the righteous man is God's son, He will uphold him and He will deliver him out of the hand of his adversaries " ($2^{18}$). But such men are blinded by their wickedness, and know not the mys-

* Speaker's Comm., p. 410.
† Ibid., p. 439, note on ver. 7.

teries of God ($2^{21\,f.}$). He has a prize for blameless souls ($2^{22}$). The righteous dead are in peace and have a glorious future ($3^{3-9}$). So also the faithful eunuch shall be compensated in the life after death ($3^{14\,f.}$). Besides, God chastens good men, trying them as gold in the fire ($3^{5\,f.}$). If they be taken away by an early death, that happens in God's mercy ($4^{10\,f.}$). Moreover, the faithful enjoy the solid good of life, possessing here and now its best prizes. It is better to be childless and virtuous than to be an adulterer, for the righteous win the approval of God and man ($3^{16}-4^{1}$). It is better to possess wisdom than all rank, beauty, riches, or health ($7^{7-10}$). Such an one finds alleviations in the midst of all cares and griefs ($8^{9}$).

To sum up, then, Ps. Solomon recognises that the saints are sorely tried indeed, but teaches that (1) God gives them now life's most solid good, that (2) He chastens them, that (3) when He shortens their days He acts in mercy, and that (4) in the unseen world He punishes the wicked and recompenses all the saints.

*Moral Evil.*—"Court not death in the error of your life," says Ps. Solomon, "neither draw upon yourselves destruction by the works of your hands. Because God made not death ; neither delighteth He when the living perish. For He created all things that they might have being : and the generative powers of the world are healthsome, and there is no poison of destruction in them, nor hath Hades royal dominion on earth. For righteousness is immortal " ($1^{12-15}$). This appears to be an account of the origin of spiritual death. It is argued, indeed, by some that Ps. Solomon here teaches the doctrine that physical death came into the world by sin. But scholars point out that his philosophical opinions—his belief in the soul's pre-existence ($8^{19\,f.}$), its being " weighed down

by a corruptible body " ($9^{15}$), and its immortality
($3^{1-4}$)—make it probable that he thought of physical
death as a boon, and therefore as of God's making.
In view of this, Tennant's interpretation is most
feasible : " Just as God appointed to man a destiny
of happy immortality and did not Himself ordain
the eternal death by which that destiny is forfeited,
so the world of lower created things was endowed
with the power to perpetuate and maintain itself,
each thing enjoying its natural span, without any
inherent element of destruction to disturb the Creator's
original appointment." * $2^{24}$, like $1^{12-15}$, is perhaps
an account of spiritual death. " By the envy of the
devil, death entered into the world, and they that
are of his portion make trial thereof." Gregg argues
that in this verse the entrance of physical death into
the world is the matter in question, and that the
death of Abel by the hand of Cain is here described.
He cites Clemens Romanus and Theophilus as taking
this view of its meaning. He also argues that " the
identification of the serpent with the devil is not
known in Alexandrian literature of this date," and
that " there is no Scriptural authority for the idea
that the serpent was jealous of Adam and Eve, nor
does the identification of the serpent with the devil
belong to the O.T." † But the Alexandrian Jew
who wrote Slavonic Enoch has a passage in which he
seems to suggest envy of Adam on Satan's part, for
he says that " the devil took thought as if wishing to
make another world, because things were subservient
to Adam on earth " ($31^3$), and the same writer describes
Satan as acting like one who envied Adam the possession of Eve (Ibid. [6]). Moreover, in 4 Maccabees $18^8$

* Op. cit., p. 125 f. and p. 126 n[3].
† Op. cit., p. 22, and I.J.A., October 1910, p. 77.

the serpent is identified with the tempter, as Gregg himself notes. It is also to be observed that Azazel is described in the Apocalypse of Abraham as " like a serpent in form, but having hands and feet like a man and wings at his shoulders " (23). Tennant shows that the idea of the devil's jealousy was current in various forms among the Rabbis of the early Christian centuries.* It is thus clear that there is no ante-cedent improbability in the idea that this writer should attribute spiritual death to the jealousy of the devil. It must be admitted, however, that there is nothing in the context to aid us in coming to a decided opinion on the question. The death spoken of in $2^{20}$ is obviously physical. Yet the contrast in verses 23 f. between the " incorruption " for which God made man and the " death " which the devil introduced, and the statement in $3^2$ that the righteous only seemed in the eyes of the foolish to have died, appear to indicate that spiritual death is here spoken of.

In $9^{15}$ Ps. Solomon speaks of the corruptible body as weighing down the soul, and Bishop Ryle says : " The view that the body is the seat of sin is shared by the writer." † But the context makes it clear that Ps. Solomon only means that the body is a hindrance to thought or knowledge.

### Part 2

*Israel and the Gentiles.*—It is in this part of the book that we find the noblest statements as to the attitude of God to the nations. "Thou hast mercy on all men because Thou hast power to do all things, and Thou overlookest the sins of men to the end they may repent. For Thou lovest all things that are, and abhorrest none of the things which Thou

* Op. cit., p. 152.          † I.J.A., January 1908, p. 7.

didst make " ($11^{23\,f.}$). The creation and preservation
of God's creatures are proof of this ($11^{24\,f.}$). He gave
even the wicked Canaanites " a place of repentance "
($12^{10}$). Even of the Egyptians this writer says :
" Thou didst take vengeance with so great heedful-
ness and forbearance, giving them times and place
whereby they might escape from their wickedness "
($12^{20}$). They had a " judgment to mock them," a
" mocking correction as of children " ($12^{25\,f.}$) ; but it
was for admonition, and the worst penalties were only
inflicted when they would not be corrected by Him
who is the " Lover of men's lives " ($11^{26}$). If men do
not know Him, it is their own fault. He is to be seen
in His works ($13^{5}$), but the ungodly refused to know
Him ($12^{27}$, $16^{16}$). The same broad doctrine is taught
in $18^{4}$, where Israel is described as those " through
whom the incorruptible light of the law was to be
given to the race of men." There are other passages,
however, in which our author falls away from this
lofty thought of God. He tells us that God as a
father admonishes Israel, but as a stern king he condemns Egypt ($11^{9\,f.}$). Israel is chastened by Him,
but He scourges Israel's foes ten thousand times
more ($12^{22}$). The writer affirms that it is alien from
God's power to condemn unrighteously ($12^{15}$). But
it is not alien from Him, according to this book, to
rule the world with a most marked favouritism for
His own people, though this is concealed by the writer
from his own eyes by his habit of styling Egypt the
ungodly and Israel the righteous.

*The Problem of Prosperity and Adversity.*—In $10^{1}$–$11^{1}$
the writer offers a series of illustrations of the fact
that Wisdom guarded the fathers and the nation in
past days and punished the wicked in the Flood and
in the Red Sea.

Unlike the writer of Part 1, this author does not dwell on the blessed compensations of the future life. Rather, as we have seen, he emphasises the truth that God's punishments are of a remedial character, and his doctrine further differs notably from that of Part 1 in that the ungodly as well as the righteous are, according to him, chastened in mercy. Unfortunately, as we have observed, this teaching is not consistently maintained throughout the work.

*Moral Evil.*—In $10^8$ it is recognised that sin is punished by moral deterioration. The writer speaks of those who, " having passed Wisdom by, were disabled from recognising the things which are good." Again, in $19^4$ it is said that the doom of the wicked was to " forget the things that had befallen them " that they might fill up their punishment. It was " doom." There seems no good reason to say, with C. H. Toy, that we have here " the O.T. idea of divine Predestination." [*] Gregg's view is better. It was, he says, " not a fate predetermined and laid upon men by an arbitrary exterior power, but the inevitable sequence of cause and effect " [†] The writer thus differs from the author of Jubilees, with his doctrine of a spiritual ruin of men caused by the simple fiat of the Supreme.

### THE BOOK OF BARUCH

This book contains no teaching as to the origin or the permission of moral evil.

### $1^{1-14}$

The only matter to be observed here is the confession that Israel has suffered the exile for sin ($13$).

[*] E.B., art. " Wisdom," 5340.   [†] Op. cit. in loc.

$$1^{15}-3^8$$

*Israel and the Gentiles.*—The teaching is that Israel is God's people for ever. " I will make an everlasting covenant with them to be their God, and they shall be My people, and I will no more remove My people of Israel out of the land that I have given them " ($2^{35}$). This, however, is because Israel in the exile will become a converted people ($2^{31-3}$). The Gentiles are not mentioned, save in a prayer that " all the earth may know that Thou art the Lord our God for ever " ($2^{15}$).

*The Problem of Prosperity and Adversity.*—The punitive justice of God is recognised ($1^{19}-2^{10}$). In His judgment, Israel's dead and living are a unity. The fathers " hearkened not unto the voice of Thee, their God, for the which cause these plagues clave unto us " ($3^{4f.}$). But it is confessed that the living members of the race share the guilt as well as the penalty. Thus the pentitents say : " Since the day that the Lord brought our fathers out of the land of Egypt unto this present day we have been disobedient unto the Lord our God " ($1^{19}$) ; and again, referring to the exiles, they say : " Thus were they cast down and not exalted, because we sinned against the Lord our God " ($2^5$). The author does not impugn the principle of solidarity when he makes the exiles say : " We do not present our supplication before Thee, O Lord our God, for the righteousness of our fathers and of our kings " ($2^{19}$). His teaching is that the fathers were not righteous.

H. M. Hughes says : " The writer looks for the redemption of Israel, but there is a note of urgency and perplexity in his prayer. Why does not God redeem the people ? However guilty the fathers may have been, his own generation is not guilty, but the chastisement still continues " * This clearly is an erroneous view of the position of the suppliants in this section, as the confession in 1$^{19}$ shows. They confess their own sin as well as that of their fathers. A note of urgency there is in the prayer indeed, but not one sign of perplexity. Rather, the trouble of Israel is clearly seen to be God's most just punishment of the sins of the dead and living members of the race. "To the Lord our God belongeth righteousness, but unto us confusion of face as at this day," say both sets of exiles (1$^{15}$, 2$^{6}$), and clearer statement of an unperplexed consciousness of God's justice in Israel's sorrows could not well be imagined. Nor do we think that Hughes is justified when he says : " This writing is marked by an absence of the sense of personal demerit. It is true that sin is confessed with contrition, but the term ' we ' is used in a national, not a personal sense." † For this general confession no more excludes the possibility of individual acknowledgment of sin than does that in the Book of Common Prayer, and in 2$^{8}$ each man seems to make the confession his own. " We have not entreated the favour of the Lord our God in turning every one from the thoughts of his wicked heart." Moreover, the implication of the teaching in 2$^{30}$ is a disciplinary purpose of God in Israel's sorrows. " In the land of their captivity they shall lay it to heart, and they shall know that I am the Lord their God." Israel's troubles are thus no cause of perplexity for this writer. He sees in them the justice and the mercy of God. And, though he does not dwell on any hope of eternal life, he finds consolation in the idea of a blessed future for Israel in this world (2$^{35}$).

* Op. cit., p. 45 f.    † Idem, p. 155.

$$3^9-4^4$$

*Israel and the Gentiles.*—To the mind of this writer God is one who exclusively favours his own race. He has given the way of knowledge only to Israel. Other nations have not wisdom ($3^{20\ ff.}$). God did not choose the giants of old time, nor give them wisdom, and so they perished ($3^{27\ f.}$). At the close of his work the writer says : " Give not Thy glory to another, nor the things which are profitable to Thee to a strange nation " ($4^3$). This may be directed against new Christian ideas.* At least, on that view of it, the verse is in harmony with the general tenor of his thought. As we have noticed in Chapter I., it is possible that $3^{35}$ is a further illustration of his narrowness. Unlike the author of Jubilees, he feels no compulsion to attempt to vindicate God for giving Israel a position of exclusive privilege. He is content to assert it and rejoice in it.

*The Problem of Prosperity and Adversity.*—Israel is in the strange land, because he has forsaken the fount of wisdom. But for this he would have dwelt in peace for ever ($3^{10-13}$).

$$4^5-5^9$$

*Israel and the Gentiles.*—The fortunes of Israel so entirely absorb the attention of this writer that he makes no reference to other peoples, save in asserting the coming judgment on Israel's foes ($4^{25,\ 31-5}$). Israel he regards as God's own for ever. The name of Jerusalem " shall be called of God for ever ' the peace of righteousness ' and ' the glory of godliness ' " ($5^4$).

*The Problem of Prosperity and Adversity.*—Israel's exile was for sin, but they were not sold for destruction

---

* Cf. Marshall, D.B., " Baruch," p. 253.

(4⁶ᶠ·). Let them cry unto God and He will deliver them (4²¹, ²⁹). Their sorrows shall have abiding blessing as their sequel. Possibly the writer regarded this as God's end in punishment.

## THE ASSUMPTION OF MOSES

*Israel and the Gentiles.*—Israel is God's permanently according to this writer. He has pledged Himself to it. He has sworn that their seed shall never fail in the land which He gave them (3⁹). He has made the world on their behalf (1¹²). When God's kingdom is set up the business of the angel-chief will be to avenge Israel of its foes (10²). When God appears He will be simply Israel's great Patron. " His wrath will burn on account of His sons " (10³). He will appear to punish the Gentiles (10⁷). Our author observes that God's " kingdom will appear throughout all His creation " (10¹), but he does not dream of Gentile conversions. It is Israel only that will be exalted to heaven, and they will look rejoicingly on their foes in Gehenna (10⁹ᶠ·). If Charles's critical reconstruction of the corrupt Latin text is correct, the writer teaches that God keeps the Gentiles in ignorance with a view to their condemnation. " He was not pleased to manifest this purpose of creation from the foundation of the world that the Gentiles might thereby be convicted, yea, to their own humiliation might by their arguments convict one another." God rules all the world, says the writer, with compassion and righteousness (11¹⁷), but the general tenor of his teaching is that it is only for Israel that He is concerned.

*The Problem of Prosperity and Adversity.*—Israel is, according to this author, under a divine government in which justice is meted out strictly. The law of

14

God's action in Israel is : " Those who do and fulfil
the commandments of God will increase and be prospered. But those who set at nought the commandments will be without the blessings before mentioned,
and they will be punished with many torments by the
nations " ($12^{11}$). Righteous men suffer indeed under
this divine government. Taxo is described as affirming of his own family and their forbears that they have
not transgressed, though they are in the direst affliction ($9^4$). But then the nation is a unity. Judah,
for example, suffers for the sins of the northern tribes,
and this is regarded as strict justice. " Righteous
and holy is the Lord," they say, " for inasmuch as ye
have sinned, we too, in like manner, have been carried
away with you, together with our children " ($3^5$).
The punishment, which is " ruthless " and " merci-
less " ($9^2$), is regarded as God's penalty ($8^1$), and it is
confessed that Israel is punished more severely than
the Gentiles are. " For what nation or what region
or what people of those who are impious towards the
Lord, who have done many abominations, have
suffered as great calamities as have befallen us ? ($9^3$)
But this seems to occasion no problem. The day of
punishment for the impious Gentile is surely coming
($10^{10}$).

### THE APOCALYPSE OF BARUCH

#### A[1]

*Israel and the Gentiles.*—This writer looks forward
to a Messianic kingdom to which only Palestinian
Jews will be admitted. " At that time," says God,
" I will protect only those who are found in those self-
same days in the land " ($29^2$). When Messiah, at the
close of His reign, returns in glory, " all who have fallen

asleep in hope of Him [or perhaps of the future life]
shall rise again '' (30$^1$).* Nothing is said of any
ethical demand on the saved.

*Moral Evil.*—The misfortunes which are to befall
men in the last times will be of God's appointment,
and even the rapine, wickedness, and unchastity of
those times (27$^{11f.}$) are ordained by Him. Perhaps,
therefore, the writer conceived of sin as the fruit of
sin by God's appointment. Demons are mentioned
in 27$^9$, and it is said that they will make incursions
in the last days ; but it is not said or implied that they
are permitted to tempt mankind.

## A$^2$

*Israel and the Gentiles.*—Nothing that is said by A$^2$
implies hope for the Gentiles. We are only told that
Messiah will judge and slay an unnamed last leader
and put the multitude of his hosts to the sword, while
He will protect the rest of God's people who shall be
found in the place which He has chosen (40$^{1f.}$). Here,
as in A$^1$, God is apparently the partial Deity.

*The Problem of Prosperity and Adversity.*—As we
have observed in Chapter I., A$^2$ recognises an operative
justice of God in the happenings of history. In his
prophetic character, he announces the divine judgment on four successive empires, beginning with
Babylon and ending with Rome (36, 39).

## A$^3$

*Israel and the Gentiles.*—According to A$^3$, when the
times of the end come, " the Holy Land will have
mercy on its own and it will protect its inhabiters ''

* Charles (Apoc. Bar., p. 56) says that the words " of
Him '' cannot be original.

(71[1]). But he also says : " At the consummation of
the world there will be vengeance taken upon those
who have done wickedness according to their wickedness, and Thou wilt glorify the faithful according to
their faithfulness. For those who are among Thine
own Thou rulest, and those who sin Thou blottest out
from amongst Thine own " (54[21 f.]). Thus, unlike A[1]
and A[2], our author makes it clear that not all Israel
will be among the accepted when the kingdom is set
up. He regards the Gentiles as altogether corrupt :
" It were tedious to tell how they always wrought
impiety and wickedness and never wrought righteousness " (62[7]). They will be judged by Messiah, who
will " summon all the nations, and some of them He
will spare, and some of them He will slay " (72[2]).
Their fate depends on their attitude to Israel. " Every
nation which knows not Israel and has not trodden
down the seed of Jacob shall indeed be spared. And
this because some out of every nation will be sub-
jected to Thy people. But all those who have ruled
over you or have known you shall be given up to the
sword " (72[3-6]). A[3] thus teaches that there will be conversions to Israel's faith among the Gentiles. " Some
out of every nation " will turn to God. His God is
the partial Deity who makes Israel His favourite and
who judges the nations on a crude principle of justice.
Yet within Israel he does not tolerate the unfaithful,
and among the Gentiles He will accept those who
turn to Him.

*The Problem of Prosperity and Adversity.*—A[3] teaches
that God judges mankind as a unity. Adam's sin
brought on the race untimely death, grief, anguish,
pain, and trouble (56[6]). The general principle of
God's government is that Israel is prospered or in
adversity in strict accordance with conduct. When

the nation did not sin the " land was beloved " and " glorified beyond all lands, and the city Zion ruled then over all lands and regions " (61⁷); but, in Jezebel's time, was the " withholding of rains and famines " (62⁴). In 67³ ᶠ. A³ declares that Zion's downfall causes anguish to the angels, and he represents Ramiel himself as being perplexed about it. " Dost thou think," Ramiel says, " that in these things the Most High rejoices or that His name is glorified ? But how will it serve toward His righteous judgment ? " But, though our author here gives indication of being himself perplexed by the problem of pain, he makes no attempt to answer the question which he raises. He looks forward to the eternal life in which the righteous will " receive an eternal reward " (66⁶ ᶠ.), and the wicked will be tormented (54¹⁴ ᶠ., 55² ⁷, 59² ¹¹).

*Moral Evil.*—A³ stoutly maintains man's moral freedom. " Though Adam first sinned and brought untimely death upon all, yet of those who were born from him each one of them has prepared for his own soul torment to come, and again each one of them has chosen for himself glories to come " (54¹⁵). " Adam is, therefore, not the cause save of his own soul; but each one of us has been the Adam of his own soul " (Ibid. ¹⁹). However, notwithstanding this emphatic assertion of man's liberty, our author appears to teach that man was spiritually imperilled from the beginning by his physical constitution: " Adam was a danger to his own soul; even to the angels was he a danger " (56¹⁰). Moreover, the primitive fall affected man's constitution adversely, for, " when he transgressed, the begetting of children was brought about, and the passion of parents produced, and the greatness of humanity was humiliated, and goodness languished "

(56[6]). Charles, who thinks that in this book spiritual death is traced to Adam only in 48[22], says : " In A[3], according to 54[16, 19], the effects of Adam's sin are limited to physical results : his descendants must die prematurely." * But, while A[3] does not teach that man dies spiritually through Adam, he does attribute " certain derangements of human nature, disposing mankind towards sin, expressly to the Fall." † The race does not lose its freedom through Adam ; 54[19], as Tennant justly observes, is " as stark a repudiation of what is commonly meant by original sin, i.e. the heredity of moral incapacity caused by Adam, as could be expressed." ‡ On the other hand, it is clearly the teaching of A[3] that, through Adam's transgression, mankind runs the greater risk of incurring spiritual death. In the last days, " when the time of the age has ripened and the harvest of its evil and good seeds has come," God, our author says, " will bring upon the earth and its inhabitants and upon its rulers perturbation of spirit and stupor of heart, and they will hate one another and provoke one another to fight " (70[2 f.]). The corrupt world will, in fact, become more corrupt, and this is the divine penalty for its sin.

## B[1]

*Israel and the Gentiles.*—In one passage of B[1] God is represented as saying : " I will scatter this people among the Gentiles, that they may do good to the Gentiles " (1[4]). He gives no other allusion to God's purposes for the nations. He is absorbed in the thought of Israel's sad estate. He announces the coming permanent restoration of Jerusalem. It " will

* Ap. Bar., p. 93.　　　　　‡ Op. cit., p. 217.
† Tennant, op. cit., p. 215.

be delivered up for a time until it is said that it is again restored for ever " (6⁹). Still, perplexed by the fall of Zion and asking God, " What wilt Thou do for Thy great name ? " B¹ has learned by a divine revelation that God's name and glory are eternal. He can dispense with Israel (51 f.). The nation's position is entirely conditional. They will see the consolation of Zion, if they endure and persevere in His fear and do not forget His law (44⁷). God has made the promise that He will never " forget or forsake " His people, but " will gather together again those who were dispersed." But this is no absolute promise. He will continually remember Israel, if they destroy from their hearts the vain error on account of which they were exiled; but, if they fail to do this, they will " finally be condemned and tormented " (78⁶ᵗ·). The teaching of the writer on the subject is well summed up in 84⁶: " Lo ! I say unto you, after ye have suffered, that, if ye obey these things which have been said unto you, ye will receive from the Most High whatever has been laid up and reserved for you " (84⁶).

*The Problem of Prosperity and Adversity.*—B¹ is deeply moved by those sorrows of Israel in which he sees the signs of God's punitive justice. He would rather die than see the destruction of Zion (3²ᵗ·). But he is by no means utterly perplexed by the facts. He feels, indeed, that the judgments of God are past finding out, but he avers his conviction that they are right (44⁶). He cannot reconcile the destruction of the city with God's promises to Israel (3⁹). But he is content to know that God's " people will be chastened and the time will come when they will seek for the prosperity of their times " (1⁵). He tells the nine and half tribes that they have now suffered for their good (78⁶). He holds that Israel is such a unity in the judgment of God that the whole suffers for the sin of a part. " Because your brethren transgressed the commandments of the Most High, He brought vengeance upon you and upon them, and He spared not the former and the latter also He gave into captivity " (77⁴). The converse also is true. The works and prayers of Jeremiah and his like are as a firm pillar to Jerusalem, though this is limited to the time of their stay therein (2²). He is far from tolerating such an idea as that which appears in Ethiopic Enoch 83–90, where it is taught that men suffer more than they deserve. On the contrary, he affirms that the northern tribes should justify God's judgment in carrying them away captive. " What ye have suffered," he says, " is disproportioned to what ye have done " (78⁵). Likewise the two and half tribes have not been chastened as they have deserved (79² ᶠ·).

Little is said of the life beyond, but Baruch is told by God that for him there will be " many eternal consolations " (43¹).

## B²

*Israel and the Gentiles.*—Unlike B¹, the writer of these sections looks for no theocratic kingdom on earth. His hopes are set on the future life, and Israel's happiness therein depends on submission to God (75⁷ ᶠ· *). If they prepare their hearts to sow in them the fruits of the law, it will protect them when God shall shake the creation (32¹). " Do ye prepare your hearts," says Baruch, " for that which before ye believed, lest ye come to be in bondage in both worlds,

* Chapter 75 may, however, belong to B¹ ; vide Chapter III. of this work.

so that ye be led away captive here and be tormented there " (83⁸).

A very important passage in chapters 13 and 14 is as follows :

" xiii. 4. If ever those prosperous cities say, ' Why hath the mighty God brought upon us this retribution ? '

" 5. Thou and those like thee may say to them, (even) ye who have seen :  ' This evil and (these) retributions are coming upon you and upon your people (are sent) in its time that the nations may be perfectly chastened.'

" 6. And then they will expect.

" 7. And if they say at that time ' When ? '

" 8. Thou wilt say unto them :  ' Ye who have drunk the strained wine, drink ye also of its dregs, the judgment of the Lofty One who has no respect of persons.'

" 9. On this account, He had before no mercy on His own sons, but afflicted them as His enemies because they sinned.

" 10. They were therefore chastened then that they might receive mercy.

" 11. But now, ye peoples and nations, ye are debtors because all this time ye have trodden down the earth and used the creation unrighteously.

" 12. For I have always benefited you and ye have always denied the beneficence.'

" xiv. 1. And I answered and said :  ' Lo ! Thou hast shown me the methods of the times and that which will be after these things.  And Thou hast said unto me that the retribution which has been spoken of by Thee will be of advantage to the nations.

" 2. And now I know that those who have sinned are many, and they have lived in prosperity and departed from the world ; but that few nations will be left in those times to whom these words shall be said which Thou didst say.' "

In some of these statements we have the clearest assertions of divine purposes of grace towards the Gentiles. They are to be "chastened," and Charles says that the Syriac word so rendered is never used, so far as he is aware, of a vindictive punishment. He suggests that possibly the word is corrupt, but adds that, even if it is, we still have the clear statement in $14^1$ of God's merciful purpose to "the nations." He thinks, however, that the word rendered "nations" may, as in $42^5$, mean Israel. But he doubts whether in $42^5$ the text is sound, for "it would be strange to speak of Israel as 'the peoples' or 'the nations.'"[*] We may take it, then, that $14^1$ refers to the Gentiles. Were it otherwise the passage would mean that the "prosperous cities," which are clearly Gentile cities, are to be punished for the chastening of Israel. The teaching seems to be of a type similar to that of the noblest passages in the second part of Wisdom. God will chasten the Gentiles for their ultimate advantage ; He will act toward them as he does toward Israel. But verses 8–11 contradict all this. The nations must drink the dregs of the cup. Israel was chastened to receive mercy, but now the nations are debtors. Moreover, in $14^2$ Baruch laments that many prosperous sinners will die and escape the penalty, though this complaint is made immediately after a verse in which the largest view of God's purposes is taken. Charles concludes that "the vindictive punishment of the Gentiles is dealt with in this chapter," and this is clearly the fact. But the whole truth is that the section gives us contradictory doctrines,

[*] Ap. Bar. in loc.

and the text is, as Charles says, in a bad state of disarrangement.  Two hands are apparently in evidence in these verses, one that of a narrow Jew whose God is simply Israel's Partisan, the other that of a Jewish believer in the God who has purposes of mercy for all mankind.

In another important passage, which apparently belongs to B², the fate of apostate Jews and Gentile proselytes seems to be in question.  Baruch has seen many of God's people withdrawing from the covenant and casting off the yoke of the law, as well as others who have forsaken their vanity and fled for refuge beneath God's wings (41³˙⁴·).  As Charles observes, this last expression is parallel to that in Ruth 2¹², " The God of Israel, under whose wings thou art come to take refuge," and suggests that Baruch here concerns himself with the ultimate fate of proselytes. " What therefore shall be to them," he asks, " or how will the last time receive them ?  Or perhaps the time of these will assuredly be weighed, and as the beam inclines will they be judged accordingly " (Ibid. 5 f.).  The question seems to be whether each will be judged strictly by his own merit or demerit, and the writer clothes his answer with divine authority. " He answered and said unto me, ' These things will I also show unto thee.  As for what thou didst say, " To whom will these things be and how many [will they be] ? "  To those who have believed there will be the good which was spoken of aforetime and to those who despise there will be the contrary of these things ' " (42¹).  " As for those," says God, " who before were subject and afterwards withdrew and mingled themselves with the seed of mingled peoples, the time of these is the former . . . and as for those who before knew not, but afterwards knew and mingled [only] with the seed of the people which had separated itself, the time of these is the former" (Ibid. ⁴ᴸ·).

As the text of this latter oracle now stands, both classes are said to be destined to be saved, apostates and proselytes. But this is certainly a textual corruption. It contradicts 42¹, and we should correct the word "former" in the first part of the sentence into "latter." * It is, then, clear that B² teaches the damnation of Jewish apostates and the blessedness of proselytes. The doctrine as to the fate of Jewish apostates in this passage is thus in harmony with that in the passages cited above (75⁷⁴, 32¹, 83⁸).† In a passage which Charles inclines to regard as of the same author we have a statement concerning the destiny of prosperous and impious Gentiles. It is affirmed that they will pass away like smoke and "will be accounted as spittle" (82²⁻⁹). This statement is like one which is made in 4 Esdras 6⁵⁶. But our author does not say of all Gentiles, as Ps. Esdras does, that they are to be accounted as spittle. His affirmation is only made of those great ones of the earth who are marked at once by strength and cruelty.

*The Problem of Prosperity and Adversity.*—This writer is of a temper very different from that of his compatriot who wrote the sections B¹. The problem of the sufferings of the righteous is to him most urgent and exasperating, or, perhaps we ought to say, it is that to the men whose views he is expressing. Right doing, he says, is of no profit to men.

Elsewhere B² teaches that the entire race has solidarity, in God's judgment in one important respect, namely, that He has decreed death for all men on account of the sin of Adam (23⁴). But he or his

* Cf. Edition of Ap. Bar. in loc.  † Cf. pp. 216 f.

compatriots felt that this principle ought to operate beneficially, while, as a matter of fact, it was not so. " It was due to Zion that, on account of the works of those who wrought good works, she should be forgiven, and not overwhelmed, on account of the works of those who wrought unrighteousness " ($14^{5-7}$). But indeed, God's way is incomprehensible (Ibid. 8 f.). Man is but a temporary creature (Ibid. $^{10 f.}$), and our author, in the manner of Koheleth, complains that the world which God said was made for man is abiding while he passes away (Ibid. $^{18 f.}$). He is gently reproved by God for his daring suggestion, and assured that not only is it true that this world was made for the righteous, but " more, even that which is to come is on their account. For this world is to them a trouble and a weariness, with much labour, and that accordingly which is to come a crown with great glory " ($15^{7 f.}$). Does our author here intend to teach that the painful present is a moral discipline for the glorious future ? It seems very clear that this is his thought. For he objects, against the divine reply, that life is too brief for man to acquire that which is measureless (16), and God tells him that Moses did it in his 120 years, though Adam failed with his longer span of days (17). We have already seen that, in $13^{10}-14^1$, B$^2$ clearly teaches the doctrine of the God who in mercy chastens men. The Divine Speaker proceeds to admonish him that what really concerns a man in any matter is the final upshot of things, what signifies is that he should be right in the end ($19^{5-8}$). That end is at hand (20). But Baruch is impatient for its coming. He cries to God to reprove the angel of death and let His glory appear. He implores God not to defer that which has been promised ($21^{23-5}$). Against his haste, God urges that time must be allowed for all things to develop (22), and reminds Baruch that he is ill at ease because he is ignorant (23²). Baruch is assured that God is mindful of the living and the dead and of those who are yet to be (23³; cf. 48⁶). God has determined the number of those to be born, and only when His purposes are fulfilled will the great consummation be (23⁴ᶠᶠ·). Baruch appears to be expressing in his complaints the common thoughts and feelings of his fellows, and he is desirous to give them a comforting answer to their troubled questionings. He is so convinced that he has God's own authority for this answer that he gives it forth as God's speech. As De Faye rightly observes : " Baruch a eu soin de couvrir d'une autorité incontestée, celle du Dieu même, la solution du grand problème qu'il prêche a ses frères affligés. C'est la voix divine qui la lui communique." * To sum up, the divine answer is : (1) that God's ways are not known to man, hence man must be patient ; (2) that time must be given for the completion of great divine purposes ; (3) that to-day is God's discipline of men for His great to-morrow, and (4) that, in the world to come, there is compensation for all the present sorrows of righteous men. On that world to come B²'s whole hopes are centred. Of this world he has no hope whatever (44⁸⁻¹⁵). It is only the consummation of this life in the next which saves it from being unmingled bitterness and vanity (21¹³· ¹⁷). But in that future he has perfect confidence. God has revealed to him that it will make manifest how long-suffering He has been to all mankind, whether righteous or sinful (24²). The end will be the torment of the wicked (30⁴ᶠ·, 51²) and the perfect bliss of the faithful in Paradise " delivered from this world of tribulation "

* " Les Apocalypses Juifs," p. 79.

and " having laid down the burthen of anguish " (51). Therefore B² exhorts his readers not to look at the delights of the Gentiles in the present, but to remember what has been promised to them in the end (83⁵).

Thus, in the face of terrible questionings, our author holds fast his confidence in the God who is faithful to His own, assured that God's ways with man will be vindicated perfectly in the great coming consummation of all things.

*Moral Evil.*—The only allusion to effects of the Fall on mankind is in 48⁴²ᶠ·: " O Adam, what hast thou done to all those who are born from thee? and what will be said to the first Eve who hearkened to the serpent? For all this multitude are going to corruption, nor is there any numbering of those whom the fire devours." Charles says that spiritual death is here traced to Adam.* If so, it is only in the sense that Adam set the race a bad example. We cannot infer any more than that from this passage. The mischief which Adam did the race is that " many have taken from the darkness of Adam and have not rejoiced in the light of the lamp " (18²).

### B³

*Israel and the Gentiles.*—B³ says nothing as to the Gentiles. He urges Israelites so to act that, in the future life, they may hope and not be put to shame, that they may rest with their fathers and not be tormented with their enemies (85⁹). They are to prepare their souls that, when they sail into the unknown, they may have rest and not be condemned (Ibid. ¹¹).

* Edition of Ap. Bar., p. 93.

## S

One brief section of this book contains doctrine which differs absolutely from all the rest. This is $10^6$–$12^4$. The writer of this, " the saddest dirge in the Jewish literature of the time," as Dr. Charles calls it, expresses indeed his belief in coming retribution on Israel's oppressors ($12^4$); but Israel, according to him, has no future in this world or the next. Offerings will never be made again in Zion ($10^{10}$). Beyond the grave there is neither reward nor retribution. The dead in Sheol are more blessed than the living ($11^{6f.}$). God has forsaken the elect people.

### 4 ESDRAS

#### The Salathiel Apocalypse (S)

*Israel and the Gentiles.*—Esdras cites the covenant with Abraham in which the divine promise was that His seed should never be forsaken ($3^{15}$). But the apocalyptist's hopes are centred upon the unseen life, not at all upon any theocratic kingdom on earth. When Esdras asks what shall be the indication of the end of the first age and the beginning of the second, the answer is : " The heel of the first age is Esau ; the hand of the second is Jacob. The beginning of a man is his hand, and the end of a man is his heel. Between heel and hand, seek nought else, Ezra " ($6^{7-10}$).*

Here, as Mr. Box says, he indicates in allegorical language " that the present corrupt Age (symbolised by Esau) will be succeeded immediately, without a break, by the glorious future Age of incorruption (symbolised by Jacob). . . . Just as there is no room

---

* This is the version of the Syriac given by G. H. Box. The Latin is defective.

in the divine acts of creation and judgment for a mediatorial Messiah, so in the transition from the present to the future there is no room for a Messianic interim." * In that future on which the Prophet's hopes are set it is, according to him, only Israel's obedient sons who will be the blessed. We shall set forth at length in Chapter III. our reasons for concluding that this is clearly his teaching. His doctrine is that God cares only for Israel. There are passages indeed in which he shows himself concerned as to the destiny of mankind in general. He laments that men are sinners, and " that, not a few only, but well-nigh all that have been created" (7⁴⁸). " Let the race of man lament," he says, " and let all the beasts of the field be glad " (7⁶⁵). But the divine answer is not only a vindication of the justice of man's condemnation as being the result of disobedience to known commandments (7⁷²) ; it is also an assertion of God's unconcern about the perishing majority of mankind. For while, on the one hand, it is declared in 8⁵⁹ that God did not will man's destruction, yet, on the other hand, in 7⁶⁰ᶠ· He says : " I will rejoice over the few that be saved . . . and I will not grieve over the multitude of them that perish." De Faye, following Hilgenfeld, argues that some Christian has retouched the passages in which Esdras speaks of the ill fate of mankind." †  But this is, in the judgment of the present writer, improbable, for the drift of these passages as a whole is strongly opposed to any catholic idea of God's mercy. He is represented as indifferent to the fate of the vast multitude of men: " Thou hast said that for our sakes Thou madest this world. As for the other nations which also come of Adam, Thou hast said that they are nothing, and are like unto spittle ; and Thou hast

* Op. cit., pp. 67 f. † Op. cit., p. iii.
15

likened the abundance of them unto a drop that falleth from a vessel" (6⁵⁶ᴸ·). This elicits no rebuke from Uriel. His only comment is : "For their sakes [Israel's] I made the world" (7¹¹). Mr. Box notes the fact that this passage is based on Isaiah 40¹⁵, and that the LXX ὡς σίελος λογισθήσονται arose from a misreading of the Hebrew. רק (small dust) was written, and רק (sputum) was read. He thinks that a similar error was made here by the Greek translator.* Yet, if it be so, if consequently we must not attribute to S the use of the word "spittle," his general idea is not affected by the omission. It clearly is that God's concern is only for Israel's righteous, that He will not grieve over the rest of mankind, that the Gentiles as a whole are nothing to Him.

*The Problem of Prosperity and Adversity.*—The great subject of the repeated questions of Esdras is the troubles of Israel. The city has been punished, he says, for its iniquity ; but then Babylon is wicked also, yet she is not punished. Greatly daring, Esdras complains that God destroys His people and spares His enemies. He has not signified to any how His way may be comprehended (3²⁶⁻³¹). To this question thus raised in the first talk with the angel Esdras recurs at the commencement of the second conversation (5¹³ᵇ-6¹⁰). Why has God given over His beloved people to their foes ? It seems as if He hates them. They ought to have been punished by His own hand. This last, said in the heat of feeling, is apologised for a moment later (5²⁸⁻³⁰, ³⁴). In the third talk the question again comes up immediately (6¹⁰-7¹⁵, 7¹⁵-8⁶², 9¹³-10⁵⁷). Why is God's chosen people given into the hand of the Gentiles, when they ought to possess the world ? God has said that for Israel the world was

* Op. cit. in loc.

made, but the hopes aroused by His word have been
falsified. It is the dominant insistent question that
runs right through S, revived in every conversation,
and our author offers an authoritative reply. This he
does by representing his solutions as invested with
the authority of God's word through Uriel.

The first point made by the angel is that man, who
cannot comprehend lower things, cannot hope to
understand loftier matters. Like the woods and the
sea, he has limits which he cannot transcend. Esdras
is "worn out with the corrupted world," and cannot
" understand incorruption." * ($4^{1-21}$). He will obtain
the answer to his question if he is alive at the end
($4^{26}$). For that end God and the righteous are eager,
but God has fixed the hour and sin cannot postpone
it ($4^{34-43}$). Esdras is exhorted to fast and pray for a
fuller revelation ($5^{13}$). Then he is assured of a love
of God for Israel which is greater than his own, and
once again reminded that he cannot fathom the
mystery of God's dealing ($5^{33-40}$). He is eager to know
the fate of Israel's dead, and the answer apparently
is an assurance that they are not forgotten of the
Lord. " I will liken My judgment to a ring : like as
there is no slackness of them that be last, even so
there is no swiftness of them that be first " ($5^{41t.}$).
He desires to know why the agony of man is so long-
drawn-out, when all whom God intends to create
might be produced at once and judgment shown the
sooner. To this Uriel replies that man must be as
patient as God is, and that the world could not contain
all at once. But Esdras answers that all will be

* Mr. Box suggests that $4^{11}$ might be retranslated into
Hebrew so as to mean : " How should the son of change, i.e.
the transient, in a changing world, be able to understand the
ways of the changeless One ? " (Op. cit. in loc.).

alive together at the judgment and the creation will therefore sustain all at that time. To this Uriel makes no reply. He is beaten in the argument. He can only take refuge in the statement that God has so ordered His universe, even as He has ordained that a woman shall not bear all her children at one birth (5⁴³⁻⁹). Esdras seems to represent in his own person current questionings and he offers the orthodox reply—the only reply which he feels he can make as the foiled argument shows—which is that things are as they are by the fiat of the Supreme.

In the third conversation Esdras is told that his righteousness is to be rewarded with new knowledge (6³¹). It is now revealed to him that Adam's sin has made Israel's experiences hard and toilsome. It is the way by which they will pass into the fuller life of the world to come (7¹⁻¹⁵). Comfort will come by considering what is to be in the future (Ibid. ¹⁶). But Esdras expresses himself as feeling that it is unjust that the wicked of Israel should be involved in penalty on Adam's account, while yet they will not share the compensation. They " will suffer the strait things and yet not see the wide " (Ibid. ¹⁸). He has previously asserted the doctrine of solidarity: " Adam transgressed, and immediately Thou appointedst death for him and in his generations " (3⁷). Later in this book he pleads with God to have regard to that principle in mercy, sparing sinners by reason of the merits of Israel's godly folk (8²⁶⁻³⁰). But, in the passage before us, he appears to make himself the spokesman of contemporaries who fret against the law of solidarity as it involves man in penalty, though naturally entertaining no objections to it when it confers benefit. But the answer is stern. If men are lost, it is by their own disloyalty to the light (7²¹⁻⁵).

Besides, "Thou art not a judge above God, neither hast thou understanding above the Most High " (7¹⁹). In fact, to men who hotly impeach the order of things as it involves them in penalties for sins not their own, the author can only reply by making the angelic ambassador assert God's sovereign wisdom and the wilful fault of those who miss the compensations of the hereafter. The conversations close with the vision of the new Zion which shall be "the work of no man's building " (10⁵⁴).

To sum up, therefore, the answer which Esdras thinks himself divinely commissioned to make to the cry of a distressed and sorely perplexed people is (1) that man, by reason of his corruption, cannot fully comprehend God's ways ; (2) that God rules the course of things and has fixed the time of a great consummation which none can retard ; (3) that He has a love for Israel transcending that of His servant ; (4) that He does not forget Israel's dead ; (5) that the sorrow of the nation is the consequence of the sin of Adam and is the way to a nobler life hereafter ; (6) that any Israelite who suffers and misses the future compensation has himself to blame for it ; (7) that God is wiser than man, and man must not impeach His justice ; and (8) that for righteous Israel there is in store the New Jerusalem above. He does not expressly suggest the idea that sorrow may have a chastening purpose, but that is perhaps the thought when he speaks of Israel's sorrows as the necessary way to the future glory (7¹²⁻¹⁴).

*Moral Evil.*—Sin is traced to God's own action in endowing man with the Yetzer Hara. "A grain of evil seed was sown in the heart of man from the beginning " (4³⁰). Of the righteous, God's testimony is that "they have striven to overcome the evil

thought which was fashioned together with them "
(7$^{92}$). "Adam," we read, "bearing a wicked heart,
transgressed" (3$^{21}$). In the last passage, instead of
the Latin "baiolans," the Syriac and Ethiopic versions have the equivalent of "cum vestivit." Charles
consequently holds that the teaching is that the
original evil impulse was developed by Adam's sin
into the evil heart.*

The expression in 3$^{22}$—"disease was made permanent"—may mean that man was permanently enfeebled by Adam's fault, and perhaps 7$^{118}$ implies the
same idea : " O thou Adam, what hast thou done ?
for, though it was thou that sinned, the evil is not
fallen on thee alone, but on all of us that come of
thee." But, be this as it may, it is clear that the
writer ascribes to God the origin of the germ of evil
in man, and the " cor malignum " may be, as Tennant
thinks, identical with the grain of evil seed originally
implanted in man by God.† Nor does S find relief
in the thought that " the evil nature is in a sense
good." ‡ On the contrary, he chafes at it. He complains that God did not restrain nations from sinning
(3$^{8}$), that He did not take away the wicked heart from
man so that His law " might bring forth fruit in
them " (3$^{20}$). With characteristic daring he argues
that, just as the farmer's harvest may fail by reason
of a too slight or too heavy fall of rain, so man's moral
failure springs from the fact that God has not supplied
him with that which he needs (8$^{42}$). The apocalyptist
is probably here making himself the mouthpiece of his
compatriots, and the divine reply is of the usual
character. It is impious to suggest such ideas.
" Thou comest far short that thou shouldest be able

---

* Edition Ap. Bar., p. 93.　　　　　　‡ Ibid.
† Op. cit., p. 226.

to love My creatures more than I. But thou hast
brought thyself full nigh unto the unrighteous " (8⁴⁷).

G. H. Box observes that S differs fundamentally
from the Rabbis in "the emphasis he lays on the
ravages of the evil yeser upon human nature generally." "The enfeeblement of man's nature is such
that practically no one has been able successfully to
withstand the yeser : the whole race has fallen into
corruption. The Rabbis insisted, on the other hand,
that human nature is not, by any means, in such a
hopeless condition. Man can, by moral effort, and
assisted by the grace of God, successfully resist the
suggestions of the evil impulse." * But the fact is
that, labouring under the great stress of his emotion,
S is not always consistent with himself. "All that
are born," he says, "are defiled with iniquities, and
are full of sins and laden with offences " (7⁶⁸). "In
truth there is no man among them that be born but
he hath dealt wickedly " (8³⁵). Yet he also speaks of
"the just, who have many good works," for whom
he does not need to plead (8³³) ; he declares that they
are blessed "that be now alive and keep the (statutes)
ordained " of God (7⁴⁵) ; it is "well-nigh all that
have been created," but yet not *all* that have been
brought into corruption by the evil heart (7⁴⁷) ; and
in the end God will testify of some men that they
have kept His law (7⁹⁴). Esdras himself will be one
of that blessed company (7⁷⁶). S feels intensely that
the battle is hard, that most men are corrupted, that
the origin of sin is in that nature which God has
given to man, but he does not consider that God has so
made man that the conflict is hopeless. Neither by
his original constitution, nor by the Fall, is man made
incapable of moral victory.

* Op. cit., p. xli.

## The Esdras Apocalypse (E)

*Israel and the Gentiles.*—The idea of any salvation for the Gentiles is absent. They who are to see God's salvation are such as escape in the final crisis, and they will see it in God's land and within the borders which He has sanctified from the beginning (9⁷). Yet not all Israelites will be among the blessed, only they who escape by works or faith (Ibid.). As for the world in general, it will become more and more corrupt, so that vain search will be made for a righteous man (5¹¹). The nations are to be raised from the dead, but only to a general condemnation (7³² ᶠ.).

*The Problem of Prosperity and Adversity.*—The great hope and consolation of the writer is that coming day when God " shall make inquisition of them that have done unjustly " and the affliction of Zion shall be fulfilled (6¹⁸ᶠ.). Beyond that, he looks for the time when God's people shall enjoy the paradise of delights and the sinners shall be tormented (7³⁶).

## The Vision of the Eagle (A)

*Israel and the Gentiles.*—In 12³⁴ there is a prophecy of a temporary kingdom of God to be followed by " the end, even the Day of Judgment." This is probably a verse inserted by the editor, as it does not harmonise with the statement of A in 11⁴⁴ᶜ, where the end is identified with the downfall of the Roman Empire : " The Most High hath looked upon His times, and behold they are ended and His ages are fulfilled."

Then, according to A, will begin the new age in which " all the earth will be refreshed and be eased " from the violence of the oppressor and " may hope for the judgment and mercy of Him that made her " (11⁴⁶). As Box, following Kabisch, suggests, " judgment " probably translates משפט and denotes " the just and mild rule of the theocratic king, i.e. God Himself. The overthrow of the Roman Empire by the Messiah is to be followed by the rule or sovereignty of God." *

*The Problem of Prosperity and Adversity.*—A looks out on a world in which the righteous are great sufferers, and his one consolation is that God is going to punish their oppressors and set up a new age of peace (11⁴⁰⁻², 12³²ᶠ·). Of the life after death he has nothing to say.

### The Vision of the Son of Man (M)

*Israel and the Gentiles.*—In 13⁹⁻¹¹ it is prophesied that the supernatural Son of Man will be assaulted on His appearance by an innumerable multitude of men, whom He will destroy. Then, it is added, the Son of Man will call to Himself another multitude. These are men disposed to peace, some glad, some sorrowful, some in bonds, some bringing others " who should be offered " (13¹²ᶠ·). Obviously these last are, as in Isaiah 66²⁰, heathen who bring Jews as an oblation to the Lord, and it may be that, as Box thinks, the glad and the sorrowful are Jews and heathen, pious and godless.† If this is the correct view, A has here made use of old material and has either missed the idea or designedly transformed it so as to teach that no heathen are to be spared when Messiah appears. For, in his interpretation, he explains that the peaceable multitude in the vision are the ten exiled tribes of Israel (13³⁹ᶠ·), and that, when Messiah destroys the multitude of the nations that war against Him,

* Op. cit., p. 247.                    † Op. cit. in loc.

He " will defend the people that remain," i.e. all Israel now found within His holy border (13⁴⁸ᶠ·). G. H. Box suggests that possibly proselytes were intended to be included, but no hint as to this is given by the writer.

### The Additions of the Editor (R)

*Israel and the Gentiles.*—Kabisch assigns to R the following passages prophetic of the Messianic kingdom :

(1) " The rest of My people shall He [Messiah] deliver with mercy, those that have been preserved throughout My borders, and He shall make them joyful until the coming of the end, even the day of judgment " (12³⁴).

(2) " He that shall endure the peril in that time [i.e. the Messianic woes] shall keep them that be fallen into danger, even such as have works and faith toward the Almighty " (13²³).

(3) " They [i.e. those who survive a preliminary judgment] shall see the men that have been taken up, who have not tasted death from their birth, and the hearts of the inhabitants shall be changed and turned into another meaning " (6²⁶ᶠ·).

In regard to (2), the R.V. reading given above is based on the Syriac ; but the Latin reads, " qui adferet periculum." If we accept this, the passage is more intelligible, and it would seem that R's doctrine is that Palestinian Jews who have works and faith will be preserved by the Messiah and inherit the joys of His kingdom. But, as (3) shows, this editor apparently cherished the conviction that, through the missionary activity of such saints as Enoch and Elijah, returned to earth for the purpose, the surviving members of the human race would be converted.

### 3 MACCABEES

*Israel and the Gentiles.*—This book contains little as to God's attitude towards the Gentiles. The writer affirms, however, that God governs " the whole creation in mercies " ($6^2$), and that He is the " Protector of the Universe " ($6^9$). He is Israel's Saviour and Patron, who fights on their behalf ($6^1$, $7^{6, 16}$).

*The Problem of Prosperity and Adversity.*—God's punitive acts are to be seen in history, and He delivers His faithful servants from trouble ($2^{16}$, $2^{4-8}$, $2^{12}$, $4^{21}$, $5^{11 f., 28}$, $6^{4-8, 18}$). True, Israel suffers, but the sufficient explanation of this is Israel's sin. " Lo ! now, O holy king, we are afflicted on account of our many and great sins " ($2^{18}$).

### 4 MACCABEES

This work contains nothing as to God's attitude to the nations. The writer teaches that sinners are punished in this world, and tells how once Providence shielded the Temple by a miraculous intervention ($4^{11}$, $18^{5, 12}$, $14^{10}$). But it is confessed that, under the " divine justice " ($4^{21}$, $18^{22}$), righteous men are terrible sufferers. This, however, is no cause of perplexity to the author. His teaching is that they who have received from God the great gift of life owe it to Him that they should be willing to endure suffering for His sake ($16^{18 f.}$). " It is," he says, " an unreasonable thing that those who are acquainted with piety should not bear up against troubles " ($16^{23}$). Such troubles have abundant compensations in the eternal life. Like the patriarchs, the martyrs live " unto God " ($7^{19}$). " For we," says a martyr, " through this suffering and endurance, shall bear the prizes of virtue, and we shall be with God, for whose sake we suffer " ($9^8$).

The martyrs are "now standing about the divine throne and are living the happy life" (17[18]). These "sons of Abraham, with their victorious mother, are gathered to the land of their fathers, having received from God pure and deathless souls" (18[23]). In like manner, the wicked shall receive in that world the due reward of their deeds (10[11, 21], 12[12], 18[22]).

The death of the martyrs is regarded as a sacrifice offered to God by which the whole nation benefits. "Be propitious to Thy nation," cries Eleazar, "being satisfied with our punishment on their behalf. Make my blood their propitiation, and receive my life an offering for them" (or "instead of theirs") (6[28]). So also the eldest of the young martyrs says: "War a holy and noble warfare for piety, through which our just and paternal Providence, becoming propitious to our nation, may punish the execrable tyrant" (9[24]). The result of their sacrifices was that "the country was cleansed as by an offering made for the sin of the nation, and, through the blood of those pious men and their propitiatory death, the divine Providence saved Israel, which before was evil entreated" (17[21 f.]). Perhaps the same thought is in 1[11], which Cotton translates: "Their country was purged and cleansed by the expiatory sacrifice which they offered." But nothing is said in the Greek of an "expiatory sacrifice." The words are: ὥστε καθαρισθῆναι δι᾽ αὐτῶν τὴν πατρίδα.

*Moral Evil.*—"When God made man," says this author, "He planted round him the passions and the moral feelings. And then over all, He enthroned the mind as a holy director by means of the inward feelings" (2[21 f.]). As Tennant says, the writer here "seems to teach that we have an inward bias to evil in virtue of our being endowed with passions; but

such original sin as this we owe to God and certainly
not to Adam." *  In another passage, a speech of the
mother of the martyrs, reference is made to the devil.
" The deceiver, the deceitful serpent, did not corrupt
the holiness of [my] virginity " (18⁸). The author's
belief in man's power to conquer evil is expressed in
3⁴: " None of you can eradicate malignancy
(κακοήθεια), but principle can fight with him so that
he shall not be bowed down by malignancy."

SLAVONIC ENOCH

*Israel and the Gentiles.*—The one passage in this
work about Israel's destiny is as follows : " And I
will leave a righteous man (of thy race) with all his
house who shall act according to My will.  From their
seed (after some time) will be raised a numerous †
generation, but (of these many will be) very insatiable.
Then on the extinction of that family I will show
them the books of thy writings, and of thy fathers,
and the guardians of them on earth will show them
to the men who are true (and please Me, who do not
take My name in vain).  And they shall tell it to
another generation,‡ and (these having read them)
shall be glorified at last more than before " § (35).
Our author thus foretells the future glory of faithful
Israelites, but there is no trace of particularism in his
work.  No specific allusion is made to the Gentiles,
except in the statement that all idolaters are destined
to have their eternal inheritance in the place of penalty

---

* Op. cit., p. 144.
† " Another " (Sok).
‡ " That generation " (B).
§ B omits the passages in brackets.  The first of them is
also omitted in A.

($10^6$). But the ethical teaching of the book is as broad as it is severe. Man must not injure man, or he commits high misdemeanour in the sight of God. The final judgment, moreover, is to be by conduct. "There is a special place for all mankind, for all the souls of men according to their number . . . and not one soul shall perish which God has made till the great judgment" ($58^{5\text{-}6}$). "Every man shall come to the great judgment of the Lord" ($65^6$).

If Sok is right, this author teaches that "the Lord contemplated the world for the sake of man and made all the creation for his sake" ($65^6$). A does not contain this, but B has the latter portion of the sentence,

*The Problem of Prosperity and Adversity.*—Our author teaches that physical death was appointed on account of the sin of Adam ($30^{16}$, cf. $32^1$). He states the doctrine of retribution in this world somewhat crudely in one passage: "Assist the honest man in his afflictions, and affliction shall not come upon you in the time of your labour" ($51^2$). B, however, omits this, and it is inconsistent with the facts on which our author dwells. He shows himself very conscious of the injustices which are permitted on earth ($10$). In one curious passage he tells how God made trial of His servants in heaven, by assigning to Enoch a great and eternal place of honour ($22^6$); but he makes no allusion to His trying the righteous on earth, unless this is an obscure reference thereto. It is to the future life that he looks for God's awards of justice. The good will receive their "reward in the day of judgment" ($51^3$). The place of torture is prepared for the wicked, and the third heaven for the righteous ($10^{1\text{-}6}$, $9^1$).

*Moral Evil.*—The author alludes to the story of the

watchers who made the earth foul with their deeds,
and to the seduction of Eve by Satan in the garden
(18¹, 31⁶); but he does not teach that men are continually exposed to demonic assaults upon their
virtue.   He represents God as saying of Adam : " I
gave him his will and I showed him the two ways, the
light and the darkness.   And I said unto him, ' This
is good and this is evil,' that I should know whether
he has love for Me or hate, that he should appear in
his race as loving Me.   I knew his nature; he did not
know his nature.   Therefore his ignorance is a woe
to him that he should sin " (30¹⁵ᶠ·).   We have here a
similar idea to that which appears in Jubilees, where
it is taught that Abraham's trial was designed to show
that God has faithful servants on earth.   Yet the
freedom of Adam, according to this passage, was of a
very limited kind.   It seems that our author thought
it almost inevitable that Adam should sin.   The text
of the last sentence in our citation is, however, dubious.
Sok has :   " His ignorance is worse than sinning."
An important passage is 41¹: " I saw all our forefathers from the beginning with Adam and Eve, and
I sighed and wept and spake of the ruin (caused by)
their wickedness: ' Woe is me for my infirmity and
that of my forefathers.' " *   Tennant thinks that the
passage implies the doctrine of an inherited depravity
and infirmity transmitted to the posterity of Adam
as a result of his sin.†   But conceivably the passage
may mean no more than that the bad example of the
forefathers has ruined mankind because it has been
universally imitated.   *Ruin* is said to have been
caused by ancestral wickedness, but not moral weak-
ness.

* B substantially omits this verse.      † Op. cit., p. 210.

### THE APOCALYPSE OF ABRAHAM

*Israel and the Gentiles.*—This writer's teaching as to the ultimate destiny of Israel is clearly expressed in chapter 29. Israel will, in the last times, execute God's judgment on the Gentiles. "Before the æon of the righteous begins to increase, My judgment comes upon the ruthless heathen through the people separated unto Me of thy seed. . . . Then there will be righteous men of thy seed left over in the number reserved through Me, hastening in the glory of My name to the place prepared for them beforehand, which thou sawest devastated in the picture, and they, living there, will be established by offerings and gifts of righteousness and truth in the æon of the righteous, and they will ever rejoice over Me."

The subject is recurred to in chapter 31. "I will have a trumpet sounded out of the air and will send to My chosen one, having in him all My power, a measure, and he shall call to him My scorned people from the nations." Then the righteous will "rejoice greatly over the downfall of the men who have forsaken Me and have gone following their gods, and following their murders." The sinners alluded to in this last sentence are apparently not Gentiles but Jewish apostates, for the divine speech proceeds: "They will be rotting in the body of the evil worm, Azazel, and burnt with the fire of Azazel's tongue, because I awaited that they might come to Me and not love and praise the stranger and cleave to him to whom they were not allotted, but the mighty Lord they have forsaken." Bonwetsch rightly sums up the teaching of our book thus: "The righteous out of Israel will become sharers of salvation." *

* Bonwetsch's Edition of this Apocalypse, p. 61.

As to the Gentiles, the teaching is that they are subject to the evil influences of Azazel. That is apparently not what is referred to in chapter 14, where Javel says to him : " Go, Azazel, into the unapproachable parts of the earth, for thy portion is over those whose being is with thee . . . with the men whose portion thou art, and through thy being they are." The last words seem to indicate that the author is here referring to the sons of the watchers. But, in chapter 13, Javel, addressing Azazel, says : " The strong Ruler . . . made thee an inhabitant of the earth, and through thee every spirit of lies and through thee wrath and disturbances (come) upon the races of godless men " (13). In chapter 23, where our author shows himself, as Tennant says, " somewhat concerned with the problem of evil and theodicy," * Abraham asks the question, " O Eternal, Mighty One, why hast thou granted him [Azazel] such power to ruin the human race in its [his ?] works on the earth ? " To this God replies : " Listen, Abraham : those that do evil, and so many as I hated among them that practise it, over them gave I him power to be loved by them." Abraham then asks : " Why hast Thou willed to cause that evil is desired in the hearts of men, since Thou art angry at that which has been willed by Thee, with him who acts frowardly with Thy decrees ? " To this question the divine answer is : " Angry with the nations for thy sake, and for the sake of the separated people of thy race after thee, as thou sawest them in the picture burdened thereby."

The doctrine of this work has thus some affinity with that in Jubilees. The nations become subject to the influences of the tempter as the result of their

* Op. cit., p. 193.

own evil doings. Here, however, their specific offence is ill-treatment of Israel, and the penalty is described as falling in arbitrary fashion not on all Gentiles, but on those among them whom God hates. The doctrine of this author as to the ultimate fate of the Gentiles is, however, apparently broader than that of Jubilees. We cannot use the earlier part of chapter 29 in this connection, because the unquestionable references to our Lord betray the hand of a Christian interpolator here. But in chapter 22 it is taught that not all the Gentiles are destined to be lost. "Those who are on the left side are the multitude of the races who have been and those after thee, who are prepared, some for judgment and order, and the others for vengeance and destruction at the end of the world. But those which are on the right side of the picture are the people separated to Me from the peoples with Azazel." In chapter 31 there is a prophecy of the destiny of those peoples who have treated Israel with obloquy to be burned with fire, together with their rulers. Again, in chapter 29 it is said that Israel, restored to the land, will ruin those who have ruined them and will treat with obloquy those who have so treated them." But this unquestionably Jewish passage contains also what looks like a prediction of the conversion of some of the heathen. "These, full of joy, will look to Me, rejoicing with My people and receiving those who in conversion to Me are converted."

*The Problem of Prosperity and Adversity.*—Punitive acts of God are referred to by this author, as we have had occasion to note in Chapter I. of this work. His belief in a future judgment of mankind is clear from what has just been said. But our author makes no contribution whatever to the problem of the sorrows of righteous men. That problem indeed seems to be

non-existent for him. Since he conceived of an ultimate restoration of righteous Israel, it would seem
that he thought of God's punishments as disciplinary
in their intention, though he does not say this.

The idea, found in Enoch 1–36 and the Testaments,
that evil spirits are a cause of trouble to mankind,
appears in this book. But, as in the Testaments, so
here, troubles from this source come only on the unrighteous. Disturbances, it is said, come through
Azazel on the races of godless men ; but God does not
permit that the bodies of righteous men should be in
the hands of Azazel (13).

*Moral Evil.*—Sin, according to this writer, had its
origin in the garden where Azazel tempted Eve (23).
Azazel was also the cause of Cain's transgression (24).
He " scattered upon the earth the secrets of heaven "
and " took counsel against the Strong One " (14).

According to chapter 13, Azazel has no power at
all to tempt the righteous. " Listen, tempter ; be
confounded by me," says Javel, " for it is not given
to thee in relation to all the righteous to tempt them ;
depart from this man, thou canst not lead him astray."
Thus the teaching is that Azazel only has power over
men when they have become sinful. But this is, of
course, quite inconsistent with chapter 23, where the
devil is represented as having power to tempt the
unfallen in Eden. It is also contradicted in chapter 14,
where Javel warns Abraham not to answer Azazel,
" lest in some way or other his will should pass over
to thee."

In chapter 26 there is a strong assertion of free-
will. In the previous chapter Israel's sin has been
foretold, and Abraham asks : " Why hast Thou
appointed that it should be so ? " To this God
replies : " Why did thy father Tharah not listen to

thy voice, and not forsake the demon of the gods until he was destroyed and his whole house with him ? " Abraham answers : "Certainly, because he did not choose to listen unto me ; but also I did not follow his works." And God's reply is : "As the decision of thy father is in himself, and as thy decision is in thyself, so is also the decision of My will in Me."

H. M. Hughes thinks that the reference in chapter 23 " is probably to the Yetzer Hara, so that moral evil is connected both with the Fall and with the evil impulse implanted in man at the beginning." * But against this it is to be observed that the evil impulse is not regarded as implanted in all men or from the beginning. It is only implanted in those sinners whom God hated.

## THE SIBYLLINE ORACLES, BOOK 4

*Israel and the Gentiles.*—This book is a missionary treatise addressed to the Gentiles, with the object of persuading them to become proselytes, by assuring them of God's willingness to receive them, and by appealing to their hopes and fears. The oracle is addressed to the "people of boastful Asia and of Europe " (1). Men may continue in disobedience and pay the penalty in the destruction of the whole race and in subsequent judgment (171–85), or they may accept the alternative to that fate, which is proselytism.

> " Wash your whole body in perennial streams,
>      And, lifting up your hands to Heaven, seek pardon
>      For former deeds : and expiate with praise
>      Bitter impiety, and God will give
>      Repentance : He will not destroy, and wrath
>      Will He again restrain, if in your hearts
>      Ye all will practise honoured piety " (165–70).

* Op. cit., pp. 211 f.

Israel is described as " the nation of the pious " (136.) But it is not of a predominant Israel that the Sibyl dreams ; she thinks of the bliss of the pious in which Gentiles may share.

*The Problem of Prosperity and Adversity.*—The Sibyl sees in convulsions of nature like the eruption of Etna or Vesuvius the results of " the anger of the God of Heaven " (130–6 ; cf. 80 f.). Nations are punished as entities, as when Antioch falls because of her own follies (140 f.). Besides this, the writer looks forward to a final judgment, when God will fashion again " the bones and ashes of men," and " will again raise up mortals as they were before " (181 f.). He shall " send the ungodly back to lower darkness ; but the pious shall still remain upon the fruitful land " (43–5).

### THE ASCENSION OF ISAIAH

The ill-doing of Manasseh is traced to its cause, when it is said that " Sammael abode in Manasseh and clung fast to him " (2¹). It was Beliar who made the king " strong in apostatising (Israel) " (2⁴). " Beliar dwelt in the heart of Manasseh and in the hearts of the princes of Judah and Benjamin and of the eunuchs and of the councillors of the king " (3¹¹, cf. 5¹).

### THE REST OF ESTHER

In these additions Israel's position as the chosen people of God is much dwelt upon, and Esther is made to celebrate the fact that Israel has been taken by God for " a perpetual inheritance " (14⁵). The object of the work was to illustrate the fact that it is God who punishes sinners and delivers Israel.

## SUMMARY

(1) *The Justice of God in His Attitude to Israel and the Gentiles.*—(A) A number of these writers prophesy confidently the future of Israel as God's elect people in this world. In Baruch $1^{15}$–$3^8$ they are all to be regenerate and dwell for ever in the land. In E and R of 4 Esdras and $A^2$ of Apoc. Baruch it will be an Israel purged of unworthy elements that will be saved when the kingdom is set up. In the Apocalypse of Abraham it is a righteous nation that is to be finally established. In Slavonic Enoch it is a faithful Israel that is to be glorified in the last time. The Sibyl also teaches that a pious nation will be at last blessed. Apparently that is the idea in Baruch $4^5$–$5^9$. $B^1$ of Apoc. Baruch makes Israel's future to be entirely conditional on obedience, insisting that it may be forfeited by unfaithfulness. None of these writers, therefore, speak of God as continuing to favour permanently an unworthy people. We cannot say the same of M in 4 Esdras, or $A^1$ $A^2$ in Apoc. Baruch, for these writers appear to teach that all Palestinian Jews will form part of the Messianic kingdom.

Some writers in this century cherished no hopes of a worldly future for Israel. They looked exclusively to the future in the unseen life. Such are the authors of S in 4 Esdras, $B^2$, $B^3$ in Apoc. Baruch, and the Assumption of Moses. The last of these teaches that all Israel will go penitent to heaven. The others insist that a blessed future for Israelites depends strictly on their conduct.

We have thirteen writers who speak of a life after death—the authors of Wisdom (Part 1), the Assumption of Moses, Apoc. Baruch ($A^1$, $A^2$, $B^1$, $B^2$, $B^3$), E and S of 4 Esdras, 4 Maccabees, Slavonic Enoch, the

Apocalypse of Abraham, and the Oracles. B[1] only prophesies Baruch's bliss in that life. The Assumption only speaks of the salvation of the whole penitent nation. All the others, except A[1], teach the ultimate bliss or woe of men according to conduct.

In one book only does despair of Israel's future find expression. S of Apoc. Baruch bewails the fact that God has for ever forsaken His people.

(B). Some writers neither say nor imply anything as to God's ultimate intentions as to the Gentile world. These are the authors of 3 and 4 Maccabees, Baruch 1[15]–3[8], 4[5]–5[9], and B[1], B[2], in Apoc, Baruch. Baruch 1[15]–3[8] contains only the hope that all the earth may know God. 3 Maccabees has only the statement that He governs all mankind in mercy. B[1] has but one allusion to the Gentiles, and this is a declaration that God intended blessing for them when He exiled Israel.

Some writers, prophesying the establishment of the kingdom of God on earth, limit the privileges of citizenship therein to Palestinian Jews. These are A[1] and A[2] in Apoc. Baruch and M. in 4 Esdras. They think only of the destruction of Israel's foes. In these three works, together with E and S of 4 Esdras, Baruch 3[9]–4[4], and the Assumption of Moses we have the narrowest conceptions of God. Similar ideas appear in B[2] of Apoc. Baruch and in the second part of Wisdom. Baruch 3[9]–4[4] teaches that God gives the knowledge of Wisdom to Israel alone. In the Assumption of Moses damnation is said to be the destiny of the Gentiles. The conception is at its meanest in S of 4 Esdras, but in none of these works is there any hope for non-Israelites.

On the other hand, we have writers of a different temper. The editor of 4 Esdras appears to have cherished the hope of a coming general conversion of men to God and the Vision of the Eagle in that work contains the prophecy of a coming world-wide reign of righteousness. We miss, however, in most of these writers such glowing anticipations of general conversions as we find in the Testaments and in Tobit. A³ in Apoc. Baruch only expects that some Gentiles will be spared. The Sibyl hopes, but not confidently, for a converted world. In the Apocalypse of Abraham the doctrine is simply that not all the Gentiles will be condemned at last, and the implied teaching of Slavonic Enoch is similar. There are passages in B² of Apoc. Baruch, and in both parts of Wisdom, in which we have evidence of the continued existence of the larger ideas of God in His attitude to the Gentiles ; but, unfortunately, B² and the second part of Wisdom contain passages also of a very different character.

In an article in the " Encyclopædia Biblica " Charles expresses the following view : " In most works written before the fall of Jerusalem only the hostile nations are destroyed (see e.g. Ap. Bar. $40^{1\,\text{f}}$, $72^{4-6}$) ; but in later works (see 4 Esdras 13) this fate is suffered by all Gentiles. In no case have they any hope of a future life. They descend for ever into Sheol or into Gehenna. If, anywhere, they are represented as having part in the resurrection, it is only that they may be committed to severer and never-ending torment (4 Esdras $7^{36-38}$)." *

Now there are seven of our authors who probably wrote after A.D. 70. These are the authors of B² B³ in Apoc. Baruch, A, S, R in 4 Esdras, the fourth Book of the Oracles, and the Apocalypse of Abraham. Of these seven, B³ is silent on the subject and S teaches the doctrine of utter hopelessness for the Gentile peoples. But this is certainly not the teach-

* E.B., art. " Eschatology," 1372.

ing of the Sibyl, the Apocalypse of Abraham, or the A and R sections of 4 Esdras. It *is* the clearly implied doctrine of a passage in B², but is contradicted in other statements of that work. We dissent, therefore, from the statement of Charles and conclude that the larger view of God lived on in some hearts and minds after the great catastrophe.

(2) *The Justice of God in the Allotment of Prosperity and Adversity.*—(A) Most of these authors recognise the operation, within the limits of the present order, of a punitive justice of God. The idea of delivering acts of God on behalf of the righteous is not much in evidence. The writer of chapter 10 in the Book of Wisdom gives a list of such acts for the encouragement of his readers. Reference to such acts is made in 3 and 4 Maccabees. Wisdom (Part 1) also speaks of the premature death of the righteous as God's deliverance. In the other books the idea is wanting. Nor is the conception of God as normally awarding prosperity to the good and sorrows to the evil in this world common in this century. It only appears in A³ of Apoc. Baruch and the Assumption of Moses. A in 4 Esdras sees a world in which only injustice is being done. In A³ and B¹ of Apoc. Baruch the writers are men who experience some perplexity as they consider the hard facts of human life. In Wisdom (Part 1) it is confessed that the experience of the righteous gives occasion for the taunts of scorners. But none of these writers find in the facts of life that which bewilders faith and makes its maintenance hard. Only in S of 4 Esdras and B² of Apoc. Baruch do we find evidence that the course of events gave rise to a baffling problem among some of the Jews of this period. These two stand alone amongst all our writers in this respect. Others feel in varying degree

the need for explanation, but no one—not even S in Apoc. Baruch, despite his utter pessimism—expresses such perplexity as these two.

(B) Only Wisdom (Part 1) and Baruch $1^{15}$–$3^8$ contain the doctrine that God punishes the children for the sins of the fathers. The idea that all men die for Adam's sin, found previously only in Ecclesiasticus, appears in this period in Apoc. Baruch ($B^2$), 4 Esdras (S) and Slavonic Enoch, while $A^3$ of Apoc. Baruch declares that Adam's sin caused untimely death, grief, and pain to all men. That a whole nation suffers for the sin of a part is a dogma which appears in Apoc. Baruch ($A^3$, $B^1$), and the Assumption of Moses. The doctrine of benefits to children, arising from the righteousness of parents, is not in evidence in this period. But $B^1$ declares that the works of the righteous are a help to their fellow citizens, though this is only while the good men remain in their midst. The martyr deaths of Israel's faithful sons are regarded in 4 Maccabees as a cause of benefit to all Israel. In Apoc. Baruch $B^2$ declares it to be just that Zion should obtain advantage from the righteousness of her saints; but he complains that God has not given Zion her due. S in 4 Esdras objects to the idea that men should suffer by the law of solidarity.

(C) Within this period there are writers who do not dwell at all on the idea of coming compensations. These are the authors of Wisdom (Part 2), 3 Maccabees, the Esther Additions, and the Ascension of Isaiah. Some, as we have seen in a preceding paragraph, think only of coming good for Israelites. These are $A^1$, $A^3$ in Apoc. Baruch, and M of 4 Esdras. Of these three, only $A^1$ contemplates in his scheme of the future any compensation for the dead, even of Israel.

But other writers take a wider view, and predicate joy or woe to mankind generally in the unseen world. Wisdom (Part 1), the Assumption of Moses, A², B², B³ in Apoc. Baruch, E and S of 4 Esdras, 4 Maccabees, Slavonic Enoch, the Apocalypse of Abraham, and the Oracles all teach a judgment of God in the unseen world, bringing bliss to the righteous and woe to the wicked. In some of these, indeed—the Assumption and E and S of 4 Esdras—all the Gentiles are to be damned. But the rest of the writers named above teach a judgment of God on individuals without limiting its operation to Israel. In the first part of Wisdom the idea of a final justice of God is marred by Ps.-Solomon's doctrine of the ultimate fate of the children of adulterers.

(D) The conception of sorrow as a divine discipline for character appears in both parts of Wisdom and in B¹, B² of Apoc. Baruch. These writers state the doctrine explicitly. It is, moreover, the implied teaching in Baruch 1¹⁵-3⁸ and 4⁵-5⁹, the Oracles (Book 4) and the Apocalypse of Abraham. In the first part of Wisdom it is the righteous, in the other writings it is the people of Israel who are the objects of this discipline. In the second part of Wisdom and B², there are passages in which it is affirmed that God treats Gentile men in a similar manner. Perhaps the idea of S in 4 Esdras is similar, when he teaches that Israel must pass to heaven by the way of sorrows. The conception is wholly absent in a considerable number of the writers of this century.

(E) The doctrine that demons or evil angels cause distress to men appears only in the Apocalypse of Abraham, where it is said that they disturb the races who are godless.

(F) B¹ in Apoc. Baruch is the only writer to make

the suggestion that God designs to bless others through a people's misfortunes.

(3) *The Justice of God in the Permission of Moral Evil.*—(A) It is only in the Salathiel Apocalypse that we have the doctrine of the evil inclination implanted in man from the beginning, though there is something very much like it in 4 Maccabees. The idea of an evil impulse in man appears in the Apocalypse of Abraham, but in that work the Yetzer Hara is no part of man's congenital endowment. A³ in Apoc. Baruch represents the body as a cause of sin. In the Slavonic Enoch sin seems to be thought of as almost inevitable to man by reason of his ignorance. S is the only writer in the whole range of the literature to regard the existence of the evil impulse as a cause of complaint against God.

(B) There is an interpolation in Slavonic Enoch in which the teaching is that man's conduct is determined for him by God. In the Apocalypse of Abraham it is declared that some men among those who have sinned are inclined by God to desire evil.

(C) The origin of sin in this world is traced to the action of an evil spirit in Slavonic Enoch, the Apocalypse of Abraham, and the first part of Wisdom. In the last-named, and in the Ascension of Isaiah, as well as apparently in 4 Maccabees, evil spirits are regarded as active in the life of man not only at the beginning. In the Apocalypse of Abraham the teaching is that men become liable to the attacks of evil spirits as a result of their own sin.

(D) The idea that men suffer deterioration of character arising from sin appears in the second part of Wisdom and in A³ of Apoc. Baruch, perhaps also in A¹ of that work.

(E) That mankind suffer permanent hereditary

consequences in enfeebled character from the sin of Adam is a notion almost non-existent in this literature. A² in Apoc. Baruch is unique in this matter. For, although he insists that each man is his own Adam, he nevertheless asserts that the primitive fall has caused a certain derangement of human nature by which man is morally weakened and imperilled.

## Conclusions

(1) *The Justice of God in His Attitude to Israel and the Gentiles.*—(A) In their commentary on the Epistle to the Romans Sanday and Headlam say : " Among the Rabbis the idea of election has lost all its higher side. It is looked on as a covenant by which God is bound, and over which He seems to have no control. God and Israel are bound in an indissoluble marriage." * S. Schechter also says : " This paternal relationship [i.e. of God to Israel], according to the great majority of Rabbis, is unconditional. . . . The only opponent of this view is R. Judah, who limits this relation to the time when Israel acts as children should act." † Now, in the literature with which we are here concerned, the worthier view of the relations of God and Israel is commonly taken. The relation was not looked upon by most of these writers as of an unconditional nature. There are, indeed, many among them who speak of the future of Israel as God's people in language which expresses the utmost confidence on the subject. They do not give the slightest indication of entertaining a question about it in their minds. Israel, to their thinking, was God's chosen people in perpetuity. Others speak in a far less confident tone. Though at times they utter the

* Page 249.        † J.Q.R., April 1894, p. 636.

most glowing prophecies, they nevertheless make it
clear that they feared that God might annul Israel's
privileges for continued disloyalty. Yet the great
majority of those who felt assurance in their hearts
as to the future of the people either declare their
conviction that in the coming time all Israel will be
regenerate or else insist that the Israel which will be
permanently privileged of God will be a nation
purged of its unworthy sons. The exceptions to this
are writers of two classes. In the first class are the
authors of Ecclesiasticus, 2 Maccabees, and 3 Esdras.
Each of these distinctly conceived of God as judging
His people for their sin. It certainly cannot be said
of them—not even of the writer of 2 Maccabees—
that they had lost sight of " the higher side of election." We cannot, however, say this of the second
class. These are Apoc. Baruch (A$^1$, A$^2$) and 4 Esdras
(M). It would be perilous to draw positive inferences
from their silence, but at least it must be said that
they give no indications of belief in any loftier conception of God than that involved in the notion that
in the last times He will favour all Palestinian Jews
as such.

Only one of these writers entirely despaired of the
future of Israel in this world and in the next—S of
Apoc. Baruch. But in the last of the three centuries
there were several who looked for no earthly kingdom
of God, and by these as well as by all the rest—includ-
ing some in each century who taught a future of
bliss or woe after death—the fate of Israelites was
regarded as conditional. Sanday and Headlam say
that the Rabbis held that no Israelite could go to
Gehenna.* But the writers of this literature did not
hold the ultimate salvation of all Israelites. In only

* Op. cit., p. 249.

two have we anything that looks like it: i.e. Enoch 83–90 and the Assumption of Moses. In the former, we apparently have merely unguarded language. In the latter, eternal bliss is affirmed of all Israelites who survive at the time of the consummation of all things ; but this is predicated of a penitent nation.

(B) In each of the three centuries there were writers who took broad views of the attitude of God to the Gentile races. Still, it is clear that the growing tendency with the passage of time was in the direction of a meaner view. In the earliest period all the writers save one were men who were far from regarding God as excluding the bulk of mankind from His favour in an arbitrary manner ; but, in the next century, there were three writers who cherished narrow ideas, and in the last period God, to a considerable number of the authors, was the God of Israel exclusively.

Moreover, in the earliest of the three centuries there were writers who maintained that originally light was given by God to all mankind, and even so narrow a patriot as he who wrote Jubilees attempted to vindicate God's rejection of the nations. No such idea occurs in any writer whose work appeared after the close of that century except in the case of the Enoch Similitudes and the Apocalypse of Abraham. On the contrary, according to such works as Baruch $3^9$–$4^4$, and (apparently) the Assumption of Moses, the cause of the unprivileged condition of the Gentiles is God's arbitrary will. He has chosen Israel alone for privilege. Further, most of the writers of the second century B.C. confidently anticipated a general conversion of the heathen peoples to God, and some of their successors in the next age cherished the same great hope. But this notion of a coming world-wide kingdom of God on this earth, embracing in its pale the converted Gentile nations, was non-existent for most of the men who wrote in the last period. The broader ideas persisted, indeed, to some extent even within the Judaism of this century; but the general tendency was strongly in the opposite direction.

Of the non-Palestinian writers, it is only in the third book of the Oracles and in Wisdom that we find clear expression of the worthiest views as to God's relations with mankind in general. On the other hand, 2 Maccabees and some passages in the second part of Wisdom witness to the existence of the meanest conceptions among the Jews of the Dispersion. The noblest doctrine comes from two Palestinians—Ben Sira and the author of the Testaments.

(2) *The Justice of God in the Allotment of Prosperity and Adversity.*—(A) The doctrine of a divine punitive justice, actively in operation in this world, is insisted upon by the great majority of the writers. But it is mainly in the earliest of the three centuries that God is conceived of as the Administrator of a justice which is almost, if not quite, perfect within the limits of time. The thought here is that God's rule is to treat men according to their merits, though it is not forgotten that there are facts which cannot be easily harmonised with the doctrine, and that there is consequent need of explanation. That was not, however, the thought of every writer in the period, for to the Enoch writers the world was rather the scene of flagrant injustices. It disappears altogether after the close of that century, save for $A^3$ of Apoc. Baruch and the Assumption of Moses. Yet it is only in $B^2$ of Apoc. Baruch and S of 4 Esdras that we have evidence of the fact that there were Jews to whom the stern facts of experience caused the greatest perplexity for faith.

None of the apocalyptic works, in the judgment of Ewing and Thompson, " bear evidence of being the production of men whose feelings have been stirred and strained by conflict in the struggle of life." * But, in the opinion of the present writer, this is too sweeping a generalisation. The statement cannot well be made of the authors of the earliest Enoch sections, nor of B² in Apoc. Baruch. Moreover, the writer of the Salathiel Apocalypse was a man whose feelings were stirred profoundly.

(B) The doctrine that sin involves in its penalties other men besides the actual transgressors was very commonly held by these writers throughout the whole period which is under our survey. As we have seen, it is stated in various ways. The idea that the sin of Adam involves the whole race in penalties appears in several works of the first century A.D., but prior to that time it is only to be found in Ecclesiaticus.

A frequently recurring idea is that God punishes the sons for the sins of their fathers, and sometimes it is taught that remote descendants suffer from transgressions of ancestors. Unless, however, Wisdom (Part I) and Baruch $1^{15}$–$3^8$ belong to the first century A.D., this idea finds no place in writings of a date posterior to the dawn of the Christian era. A considerable number of writers teach that the whole nation is implicated in the penal consequences of the sins of a part. In some one or more, therefore, of its various forms this is a persistent doctrine of our literature. It is absent from the books of Maccabees, save the second book, and in the Ethiopic Enoch there is only one allusion to it. But it is not peculiar to any one century or to the Palestinian writers. It

* " The Temple Bible Dictionary," p. xxx.

appears in the first part of Wisdom, Slavonic Enoch, and 2 Maccabees, none of which works were probably written in the homeland. S of 4 Esdras, who makes grave objection to it as involving a miscarriage of justice, represents Uriel as unable to offer explanation of it, able only to affirm that God is Judge, and He wills it. This is, indeed, the common view in this literature. It comes about by God's simple fiat that men suffer by reason of the sins of others. But S is singular in taking exception to it. The rest find in it no difficulty, and some affirm that God is just and holy when He acts upon this principle.

S. Schechter, in his "Studies in Judaism," speaking of the idea that a man's sin is punished in his descendants, says : " Prevalent as this view may have been in ancient times, the Rabbis never allowed it to pass without modification. . . . They speak very frequently of the 'merits of the fathers,' for which the remotest posterity is rewarded, for this could be explained on the ground of the boundless goodness of God, which cannot be limited to the short space of a life-time. But there was no possibility of overcoming the moral objection against punishment of people for sins which they have not committed." *   " They interpreted Josh. 7²⁴ᶠ· as meaning that Achan's sons and daughters were only compelled to be present at his execution. They explain passages where it is implied that children suffer for parents' sin as 'referring to cases in which children perpetuate the crimes of their fathers.' " †

This, then, is a matter in which the apocryphal and apocalyptic writers differ greatly from the Rabbis. While it is manifest from such passages as Jer. 31²⁹ᶠ· and Ezek. 18²⁰ that in O.T. times there was a dis-

* P. 265.                    † Ibid., p. 267.

position to make grave objection against the justice of penalties awarded to men on this principle, it is remarkable that in these centuries it was widely asserted as a fact, and that only one among all these writers demurs to its justice.

Scarcely less remarkable is the scanty allusion in this literature to the idea of solidarity in benefits arising from righteousness. The doctrine that God rewards the faithfulness of the saints by blessing their children appears only in three writers of the second century B.C. and in one of the following period. It finds no place in non-Palestinian works. The idea that the presence of good men in Zion stays execution of judgment on the guilty city appears in one writer, and there are two works in which the death of martyrs is regarded as of benefit to the whole people. We have also in the Testaments the doctrine that Israel is beneficially affected by the sufferings of Joseph.

(C) Many of the writers comforted themselves and their compatriots in face of the trials of Israel by confident anticipations of a glorious future which God would give their race in this world. His justice and goodness to Israel would receive splendid proof in the future. Authors of this type appeared in each of the three centuries. The mental horizon of some of them was wholly bounded by this world, and they were exclusively occupied with the destiny of Israel. These, however, are a small minority and mainly belong to the last of the three centuries. Unless the Book of Baruch as a whole belongs to an earlier time, they are all of this period.

There is, however, a considerable body of writers who look out beyond the confines of the present life. They differ widely in their eschatological conceptions ; but agree in this, that there is to be after death a

future in which God will give to all mankind the due reward of their deeds. Such writers appear in each century, and included among them are Palestinians and Hellenists. " The vindication of the individual and the development of belief in his resurrection," says G. A. Smith, " are among the most signal services of the Jewish Apocalypses to the cause of religion." *
" There was," says Fairweather, " a new consciousness that at the Great Assize the question at issue would not be the supremacy of Israel over the heathen, but the moral worth or worthlessness of individual men." † These pronouncements are just. In the Apocrypha the idea of a future in which bliss or woe will be given to man according to desert is wholly wanting in such works as Tobit and Ecclesiasticus. It does make some appearance, however, in the Apocrypha, for Wisdom (Part 1) and E and S of 4 Esdras clearly teach it, and 2 Maccabees contains the doctrine of a blessed future for righteous Israelites. But each of these except Wisdom (Part 1) is marred by intense nationalism. Only, therefore, in the first part of Wisdom have we among the apocryphal books the doctrine of God as rendering rewards to good and bad men in virtue simply of their desert. There are Apocalypses in which the conception of God as the ultimate Judge is marred in a similar manner. Still, the fact remains that in a considerable number of the Apocalypses the doctrine of a final judgment of God on all men determined by conduct alone appears distinctly. Fairweather observes that, when the idea of a resurrection appeared among these writers, it " was propelled in the direction of universalism, the thought of judgment being developed until it

* " Jerusalem," vol. ii., p. 537.
† Op. cit., p. 290.

took in all men without exception.'' * If he means, as he apparently does, that the apocalyptists first apprehended the idea of a judgment and resurrection of Israel, and that, subsequently, the thought was developed so that all men came to be included in the judgment programme, the statement is, in the judgment of the present writer, a mistaken one. For the conception of a universal resurrection to judgment is in evidence in the earliest of the apocalypses, and one writer belonging to the second century B.C. even rises to the great thought that some of the Gentile dead might be superior in God's judgment to some of the chosen nation itself.

(D) It seems quite clear that the conception of God as mercifully disciplining men by sorrows had no place in the thoughts of some of these writers. The idea that trials are meant to purge and ennoble men is notably absent—it is neither asserted nor implied —in the pages of some whose aim in writing was to comfort troubled saints. Their only thought is of coming compensations for the sorrows of good men.

In a number of works the doctrine seems to be implied in what is said of the effects of trouble on character and conduct, but only in a few is it explicitly asserted. Ordinarily the idea is that it is Israel or the saints who are the objects of this merciful divine discipline. Ben Sira stands alone in his explicit teaching that God acts in this manner toward all mankind; but the author of the third book of the Oracles also implies that Gentiles are so treated by Him, and in Wisdom (Part 2) it is said that God aims to correct the Egyptians by penalties.

(E) The attempt to explain sorrow as caused by

* Op. cit., p. 290.

evil angels or spirits, whether as punishment for sin
or not, which appears in several writers of the second
century B.C., is peculiar to them, except for one subsequent author. In the Apocalypse of Abraham, alone,
does the idea find a place after the close of that
century.

(F) Only in one work—Jubilees—does the idea
appear that the trials of men are permitted in order
to instruct spirits in the unseen world. The psalmist
is alone in his suggestion that God makes the suffering which He sends on men an atonement for their
sin. The idea that He brings blessing to other men
through the sorrow of Israel or a good man appears,
the former only in $B^1$ of Apoc. Baruch, the latter only
in the Testaments. In neither is there any attempt
to define the way in which the sorrow is productive of
good.

(3) *The Justice of God in the Permission of Moral
Evil.*—(A) The conception of God as absolutely determining human character and conduct appears in some
places, but such passages contradict the tenor of the
works in which they are found. The original writers
make it clear that they firmly held the moral freedom
of man.

(B) God is not often represented as having made
man with an evil inclination in him, or as having
exposed him to moral peril by his limitations or his
physical constitution. This idea is almost purely
Palestinian. It appears in two works of the earliest
period, and in two, perhaps three, of the last century.

(C) The doctrine that God permitted an evil spirit
or spirits to corrupt man at the beginning appears in
some works of each century and in the pages of two
Jews of the Dispersion. But most of our authors do
not refer to it. A few writers in each century teach

that He permits such spirits constantly to assail human virtue. These, however, are all Palestinians, unless the idea is implied in one passage of 4 Maccabees.

(D) Two writers teach that God punishes sin by handing men over to the seductions of evil spirits, and the idea that His penalty for transgression is deterioration of character appears in four, perhaps five, writers, all save one of whom are Palestinians.

(E) Only one author—a writer of the first century A.D.—teaches expressly that the race is morally weakened by the primitive fall.

# CHAPTER III

## THE GRACE OF GOD

IN this chapter it is intended to discuss the following questions : Do the writers regard God as one who is forgiving, and, if so, to what extent and upon what terms ? Do they conceive of Him as aiding man by His grace in his struggle to do what is right ? Do any of them rise to the idea of Him as being essentially love ; or, if not, do they at least teach that He loves the righteous or Israel ? These questions are partially answered of necessity in the previous chapters, but they will be dealt with in this section in a more systematic fashion and more specific statements on this matter will be considered. Some conception of what God is, is necessarily implied in the statements of the authors as to the character of the righteousness which He demands or approves. It will be convenient, accordingly, to discuss in this chapter the question : How far is God's love for man or interest in man of an ethical character ?

## THE SECOND CENTURY B.C.

### ECCLESIASTICUS

In a number of passages Ben Sira appears to teach the doctrine of the freely forgiving God. " The Lord is full of compassion, and He forgiveth sins " ($2^{11}$). " Unto them that repent He granteth a return "

264

($17^{24}$). " How great is the mercy of the Lord and
His forgiveness unto them that turn unto Him ! "
(Ibid. $^{29}$). " He has mercy on them that accept chastening " ($18^{14}$). " My son, hast thou sinned ? Add
no more thereto, and make supplication for thy
former sins " ($22^{1}$). In one passage his teaching
strikingly resembles that of our Lord : " He that
taketh vengeance shall find vengeance from the Lord,
and He will surely make firm his sins. Forgive thy
neighbour the hurt that he hath done thee, and then
thy sins shall be pardoned when thou prayest " ($28^{1 t.}$).
Edersheim regarded verse 2 with suspicion : " So far
as we know, there is not any ancient Jewish saying
strictly parallel to this verse. We therefore regard
it as a later Christian addition." * He admits, however, that there are Talmudic sayings of similar
import, and it must further be observed that this
teaching is contained in the Testaments, a work
which belongs to this century. The strongest reason,
however, for omitting the verse is that Ben Sira seems
elsewhere to be opposed to such sentiments. He
counts the man happy " that liveth and looketh upon
the fall of his enemies " ($25^{7}$). Of the father of a well-
trained son he says : " When he died he sorrowed not.
He left behind him an avenger against his enemies "
($30^{s t.}$). But the force of this is neutralised by the
fact that in $28^{1}$ and the following verses the teaching
is not really inconsistent with $25^{7}$ and $30^{s t.}$. For,
though some verses isolated from the context (e.g.
verses 1, 3, 4), seem to inculcate a universal forgivingness, the passage as a whole limits the duty to one's
neighbour. There is thus no sufficient reason for
questioning the originality of the passage, and the
clear teaching is that God requires, as a condition of

* Speaker's Comm., p. 144.

His own forgiveness, that a man should forgive his neighbour but not his foe.

In 16¹⁴ we have this : " He will make a place for all mercy. Every one shall receive according to his works." This may conceivably mean that God will show mercy yet each shall receive justice, or it may mean that God will take just account of man's acts of mercy. As Edersheim notes, ἐλεημοσύνη is rarely ascribed to God, yet it is ascribed to Him in 17⁸⁹. But the πάσῃ, he suggests, points to human acts of mercy.* The verse falls thus into line with the teaching in 28¹ᵃ.

Ben Sira insists on the fact that the forgiving God is not lax. " Concerning atonement, be not without fear to add sin upon sins, and say not, ' His compassion is great. He will be pacified for the multitude of my sins ' " (5⁵ᵇ).† " He was not pacified toward the giants of old time who revolted in their strength " (16⁷).‡ " In the O.T.," says Oesterley, " it is only sacrifices that atoned for sin, in the N.T. it is only Christ who can do this ; here (i.e. in Ecclus.) we have an intermediate conception." § That conception is that good works win God's forgiveness. " Water will quench a flaming fire, and almsgiving (Hebrew, righteousness) will make atonement for sins " (3³⁰). "To depart from unrighteousness is a propitiation " (35³). To the filial son Ben Sira says : " As fair weather upon ice, so shall thy sins also melt away " (3¹⁵). Sacrifices are regarded by him as a duty, but he

* Op. cit., p. 75.

† Hebrew : " Trust not to forgiveness to add iniquity to iniquity, nor say, ' His mercy is great. He will forgive the multitude of mine iniquities.' "

‡ Hebrew : " He forgave not the princes of old time."

§ " The Jewish Doctrine of Mediation," p. 34.

teaches that only those offered by the righteous are acceptable ($7^{31}$, $35^7$). " The Most High hath no pleasure in the offerings of the ungodly, neither is He pacified for sins by the multitude of sacrifices " ($34^{19}$).

In the endeavour after righteousness, man is assisted by God. " Strive for the truth unto death, and the Lord God shall fight for thee " ($4^{28}$). Ben Sira prays that God will take away from him pride and concupiscence ($23^{4L}$). This is insisted upon by him again in $15^{15}$, if the Hebrew be correct : " If thou trust in Him thou shalt even live," for the allusion is to man's choice of good or ill.

In $12^6$ Ben Sira says : " The Most High hateth sinners." Similar to this are two other passages. One is $27^{24}$, where, speaking of a false friend, Ben Sira says, " The Lord will hate him." The other is $16^8$ : " He spared not those with whom Lot sojourned, whom He abhorred for their pride." In this last the Hebrew has, " Who transgressed in their pride " ; but in $31^{18}$ the Hebrew has, " God hates the man of an evil eye." This the Greek and the Syriac omit. There are not wanting, however, passages in which God is spoken of as loving and lovable. " With all thy strength, love Him that made thee " ($7^{30}$). " They that love Him will keep His ways " ($2^{15}$). " Them that love her [Wisdom] the Lord doth love " ($4^{14}$). In one of his noblest passages—a passage worthy to be included in the sacred canon—Ben Sira celebrates the experience of the generations of mankind who have proved that God is faithful, full of compassion, and merciful ($2^{10L}$). He is, indeed, as gracious as He is powerful. " As His majesty is, so also is His mercy " ($2^{18}$). And, as we have seen in Chapter II., that mercy is universal in its sweep. Edersheim observes how this writer traces " the quality of *justice* in God's dealings, not only with individuals, but with nations, and especially in God's ways with Israel. . . . By the side of this quality—as its complement, and, in a sense, its other aspect—Ben Sira places that of ' Mercy.' " * " But there is not any mention of the free outgoing of divine *love*. The latter is only evoked in return for our love of wisdom." † This is most true. Ben Sira conceives that God has mercy upon man, that He will not see men wronged with impunity (e.g. 34$^{30}$, 35$^{13-17}$), that the righteous should love Him, and that good qualities in man win His love. He addresses God as " Father and Master of my life " (23$^1$ ; cf. verse 4). He declares that the benevolent man shall be as a son of the Most High, "whom God will love more than his mother doth " (4$^{10}$). But he does not rise to the thought of God as being essentially love.

Edersheim declares that throughout this work " moral questions are placed on a low level and viewed in a wrong light. Ben Sira seems to be always arguing that, after all, religion is that which profits best." ‡ H. M. Hughes also says that in this book moral evil " is viewed more from the human than the divine standpoint, and is condemned as folly." § " It is folly viewed from the standpoint of a prudential externalism and with regard to the issues and interests of the present life." ‖ It cannot be questioned that Ben Sira merits these adverse pronouncements on his ethical teaching. Yet it is but fair to him to observe that there are passages in his work in which conduct is viewed from a loftier standpoint and appeal is made to higher motives and sanctions. His conception of

* Speaker's Comm., p. 15.　§ Op. cit., p. 168.
† Ibid., note 2.　‖ Ibid., p. 188.
‡ Ibid., p. 17.

the righteousness which is acceptable to God includes
" faith and meekness " as well as humility ($1^{27}$, $3^{18}$,
$10^{18}$). What angers God, according to him, is the lack
of filial piety. What pleases Him is benevolence
toward man ($3^{16}$, $4^{10}$). Nor is his appeal made exclusively to prudential considerations. Faith and
meekness are said to be God's " good pleasure " ($1^{27}$),
and his readers are urged to benevolence by the consideration that God will love men who practise it.
His work contains much ethical teaching that makes
painful reading. Still, his doctrine of God is that He
cares for righteousness in man, and that, most of all,
He approves in His creature filial piety, benevolence,
faith, meekness, and humility.

## ADDITIONS TO ECCLESIASTICUS

In $17^{21-23}$ we have the following lines in the MSS.
248, 70, and 106 : " The Lord, being gracious and
knowing His creature, neither left them nor forsook,
sparing them . . . dividing to His sons and daughters
repentance." On the last line Hart's comment is :
" Repentance is the gift of God." *  But this is doubtful. Possibly the idea is simply that He gives opportunity of repentance. Still, that the writer or writers
taught God's gracious willingness to help man is
evident from $1^{13}$ and $13^{13}$, cited below. And in $24^{24}$
we have this doctrine very clearly expressed : " Faint
not to be strong in the Lord ; but cleave to Him,
that He may strengthen you " (MSS. 248, 70).

But the doctrine which the author or authors of
the additions most desired to emphasise, and for the
sake of which he or they apparently altered some
passages, is the lovableness of God. Thus, $1^{10}$ : " The

* Op. cit., p. 305.

love of the Lord is glorious wisdom " (70, 253, Syro-
Hexaplar under asterisk, L after 13)*; 1¹²: " The fear
of the Lord is a gift from the Lord, for upon love's
paths it setteth him " (70, 253, Syro-Hexaplar under
asterisk); 13¹³: " In all thy life love the Lord, and
call upon Him for thy salvation " (106, 248, 253, Syro-
Hexaplar under asterisk) ; 10¹⁹: " Seed of safety are
they who fear the Lord, and honoured plant they who
love Him " (70, 248) ; 19¹⁸: " Wisdom winneth love
from Him " (Ibid.); 25¹²: " The fear of the Lord is
the beginning of His love " (70, 248, L). Edersheim
rejects this last verse as a Christian insertion ; but
the same doctrine appears in 1¹². As Hart says :
" Faith and fear belong to the elementary stage of
religion ; by these stepping-stones the pupil of the
Pharisees may advance to Love of God and Union
with God." † Still, here, as in Ben Sira, it is righteousness in man that wins God's love. Nothing is
said of a love of God for man which exists and per-
sists despite his sin.

### TOBIT

Tobit prays that God will not take vengeance on
him for his sins (3⁴). He admonishes sinners to turn
to the Lord with their whole heart and soul, to do
truth before Him. Then He will turn to them and
will not hide His face from them (13⁶). Chapter 14,
in its doctrine of the end, clearly implies God's forgiving mercy for mankind. Yet, notwithstanding
the evangelical teaching of 13⁶, this author, like Ben
Sira, teaches that the divine forgiveness may be won
by meritorious acts. " Alms doth deliver from death,
and it shall purge away sin " (12⁹; cf. 4¹⁰).

* L has : " Dilectio Dei honorabilis sapientia."
† Op. cit., p. 316.

The author celebrates God's mercy and describes Him as Israel's Father for ever (6[17], 8[16], 13[4]). He teaches that a right attitude to Him on the part of the exiles will win His love, and he speaks of men "that love the Lord God in truth and righteousness" (13[10], 14[7]).

Faithfulness to Judaism—worship in Jerusalem, payment of tithes, separateness from the Gentiles— is regarded as of high importance and pleasing to God. Tobit recounts all his own fidelity in this matter and adds : "I kept myself from eating [i.e. the bread of the Gentiles] because I remembered God with all my soul. And the Most High gave me grace and favour in the sight of Enemessar " (1[11-13]). But there are also ethical elements in the conception. Wages must be paid promptly, and God will recompense the man who thus serves Himself (4[14]). "Turn not thy face from any poor man," says Tobit, "and the face of God shall not be turned away from thee " (4[7]). "Alms is a good gift in the sight of the Most High for all that give it " (Ibid. [11]). In one place the ethical conception is low, for Raphael is a liar, though he is one of the most privileged of the angels (5[12], 12[14]). Apart from this, the doctrine of our author is admirable. The God whom he pictures for us is One who above all else approves in man justice and kindness to his fellows.

## ETHIOPIC ENOCH 1–16

At 5[6] the Gizeh Greek fragment gives us the following passage : "And all the ἁμαρτοι shall rejoice and there shall be (to them) remission of sins and all mercy and peace and gentleness; there shall be to them salvation (and) good light and they shall inherit

the earth, and to all you the sinners there shall be no
salvation, but a curse shall lodge upon you all."
'Ἄμαρτοι can hardly be corrupt for ἀμαρτωλοί, for in
that case the first and second members of the sentence
would contradict each other. It is probable, as Charles
suggests, that the word we need is ἀναμάρτητοι, and
that the sentence affirms God's pardoning grace
toward those who in the main are righteous.

In the Ethiopic version there is no express mention of the idea of God as forgiving. The teaching
of the writer is that ultimate blessedness is for the
righteous and that torture awaits the wicked (1[8], 10[14],
10[17]). Yet something better than strict justice awaits
the righteous. "In the days of judgment over the
former [the sinners], they [the righteous] will bless
Him for the mercy in accordance with which He has
assigned (their lot)" (27[4]). Moreover, the implication of 10[21], where our author prophesies the conversion of the Gentiles, is that He forgives their sins.
Again, while God is described as implacable toward
the offending angels under Azazel (10[10], 12[4-6], 13[1 f.],
14[5 ff.]), He nevertheless says to them : "You should
intercede for men, and not men for you"; and this
clearly implies that God forgives sinful men (15[2]).

The writer anticipates a future when "wisdom"
will be bestowed on the elect and they will all live and
never again sin either through heedlessness or through
pride" (5[8]). But he nowhere suggests that such
grace is now given to any man.

The idea of God's love is absent from the whole work.

Hughes thinks we may infer that this apocalyptist
"defined righteousness in terms of the law" from
the "fact that those are condemned who have not
fulfilled 'the law of the Lord.'"* But the absence

* Op. cit., p. 39.

of any insistence on ritual requirements is notable.
Sexual impurity is said to be condemned by God
(10⁹, ¹⁵). It is not suggested that He cares for benevolence in man, but He is said to condemn oppression
(10¹⁶, 13²). The sin which is chiefly censured is the
utterance of unseemly words against God (5⁴, 27²).
God is not described as hostile to human advancement
in knowledge, though the information imparted by the
watchers is said to have been a cause of sin (16³).

### ETHIOPIC ENOCH 83–90

God is represented in a very unlovable light by this
writer, when he describes Him as rejoicing over a
sinful Israel " devoured and swallowed and robbed "
(89⁵⁸). The idea of His loving or being loved does
not once appear in these chapters. Nevertheless,
there is decidedly an approximation to this idea
when the author declares that God will " rejoice with
great joy " in the coming days when men will become
good and return to His house (90³³). That clearly
implies that He is forgiving, that He has gracious
interest in man.

There is little indication of the writer's conception
of that goodness which pleases God. The teaching
is that He is hostile to Israel's oppressors (89¹⁹ ⁱ,
90¹⁸), and perhaps we may infer, from Enoch's obtaining his visions as a celibate, that the writer regarded
asceticism as pleasing to God (83²).

### JUBILEES

This writer represents God as implacable toward
offenders. " I have commanded thee to say to the
children of Israel that they should not commit sin,
nor transgress the ordinances, nor break the covenant

18

which has been ordained for them, (but) that they should fulfil it and be recorded as friends. But, if they transgress and work uncleanness in every way, they will be recorded on the heavenly tables as adversaries, and they will be destroyed out of the book of life " (30[21f]). Should Israelites omit the rite of circumcision " there will be no more pardon or forgiveness unto them for all the sin of this eternal error " (15[34]). There is also " a sin unto death " (21[22], 26[34], 33[18]), and Hughes thinks that the author " probably does not refer to any particular sin, but to that habit of sin which makes for moral death." * This, however, is certainly not the case in 33[18], for the sin unto death in that passage is a specific act of immorality. Concerning it the order is given : " Do thou, Moses, command the children of Israel that they observe this word ; for it (entails) a punishment of death . . . and there is no atonement for ever to atone for the man who has committed this ; but he is to be put to death and slain, and stoned with stones, and rooted out from the midst of the people of our God " (Ibid.[10, 13]). The passage cited above about circumcision—15[34]—illustrates his notion of a sin unto death. The same idea appears when he lays it down that a man who does any work on the Sabbath " shall surely die eternally " (2[27]), when he threatens death if one should even say that he will work on that day (50[8]), and again when he declares that the sin of a fornicator will be " recorded against him in the eternal books continually before the Lord " (50[8]). As in Numbers 18[22], so in the pages of this author, the sin unto death is disobedience to a specific command of God.

Nevertheless, he teaches that God's righteousness is shown not only in the stern punishment of ill-doers

* Op. cit., p. 157.

but also in His mercy. He "is righteous and exe-
cuteth judgment on all those who transgress His
commandments" (21⁴). But also God says to Moses:
"Incline thine ear to every word which I shall speak
to thee on this mount, and write them in a book in
order that their generations may see how I have not
forsaken them, for all the evil which they have wrought
in transgressing the covenant which I establish between
Me and thee for their generations this day on Mount
Sinai. And thus it will come to pass, when all these
things come upon them, that they will recognise that
I am more righteous than they in all their judgments
and in all their actions" (1⁵ᵗ·).

Of Reuben our author teaches that he was forgiven for his ignorance (33¹⁵ᵗ·), and of Judah he says
that, by reason of earnest supplication and lamentation and ignorance, and because he turned from his
sin and did it not again, he was forgiven (41²⁴ᵗ·).
Abraham, he says, breathed for Jacob the aspiration:
"That thou mayest be forgiven all (thy) transgressions (and) thy sins of ignorance" (22¹⁴). The words
in brackets are supplied from the Latin version, and
are not in the Ethiopic. If, then, the Ethiopic is
correct, the writer is here perhaps only contemplating
sins of ignorance. In fact, none of these passages
prove that the writer believed in the possibility of
forgiveness for wilful sin. There is, however, an important passage concerning the Day of Atonement:
"Of the children of Israel it has been written and
ordained: If they turn to Him in righteousness, He
will forgive all their transgressions and pardon all
their sins. It is written and ordained that He will
show mercy to all who turn from their guilt once each
year" (5¹⁷ᵗ·). It will be observed that the ceremonial of the great Day is not regarded by our author

as of the nature of an *opus operatum*. The mercy of God is obtained on truly ethical conditions; but clearly he here widens the scope of God's forgiving grace. All sorts of sins may be forgiven to the penitent. Yet this sweeping statement is obviously limited by those cited above in which it is clearly laid down that some sins of the nation or the individual are unpardonable. Dr. Charles expresses the opinion that this passage is possibly an interpolation, though it may be only misplaced.* But, even if it be an interpolation, we have a somewhat similar passage in $34^{19}$, where it is said that the Day of Atonement " has been ordained that they should grieve thereon for their sins and for all their errors, so that they might cleanse themselves on that day once a year." The daily sacrifice, also, has for its purpose, says this author, " that they may atone for Israel with sacrifice continually from day to day, for a memorial well pleasing before the Lord, and that He may receive them always from day to day, according as thou hast been commanded " $(50^{11})$.

In another passage the angel gives commandment concerning the ordinance that Israel shall eat no blood as follows : " They shall observe it throughout their generations, so that they may continue supplicating on your behalf with blood before the altar ; every day, and at the time of morning and evening, they shall seek forgiveness on your behalf perpetually before the Lord, that they may keep it and not be rooted out " $(6^{14})$. In this latter clause the reading given—" forgiveness on your behalf "—is that of *d*. B*c* have " their " and *a* has " its "; but, as Charles points out, the reading of *d* is best because of the parallelism between the two clauses.

* Edition of Jubilees, p. 45.

It must be added that the nation is charged to clear itself from complicity with evil deeds by burning offenders in certain cases. Then God " will turn away wrath and punishment from Israel " ($41^{26}$).

To sum up, it is the author's teaching that God will never forgive some sins, that ignorance is a ground of mercy with Him, and that even wilful sin may be forgiven. Israel's status as the favoured people of God is maintained by the offering of the daily and the annual oblations. But the whole drift of the teaching as to the position of Israel makes it clear that, like Ben Sira, our author saw that acceptable sacrifice could only be offered by righteous men. He differs from Ben Sira in that he does not dream that righteous deeds can propitiate God. Often this writer expresses his belief in the operation of that grace which changes the hearts of men. He tells how God " made for all His works a new and righteous nature, so that they should not sin in their whole nature for ever " ($5^{12}$). And this occurred after the Flood! But the author could not have given utterance to such an idea in view of the facts which he chronicles. The Ethiopic translator has doubtless given us, as Charles suggests, a misrendering of the writer's Hebrew tenses and we should read the sentence as a prophecy.* Then it agrees with $1^{23}$ : " I shall create in them a holy spirit and I shall cleanse them so that they shall not turn away from Me from that day unto eternity." But this Jew believed in the possibility of obtaining such grace before the coming of the kingdom. Noah's prayer is : " Let Thy grace be lift up upon my sons, and let not wicked spirits rule over them " ($10^{3}$). Abraham says : " Deliver me from the hands of evil spirits who have sway over the thoughts of men, and

* Edition of Jubilees in loc.

let them not lead me astray from Thee, my God. And 'stablish Thou me and my seed for ever, that we may not go astray from henceforth and for evermore " ($12^{20}$). Again, we have such prayers as these : " My God and thy God strengthen thee to do His will " ($21^{25}$), and : " The God of all bless thee and strengthen thee to do righteousness and His will before Him " ($22^{10}$). The writer appears to have been deeply imbued with the spiritual teaching of such O.T. prophets as Jeremiah and Ezekiel, and evidently held a noble doctrine as to what God can and will do to save men from sin in answer to prayer. He also saw that God's purposes of grace are frustrated by man's wilfulness. Thus Moses is represented as praying : " Create in them a clean heart and a holy spirit, and let them not be ensnared in their sins from henceforth until eternity " ($1^{21}$), and the answer of God to that prayer is : " They will not be obedient till they confess their own sin and the sin of their fathers " ($1^{22}$). He will be able to confer on Israel the indefectible grace described in $1^{23}$ when they turn unto Him " with all their heart and with all their soul."

God is regarded as the loving Father of all righteous Israelites : " I shall be their Father, and they will be My children, and they will all be called children of the living God, and every angel and every spirit will know, yea, they will know that these are My children and that I am their Father in uprightness and righteousness, and that I love them " ($1^{24f.}$). " All will know that I am the God of Israel and the Father of all the children of Jacob " ($1^{28}$). " Israelites," says Charles, " are God's children according to our author by virtue of their physical descent from Jacob." *

* Edition of Jubilees, p. 7.

But, despite all the narrow and fierce particularism of this writer, the passage would be utterly contrary to his whole teaching if it meant this. As a matter of fact, God is said here to take up this attitude to an Israel all whose people are regenerate at a time when He has cleansed them and given them His Holy Spirit. Charles's view may appear more capable of justification from 22[11] : " Blessed be my son Jacob and all the sons of God Most High." But, even in this verse, it is not said or implied that all Israelites are sons of God, and Charles thinks the passage ought perhaps to read : " his sons unto the God Most High." *

Account must be taken of other passages in which God is spoken of as lovable. " I implore you, my sons, love the God of heaven " (20[7]). Abraham " was a lover of the Lord " (17[18]).

God is interested in the characters of men. " Work uprightness and righteousness before Him, that He may have pleasure in you and grant you His mercy " (20[9]). That God is gravely concerned for right conduct in Israel and intolerant of their sins is indeed a truth on which this writer repeatedly dwells. Only those who are loyal to the legal cultus are righteous in God's eyes. Repeatedly and solemnly the author recurs to this point, and its grave importance in his eyes is shown by the large amount of space which he devotes to it. The breach of the ritual law awakens the divine displeasure, and it is against this offence that our author fulminates his most awful threats. It is of the utmost importance that Israel, in conformity with divine orders, should keep a year of 364 days and so duly observe the festivals of the faith (ch. 6). Abraham's righteousness is seen in his due observance of the Feast of Tabernacles, and that makes Israel

* Edition of Jubilees, in loc.

blessed for ever (16²⁸). But Israelites who work uncleanness, i.e. intermarry with Gentiles (30¹⁴ᶠ·), " will
be destroyed out of the book of life " ; and if an
Israelite should omit the rite of circumcision it means
for him utter ruin (30²², 15³⁴). It is, however, only
fair to bear in mind the fact that these pronouncements, in which the writer attaches an exaggerated
importance to a merely ritual righteousness and
clearly implies that God cares profoundly for this,
had their cause in that widespread apostasy from
Israel's religion to which this book bears eloquent
testimony. Nor are there wanting passages in which
this writer teaches the necessity of righteousness in
the only true sense of the word. His ethical ideal is
expressed in the words which he puts on the lips of
Abraham when that patriarch commands his sons that
they should " observe the way of the Lord ; to work
righteousness and love each his neighbour and act on
this manner amongst all men ; that they should each
so walk with regard to them as to do judgment and
righteousness on the earth " (20³ᶠ·). Isaac, in like
manner, urges his sons to love one another, to act
together and to seek each other's good, for the wrong-
doer will fall into the hand of the wronged and be
rooted out (36⁴· ⁹). Noah exhorts his sons to filial
piety, to love of neighbours and to moral purity, for
disregard of these duties led to the Flood (7²⁰ᶠ·). In
one passage this writer appears to teach the iniquity
of cruelty to the beasts. He speaks of those who
" sinned against the beasts and birds and all that
moves and walks on the earth," and he adds that
" much blood was shed on the earth " (7²⁴). The
book's omissions, manifestly not made for the sake
of brevity, give us some idea of the author's ethical
ideas. He omits the lies of Abraham and Isaac, and

Jacob is not so bad a liar in his narrative as he is in that of the O.T. (26¹³, ¹⁹). Doubtless the author desired to omit whatever might reflect on the character of the patriarchs, but it is made clear by the omission that he considered truth-speaking an element in righteousness. He appears to be gravely concerned to vindicate the righteousness of the Hebrew conquest of Palestine. He invents or borrows a legend to the effect that the Canaanites were punished for the violation of an ancestral covenant. The seriousness of this matter in his eyes is shown by the great amount of space which he allots to it (8⁹–9 ᵃᵈ ᶠⁱⁿᵉᵐ). It is not clear whether he seeks to vindicate the character of God or that of his ancestors. But, on either hypothesis, the passage witnesses to his conception of righteousness as involving that nation should not wantonly attack nation. Yet the teaching about the conduct in man which pleases God is seriously marred by his own racial antipathies. He is far from supposing that God disapproves of these. Isaac is represented as praying that God will make his Philistine foes " a derision and a curse, and an object of wrath " (24²⁸). While in the O.T. the perpetrators of the deed of revenge on the sons of Shechem are condemned, our author declares that they were recorded in heaven as having done a righteous deed, and a writing was recorded in their favour on account of it (30¹⁷, ²³). They did but execute the divine decree. " The Lord delivered them into the hands of the sons of Jacob that they might exterminate them " (30⁶).

H. M. Hughes says that at times this author " realises that the noblest morality is a matter of the heart and of the soul, involving holiness of spirit and inward cleansing." In proof of this he cites the writer's great prophecy in 1¹⁵⁻²⁵. He also cites 20⁴, 1¹¹, 2²⁹,

39⁶, and 7³⁴ as "evidences of a more inward view of moral evil." * Now, 20⁴ is a charge against overt acts of impurity, "after the eyes and the heart"; 1¹¹ is a prophecy that Israel will sacrifice to "demons and to all the works of the error of their hearts"; 2³⁹ is an injunction against forsaking the Sabbath "in the error of their hearts"; 39⁶ describes Joseph, victorious in temptation, as not surrendering his soul; while in 7³⁴ we have this: "Every imagination and desire of men imagined vanity and evil continually." Undoubtedly, in these passages evil is traced to its root in the heart; but examination of them discloses nothing to make us think that the writer is condemning the inward wrong desire in itself, apart from an act. And while one would certainly not grudge meaning to the splendid prophecy of the coming regeneration of Israel in 1¹⁵⁻²⁵, the language, taken by itself, is too general to warrant the conclusion that this writer held the doctrine that God requires in man an interior self which is altogether pure. There is no approach to such lofty morality as that which is taught by our Lord in His revision of the Sixth Commandment (St. Matt. 5²⁸). Apart from the exhortations to love mentioned above, the one passage in which a quality of soul is commended is that which speaks of Abraham's patience of spirit (19⁴).

## THE TESTAMENTS OF THE TWELVE PATRIARCHS

According to this writer, the great condition upon fulfilment of which God is willing to forgive is repentance. "If He taketh away [from a man] wealth gotten by evil means, He forgiveth him if he repent; but the unrepentant is reserved for eternal punish-

* Op. cit., pp. 47 and 157.

ment " (T. Gad 7⁵). " Do you give these commands
to your children, that, if they sin, they may the more
quickly return to the Lord. For He is merciful and
will deliver them " (T. Iss. 6³). " When ye return to
the Lord, ye shall obtain mercy " (T. Dan 5⁹). Repentance, however, in the view of our author, includes
long penance. Thus Reuben, Simeon, and Judah
mourned and practised abstinence for years on account
of their transgressions (T. Reub. 1⁹, T. Sim. 3⁴, T.
Jud. 15⁴).

God's pardon is granted to men who manifest a
compassionate spirit (T. Zeb. 5³, 8⁸). He takes ignorance into account also as a ground of mercy (T.
Jud. 19⁹), but nothing is said here which suggests that
wilful sin is not pardoned to the penitent. God's
forgiveness is obtained sometimes through human
intercessors (T. Reub. 1⁷, T. Benj. 3⁶), and there are
archangels who " make propitiation to the Lord for
all the sins of ignorance of the righteous " (T. Levi 3⁵).
In two passages, cited in chapter 2 of the present
work—T. Asher 7⁷, T. Levi 15⁴—the idea of forgiveness
for Israel in part at least through ancestral merits
occurs. But this is no doctrine of the original author.
It is from the pen of a writer of the first century B.C.
A notable passage in T. Zebulun 9⁷ belongs to the
same period : " After these things, ye shall remember
the Lord and repent, and He shall have mercy on
you ; for He is merciful and compassionate, and He
setteth not down in account evil against the sons of
men, because they are flesh and are deceived through
their own wicked deeds."

Israel's regeneration is prophesied as it is in Jubilees.
" It shall be in the time of the lawlessness of Israel
that the Lord will (not) depart from them, but will
turn them into a nation that doeth His will " (T.

Dan 6⁹). But, like the author of Jubilees again, this writer teaches the possibility of such grace before that time has come. " I besought the Lord . . . that I might hold aloof from all pollution and envy, and from all folly " (T. Sim. 2¹³). " I struggled against a shameless woman, urging me to transgress with her ; but the God of Israel my father delivered me from the burning flame " (T. Jos. 2²).

That God is to be loved is taught by this writer (T. Gad 5², etc.) ; but, like Ben Sira, this Jew has no idea of a love of God for sinners. His love is for the righteous only. " If ye work that which is good . . . the Lord shall love you " (T. Naph. 8⁴). " I went not astray, but persevered in the truth of the Lord. These my brethren hated me, but the Lord loved me " (T. Jos. 1⁴). " Every one who doeth the law of the Lord shall be loved by Him " (Ibid. 11¹). But of a persistent wrong-doer it is said : " The Lord shall hate him " (T. Naph. 8⁶).

This author had a lofty idea of the righteousness which God approves. Fasting and sacrifices are alluded to (e.g. T. Levi 9⁷, ¹¹⁻¹⁴, etc.), but it is not upon these things that he puts emphasis. It is truth and just dealing that please God (T. Dan 1³). He is provoked by one who defrauds his neighbour even though he who does that is a man who pities the poor (Ibid. 2⁶). Fasting is an idle thing, if one be at the same time an evil liver and an oppressor of the poor (T. Asher 2⁸). God " delighteth in the unity of brethren and in the purpose of a heart that takes pleasure in love " (Ibid. 17³). Love to God and man is of supreme importance (T. Dan 5³, T. Iss. 5², 7⁶). A forgiving spirit is pleasing to God, and, even if an offender be still impenitent, one ought to dismiss all resentful feeling (T. Gad 6⁴). God redeems the man

from evil who puts away the desire of retaliation and
seeks to bless the offender (T. Jos. 18²). He blesses
those who are compassionate to men and to beasts
(T. Zeb. 5¹ ⁿ·).

In the midst of this insistence on the gentler virtues
it is singular to find a passage in which one reads that
the vengeance on the men of Shechem was a righteous
act for which Levi and Simeon had the command of
God (T. Levi 5³ ᶠ·). There is, however, some confusion
in the narrative, as the text now stands in all the
manuscripts, for it is said, in contradiction to 5³ ᶠ·,
that in this act the brothers sinned, since they contra-
vened the will of their father (Ibid. 6⁷). It is to be
observed also that in T. Asher 4² ᶠ· we have the statement that it may be a duty to kill and hate the wicked.

Apart from these passages, the thought of the
writer is noble. God is One who delights in right
conduct in men, approving chiefly kindly and just
human relationships. He also requires right dis-
positions : " The poor man, if free from envy, pleases
the Lord " (T. Gad 7⁶). The righteous, " fearing
lest he should offend the Lord, will not do wrong to
any man even in thought " (T. Gad 5⁵). They find
favour before God, who " make their hearts good
before Him " (T. Sim. 5²).

## THE SIBYLLINE ORACLES, BOOK 3⁴⁷⁻⁸²⁹

It as been shown in Chapter II that the Sibyl
taught the doctrine of the forgiving God. We have
only to note here the conditions on which God's pardon
is bestowed according to these Oracles. He is to be
propitiated by " hecatombs of bulls and firstling
lambs and goats as times revolve . . . if haply He

show mercy" (625–8). But this is not all. There are ethical conditions :

> " Honour justice and oppress no man,
> For these things the Immortal doth enjoin
> On miserable men. But do thou heed
> The cause of the wrath of the Mighty God " (630–2).

God is called " All-Father " (550), as we have previously observed ; but the writer only predicates love of God for Israel (710 f.).

The Sibyl anticipates a coming age when all mankind will Judaise.

> " There shall again be a holy race
> Of godly men, who, keeping to the counsels
> And mind of the Most High, shall honour much
> The great God's temple with drink-offerings,
> Burnt offerings, and holy hecatombs " (573 ff.).

Then the temple will be weighed down again with goodly wealth, and frankincense and gifts shall be brought into the house of God out of every land (657 ff., 772 f.). " All must sacrifice to the great King " (808). But the righteousness for which God cares, and on which He insists, includes also justice, benevolence, purity, and speech not deceitful. Cruelties and oppressions, and all acts of impurity He punishes (156, 182 f., 311–13, 764–6). Theft, unjust measures, and injury to the poor are censured. It is by benevolence that men fulfil the saying of the Mighty God who finished the earth a common good for all (237–47). Unjust speech, deceitful and unrighteous words, incur grave penalties (496–8).

### THE PROEMIUM

The teaching as to the Gentiles implies the doctrine of God's forgivingness, but nothing is said as to His love.

## SUMMARY

(1) *Forgivingness in God.*—Upon one point alone, in regard to the doctrine of the divine forgiveness, there is entire agreement among the writers of this period. It is that God's pardon is only to be obtained upon the condition that men amend their conduct. Otherwise, the conceptions of these writers are very various.

Only one among them—the author of Jubilees—maintains that there are some specific transgressions which God will never forgive. The idea that righteous deeds cancel past sins is peculiar to Ecclesiasticus and Tobit. Jubilees and the third book of the Oracles are the only works in which men are enjoined to offer sacrifices in order to obtain pardon. In the Testaments, but nowhere else, penance is apparently regarded as inclining God to mercy. Jubilees and the Testaments insist on the idea that ignorance is a ground for His forgiveness. In two works—Ecclesiasticus and the Testaments—it is laid down that he who would be forgiven must himself be forgiving. The former, however, only affirms that necessity so far as one's neighbour is concerned; but the latter anticipates the very teaching of Jesus Christ on the subject. In the two Enoch sections the doctrine appears to be that of the free acceptance of the penitent. The Ecclesiasticus Additions contains only a passing allusion to the fact of God's forgivingness.

The doctrine of the intercession of angels on behalf of human offenders appears nowhere save in Enoch 1–36 and the Testaments. The latter work alone speaks of an intercession for sinners by righteous men living on the earth.

It has been shown in Chapter II., to which reference may be made for a fuller statement of the facts, that most of the writers of this period did not limit the forgivingness of God to Israel. It is in Jubilees only that the narrowest views are found, and it may be that even the author of this work conceived of a pardon for repentant Gentiles in the time of the great consummation.

Each of the five writers who speak of a final judgment teaches that God will judge men according to conduct. But did they mean that in the great Day there will be no exercise of His sovereign grace? Not at all. On the contrary, in Enoch 1–36 and Jubilees it is expressly said that the accepted righteous will then be recipients of mercy. Though nothing is said to this effect in the Testaments, the writer's whole idea of God is such as to make it most improbable that he did not share this view. The Sibyl also clearly teaches that penitent Gentiles will be among the pious whose destiny is the bliss of Paradise. In Enoch 83–90 God is described as freely accepting at last the repentant Gentiles, who enter into the bliss of the kingdom because they are changed in character, although they have done no good works to merit the privilege.

(2) *God's Redeeming Grace.*—There are three writers in this century who teach the possibility and actuality of a divine redeeming grace by which men may be delivered from sinfulness. This is the clear doctrine in Ecclesiasticus, Jubilees, and the Testaments. Men obtain it in answer to prayer. In Enoch 1–36 the teaching is that such grace will be in operation in the future, and here, as in Jubilees, the idea is that of an indefectible grace. The author of this part of Enoch did not, however, conceive of God as affecting men by His grace before the time of the great consummation.

(3) *The Love of God.*—The Enoch writers of this period do not speak of the love of God. Tobit, Ecclesiasticus, the Ecclesiasticus Additions, Jubilees, and the Testaments declare that men should love Him. Tobit contains no suggestion of His love, though He is styled the Father of Israel. In Jubilees He is called the loving Father of all righteous Israelites. The Sibyl names Him the All-Father, but only predicates of Him love toward the chosen nation. Ben Sira, the author of the Testaments, and the scribe or scribes who wrote in Ben Sira's name affirm a wider love. It is love which is evoked toward all right-doers. The idea of a love of God for man as man—a love not caused by man's virtues, nor destroyed by man's sinfulness, a love that goes out to all God's creatures because He is essentially loving—did not enter into the minds of any of these writers. On the contrary, even the large-minded men who wrote the Testaments and Ecclesiasticus declare that God hates sinners.

(4) *The Righteousness Acceptable to God.*—That the righteousness which is acceptable includes the due observance of the ceremonial law is the teaching of Tobit, Jubilees, and the Oracles. In the two former of these this is regarded as a matter of the gravest importance. In Ecclesiasticus and the Testaments, on the other hand, it sinks into relative insignificance, and the Enoch writers do not make any reference to it. But no writer fails to include ethical elements in the conception.

Benevolence in men toward men is inculcated by the authors of Ecclesiasticus, Tobit, Jubilees, the Testaments, and the Oracles. Jubilees and the Testaments insist on mercy toward the beasts. The importance of truthfulness is implied in Jubilees by notable omis-

19

sions, and in the Testaments it is expressly taught. Enoch 1–36 and Jubilees denounce sexual impurity as gravely displeasing to God. We have, perhaps, in Enoch 83–90 the notion that an ascetic life is acceptable to Him.

Evil elements appear. The writer of Jubilees did not conceive of his own racial hatreds as offensive to God. The author of Tobit did not include strict truthfulness in his idea of the righteousness which pleases Him. Even in Ecclesiasticus and the Testaments revenge is regarded as permissible.

In the last-named work there is insistence on the need of an interior righteousness. Ben Sira and the author of Jubilees also make some slight reference to this thought.

## The First Century B.C.

### I MACCABEES

This writer has almost nothing to say of the divine forgivingness. He declares that Judas, by destroying the ungodly, " turned away wrath from Israel " ($3^8$). The *locus classicus* on the subject of justification— Gen. $15^6$—is treated by him in the manner of St. James: " Was not Abraham found faithful in temptation, and it was reckoned unto him for righteousness ? " ($2^{52}$). He speaks of God's mercy, compassion, and faithfulness ($3^{44}$, $4^{24}$, $2^{61}$), and in one place he describes the Israelite army as " them that love Thee " ($4^{33}$).

What displeases God is disloyalty to the law, but the conduct of a Judas in slaying transgressors wins His favour ($1^{11-15, \ 52, \ 64}$, $3^8$). Nothing is said of any demand for an ethical righteousness.

ETHIOPIC ENOCH 91–104

The teaching here is of an ultimate judgment by works. " Blessed are all they who accept the words of wisdom and understand them, and follow out the paths of the Most High, and walk in the path of His righteousness, and become not godless with the godless, for they will be saved " (99$^{10}$). God " will be gracious to the righteous, and will give him eternal uprightness, and will give him power, and he will live in goodness and righteousness and will walk in eternal light " (92$^{4}$). Men are exhorted to place their prayers as a testimony before the angels (99$^{3}$) ; but this is not in order that sinners may be forgiven, but that the wrongs of the righteous may be avenged. The writer is far from exhorting sinners to repent after the manner of the Sibyl. His teaching rather is, that there is no hope whatever for them. " Now know ye," he says, " that ye are prepared for the day of destruction ; wherefore do not hope to live, ye sinners, but ye shall depart and die, for ye know no ransom " (98$^{10}$). There is teaching in this work to the effect that sinners should be afraid of God, as a mariner is of the sea which may swallow him up (101$^{5-9}$) ; but the idea of loving God is entirely absent from the book, nor is there any reference to His mercy or compassion. Indeed, God is far from lovable, as our author pictures Him. " He who has created you will overthrow you, and for your fall there will be no compassion, and your Creator will rejoice at your destruction " (94$^{10}$). The general drift of the teaching is, therefore, such as to confirm the view which we have taken in Chapter II. of the one passage which implies that God forgives. For 91$^{14}$ contains an idea which is quite foreign to the thought of the man who wrote this apocalypse.

The conception of righteousness is not Judaistic. The writer censures those who do not separate from sinners (97⁴). He condemns the eating of blood (98¹¹). He denounces apostates and those who transgress the eternal law (99¹⁴, Ibid.⁹). But what he insists upon most frequently is the fact that they will be punished who are guilty of deceit, blasphemy, and falsehood, who acquire riches unjustly and oppress the poor (96⁷, 101³, 98¹⁵; 97⁸, ¹⁰, 99¹²ᵗ·; 96⁸, 98⁸). Nevertheless, like their God, the righteous rejoice to take reprisals. In most naïve fashion, Enoch exclaims : " Who has permitted you to practise hate and wickedness ? May judgment light upon you, ye sinners. Fear not the sinners, ye righteous, for again will the Lord deliver them into your hands, that ye may execute judgment on them according to your desires " (95²⁻⁴). " Ye will be delivered up and persecuted, ye people of injustice, and heavy will their yoke be upon you. Be hopeful, ye righteous, for suddenly will the sinners perish before you and ye will have lordship over them according to your desires " (Ibid.⁷–96¹). " Know ye that ye shall be delivered into the hands of the righteous, and they will cut off your necks, and slay you, and will have no pity upon you " (98¹²).

## ETHIOPIC ENOCH 37–70

In this work, again, the teaching is that men are to be judged by works. Enoch saw " how the actions of men are weighed on the balance " (41¹). At the last, God's " Elect One will sit on the throne of His glory and make choice among their [men's] deeds." The righteous will be satisfied with peace and the sinners will be destroyed (45³⁻⁶). The Elect One " will judge all the works of the holy in the heaven, and weigh their deeds in the balance (61[8]). Dr. Hughes, commenting on the idea in 41[1], says it "is not out of harmony with the conception of divine grace implied in salvation in His name." * The passage, however, simply affirms that the righteous "have hated and despised this world of unrighteousness, and have hated all its works and ways, in the name of the Lord of Spirits, for they are saved in His name and He is the avenger of their life" (48[7]). This apparently means only that in the name of the Lord, as His true servants, owning His authority, they have opposed themselves to what is evil and so are saved. The interpolator has indeed inserted a passage into these Similitudes in which he teaches that the heathen will be saved through the name of the Lord of Spirits, and there we have clearly the thought of God's grace to sinners (50[2]). But our author appears not to use the phrase in that way. The passage simply reasserts the doctrine of a divine judgment according to works.

But that there *is* forgiveness with God is implied more than once. It is implied in what is taught about the Gentiles (see Chapter II.), in the description of Fanuel the angel "who is set over the repentance and hope of those who inherit eternal life" (40[9]), and in the statement concerning the kings and the mighty that "thenceforward none will seek for mercy for them with the Lord of Spirits, for their life is at an end" (38[6]). For them, there *has* been a day of mercy which is now past. 39[5] should not be cited in this connection, because the angels who "petitioned and interceded and prayed for the children of men" are not said in that verse to have prayed for forgiveness for sinners, and in 47[2], where, again, the angels are described as intercessors their prayer is that judg-

* Op. cit., p. 76.

ment may be done to those who shed the blood of the saints.

Possibly, the doctrine of the grace by which men are morally strengthened is implied in the statement that the works of the elect righteous " are wrought in dependence on the Lord of Spirits " (38²).

No word is uttered which implies the idea of God's love, but His mercy is celebrated in 61¹³ : " Great is the mercy of the Lord of Spirits."

Sins denounced in these pages are ingratitude, unjust acquisitions, and oppression (46⁵, 53², 46⁷).

### ETHIOPIC ENOCH : INTERPOLATIONS

In 60¹² it is recorded that Enoch was shown " how the spirits are parted and the weighing is done," and the same idea occurs in chapter 43. But belief in the forgiving God is manifested in the passage concerning the fate of the Gentiles, which we have cited in our second chapter (50²). Of the Judgment Day it is said : " Until this day lasted the day of His mercy and longsuffering toward those who dwell on the earth. But when the day, and the power, and the punishment, and the judgment have come . . . that day is prepared, for the elect a covenant, but for sinners an inquisition " (60⁵˙⁶). Yet, though the present day of mercy will then be past, the judgment will not be strictly according to merit. Rather, it " will take place according to His mercy and His patience " (Ibid. ²⁵). In one passage objection is taken to the idea that any man can be acceptable to God purely on his merits. " After that I spake : ' Blessed is the man who dies in righteousness and goodness, concerning whom there is no book of unrighteousness written and (against whom) no day of judgment is found.'

And those seven holy ones brought me and placed me
on the earth before the door of my house and spake
unto me : ' Declare everything to thy son Methuselah,
and show to all thy children that no flesh is righteous
in the sight of the Lord, for He is their Creator ' "
(81⁴ᵗ·). But the general doctrine of the Interpolations appears clearly to be that of the God who is
merciful in His judgment of men and does not reward
them strictly according to their deserts.

It is said that He "strengthens the spirits of the
righteous in the name of His righteousness " (41⁸).

In chapter 108, which is probably an independent
addition, the idea of God as being loved by men
appears (verses 8 and 12).

God is regarded in these Interpolations as opposed
to man's advancement in knowledge. In 69⁹ᵗ· we
read that Penemûe "instructed mankind in writing
with ink and paper, and thereby many sinned from
eternity to eternity and until this day. For men are
not created to the end that they should give confirmation to their good faith with pen and ink in such
wise." Here, as Charles says, the invention of writing
is not apparently condemned *per se*, but only "so far
as it is used as a safeguard against the bad faith of
men." * In 8¹⁻³, again, the knowledge of the way to
make implements of war and personal adornment, as
well as the knowledge of astrology, communicated to
men by the spirits, is not accounted as sinful in itself,
though it is connected closely with the primitive
corruption of mankind. But in 65⁶ ᶠᶠ· man's knowledge of the secrets of the angels, of sorcery, of the
production of silver and lead and tin from the earth,
is apparently regarded as in itself sinful. "A command has gone forth from the presence of the Lord,

* Edition of Ethiopic Enoch, in loc.

concerning those who dwell on the earth, that their end should be brought about, because they know all the secrets of the angels." Elsewhere in the Interpolations sin is godlessness, impurity, oppression, and blasphemy (8², 91¹¹). In chapter 108, which is possibly Essenic, righteousness is asceticism (verses 7 and 9).

THE PSALMS OF SOLOMON

An important passage is 3⁷⁻⁹, and it will be convenient to give renderings of the Greek and Syriac versions.

*Greek.*—" The confidence of the righteous (cometh) from God their Saviour. There lodgeth not in the dwelling of the righteous sin upon sin. The righteous man maketh inquisition continually in his own house, to the end that he may put away iniquity ; with his trespass offering he maketh atonement for that wherein he erreth unwittingly, and with fasting he afflicteth his soul. And the Lord purifieth every man that is holy and his house."

*Syriac.*—" The stability of the righteous is from God their Saviour. For in the house of the righteous there does not lodge sin upon sin ; because He always visits the house of the righteous to remove the sins of his transgressions. And He delivers his soul, in whatsoever he has sinned without knowledge, by fasting and by humiliation."

Where the Syriac in this passage has the equivalent of " stability," the Greek has ἀλήθεια, and Ryle and James observe that this word is here used in the unusual sense of " confidence," or " security," probably translating one aspect of אמונה.* It will be observed that, in both versions, it is sins which are

---

* Op. cit., p. 34.

not wilful that are dealt with. In both, also, the
teaching is that fasting is a condition of forgiveness,
and the Syriac adds " humiliation " as a condition.
But on one important point the two versions radically
differ. If the Syriac be correct, the idea is that God
acts as well as man. He " visits the house of the
righteous to remove the sins of his transgressions."
The idea seems to be like that in $13^9$, cited in Chapter
II., where it is said that God blots out transgression
by chastening. But, according to the Greek, it is the
sinner who acts, making atonement with his trespass
offering and behaving with scrupulous carefulness
" to the end that he may put away iniquity." As
Ryle and James point out, the phrase is parallel to
that in Deuteronomy $17^{7, 12}$, etc., where " Thou shalt
put away evil from among you " is obviously an injunction to such conduct as shall free offenders from
guilt.

In another passage on the subject the psalmist
seems to be dealing with sin that may be wilful : " He
will cleanse the soul that hath sinned, if it make
confession in acknowledgment. For upon us and
upon our faces is shame because of all these things.
And to whom will He forgive sins, save unto them
that have committed sin ? " ($9^{12-14}$). This is the one
passage in this Psalter in which a free divine forgiveness, for all sorts of sins, and with no limitation of
class, is declared, though of course the same doctrine
is implied in the prophecy of the Gentile converts, if
we are to accept the Syriac version of it as correct.

The singer deeply realised the need of God's help
for men who would live holily, and he believed in
God's willingness to grant it : " Keep me, O God,"
he cries, " from abominable sin " ($16^7$). " Establish
Thou the works of my hands in Thy word, and pre-

serve my goings in the remembrance of Thee " (Ibid. ').
" My tongue and my lips do Thou guard about with
the words of truth. Anger and senseless wrath put
Thou far from me. Murmuring and faint-heartedness
in the time of affliction remove Thou far from me. . . .
But with good-will and cheerfulness uphold Thou my
soul. When Thou strengthenest my soul, I shall be
satisfied with what Thou givest me. For, if Thou
strengthenest not, who can abide chastisement in
poverty ? " (Ibid. $^{10-13}$).

In many passages, God is represented as a lovable
Being. He is " gracious unto them that call upon
Him in patience, to deal according to His mercy with
them that are His " ($2^{40}$). He is the hope and refuge
of the needy and the poor ($3^{13}$, $15^2$). He is gentle,
opening His hand to the humble. Man is often parsi-
monious, and it is wonderful if he repeats a gift without grudging ; but God's gifts are many and rich with
kindness ($5^{14-16}$). To Israel, when they are purified,
He will be a Father, and the Christ will know them
that are all His children ($17^{30}$). The righteous is to
Him as a beloved son, and he not only fears God but
also loves Him ($13^8$, $4^{29}$, $6^9$, $10^4$). The psalmist teaches
the love of God for Israel ($18^{3 t.}$), but he does not hint
at a love of God for mankind.

Righteousness is obedience to the ritual law. The
men who bring down wrath on Israel are such as
pollute the holy things of the Lord ($1^9$, $2^3$, $8^{12-14, 26}$).
The righteous, to whom God is faithful, are those who
walk in His ordinances ($14^1$). But ritual is not all.
The cruelty of the Roman brings down divine punishment, as does also any impurity ($2^{25, 30}$, $8^{8-11}$). God is
opposed to those who judge in unrighteousness. The
godly must guard against sins of speech and passion
($16^{10-13}$). The need for a righteous inner self seems

to be suggested when it is affirmed that God knows " the secret chambers of the heart " (14⁵).

Nevertheless, the conception of God is not such as to hinder the psalmist from invoking the most terrible curses on the foes of Israel's saints. He implores God to inflict on them the most terrible torments, and declares that " the quiet soul that hateth the unrighteous " is one who may hope that God will preserve him (4¹⁶⁻²², 12⁶).

### JUDITH

In the Greek text of this book nothing is said of the divine forgiveness, but the Vulgate has two references to it: "Whensoever they [Israel] repented that they had departed from the worship of their God, the God of heaven gave them valour for resistance" (5¹⁴).

" And who are ye who are tempting the Lord ? Your words are not such as to provoke pity, but rather to rouse anger and kindle indignation. You have fixed a time for the Lord's compassion, and according to your own will you have appointed Him a day. But, because the Lord is patient, let us repent in this very matter and crave His pardon with floods of tears " (8¹²⁻¹⁶). Of the former passage Fuller says that the whole of it bears " evident traces of the Chaldee original." *

In a beautiful passage God is called " God of the afflicted, Helper of the oppressed, Upholder of the weak, Protector of the forlorn, Saviour of them that are without hope " (9¹¹). He is merciful to them that fear Him (16¹³⁻¹⁵).

Righteousness is conformity to ritual requirements (e.g. 8⁴⁻⁶, 11¹³, 12⁷⁻⁹). There is no concern for philan-

* Speaker's Comm., p. 291.

thropy, no passion for an ethical righteousness. The heroine's thought of God is that of One who will approve her deceit for what she deems a right end. She is at liberty to pray that God will smite by the deceit of her lips and make her speech and deceit to be the wound and stripe of the foe (9[10, 13]). She asks God to give her strength to carry out her purpose (13[7]). She takes courage for her act by recalling the fact that God gave Simeon the sword to take vengeance on the sons of Shechem (9[2]). Ozias, warmly commending her, declares that she has walked a straight way before God (13[20]). Joakim, the High-priest, and the Senate say that God is well pleased with what she has done (15[10]). It is not, of course, surprising that Judith should act as she did under such circumstances; but, as André observes : " L'écrivain qui n'y trouve rien à redire ne témoigne pas une grande élévation morale." In the author's sight the end justifies the means, and the implication is that he conceived of God as passing the same judgment on Judith's deceit. The writer of the song in chapter 16 fully shared this sentiment. In 16[6], Fuller says, the Syriac gives us the following : " The mighty Lord defrauded them. By the hand of a female He destroyed them." The Greek is rendered in the English R.V. thus : " The Almighty Lord brought them to nought by the hand of a woman " ; but Fuller suggests that, as in 14[18], the ἠθέτησεν should be rendered : "The Lord of hosts cheated [or dealt treacherously with] them by the hand of a woman." The Vulgate has : " Nocuit eum et tradidit illum in manus fœminæ et confodit eum."

A remarkable passage is 16[16] : " For all sacrifice is little for a sweet savour, and all the fat is very little

* Op. cit., " Judith."

for a whole burnt offering to Thee ; but he that feareth the Lord is great continually." This verse might, of course, merely mean that the utmost sacrifice is not worthy of God ; but the antithesis suggests that the writer had conceived a loftier idea than any that entered the mind of the man who wrote the earlier part of the book, with its insistence on a merely legal righteousness. He appears to teach that what is most significant before God is the state of a man's heart.

### 3 ESDRAS

According to this writer, Israel can "turn away the wrath of the Lord," by sacrifice and amendment ($9^{13, 20}$). Nothing is said of God's love even for Israel. But His deep interest in Israel is manifest. He is "grieved exceedingly " by Israel's sin ($1^{24}$).

The righteousness that is of vital importance is the due performance of all things after the law. That stays wrath from coming upon men ($8^{21}$). The intermarriage of Israelites with alien wives is confessed as sin.

### 2 MACCABEES

The idea of reconcilement between God and Israel is one which appears in this book with great frequency (e.g. $1^5$, $2^{22}$, $5^{20}$, $7^{33}$, $8^{29}$). He never withdraws His mercy from Israel ($6^{16}$). The death of the martyrs, it is hoped, will stay His wrath against the whole race ($7^{38}$).

The unique teaching of this book is that prayer avails to obtain pardon for the sinful dead. The writer tells how, upon the discovery of the death of the soldiers of Judas, who were slain for their idolatry, " all betook themselves unto supplication, beseeching

that the sin committed might be wholly blotted out."
On their behalf Judas sent money for a sacrifice
(12⁴²ᶠ·). The author appears to be arguing in favour
of a new idea, for he proceeds to say that Judas was
" doing therein right well and honourably in that he
took thought for a resurrection. For, if he were not
expecting that they that had fallen asleep would rise
again, it were idle and superfluous to pray for the
dead " (12⁴³ᶠ·). In the next verse it is added :
" And if he (did it), looking unto an honourable
memorial of gratitude laid up for them that fall asleep
in godliness, holy and godly was the thought." There
is no manuscript authority for omitting this, but it
seems to be an intrusion on the text. If it be omitted,
the narrative ceases to be encumbered with a sentence that makes an awkward break in the thought,
and it then concludes quite naturally : " Wherefore
he made the propitiation for them that had sinned,
that they might be released from their sin." *

Once, the idea of grace to aid men in right conduct
occurs : " May God . . . give you all a heart to worship Him and do His pleasure with a great heart and
a willing soul, and open your heart in His law and in
His statutes " (1³ᶠ·).

God is described as terrible and righteous and
merciful and gracious (1²⁴ᶠ·), but the idea of His love
is absent. It agrees well with the author's conception
of a nationalistic God that, even though the dying
Epiphanes is represented as the subject of a change
of mind, it is added that " the Sovereign Lord would
no more have pity upon him " (9¹³ᶠ·).

* " The reference to such offerings is . . .without paralle·
in Jewish literature, and nothing is otherwise known of such
offerings being made in the temple on Jerusalem " (Israel
Abrahams, J.E., art. " Maccabees," 42 f.).

Naturally, this writer insists on the great importance of loyalty to Judaism. It is the Hellenisers who occasion calamities, for they do impiously against the laws of God (4¹⁰⁻¹⁷). To eat the flesh of swine is to incur God's anger (6²³). To have complicity in idolatrous practices is perilous (12²⁴). The idea appears that God is opposed to those who ill-treat His chosen people. Otherwise, there is no suggestion that He has the least concern for justice and benevolence as between man and man. On the contrary, the writer rejoices in the horrible death of Israel's foes, and he prays the vengeful prayer, " Torment them that oppress us " (1¹⁷, ²⁸).

### THE ADDITIONS TO DANIEL

In the Song Azarias expresses the hope that Israel may be accepted by God, in the absence of offerings and sacrifices, by reason of a contrite heart and a humble spirit (15 ff.). He prays : " (Grant) that we may wholly go after Thee " (17). Abraham is described as "beloved" of God (12). God is good, says Azarias, and " His mercy endureth for ever " (67 f.).

Righteousness is only described in general terms as obeying God's commandments.

In " Bel and the Dragon " we have only to note an allusion to " them that love God " (38).

### THE EPISTLE OF JEREMY

There is nothing for us to note here except verse 7 : Ὁ γὰρ ἄγγελός μου μεθ' ὑμῶν ἐστιν. αὐτός τε ἐκζητῶν τὰς ψυχὰς ὑμῶν. The verse is ambiguous, but perhaps it means that God cares for Israel.

SUMMARY

(1) *Forgivingness in God.*—The Epistle of Jeremy, the Story of Susanna, and Bel and the Dragon contain no teaching on this subject. In 1 Maccabees there is only a brief reference to the subject. In Enoch 91–104 the teaching is that God's judgment of man proceeds simply upon his deserts, and there is no hint of forgiveness, save in one passage which is so out of harmony with the tenor of his doctrine that it must be judged to proceed from the pen of an interpolator. But the mercy of God for repentent men is taught in Enoch 37–70, the Interpolations to Enoch, 2 Maccabees, the Psalms of Solomon, the Song of the Three Children, and 3 Esdras. In the Greek version of Judith there is nothing said on the subject, but there are passages in the Vulgate version in which God is described as pardoning the penitent.

The doctrine of an angelic intercession, exercised in order to obtain forgiveness for men, appears to be taught in Enoch 37–70, but only in that work. Enoch 91–104 contains the doctrine of an intercession of angels, but that intercession is not regarded as directed to this end. In 2 Maccabees departed saints are said to intercede for Israel, and possibly the writer meant that they obtained forgiveness by their prayers. He teaches also that martyrs' deaths are of advantage to the sinning nation, and that living Israelites affect by sacrifices the position of sinners in the unseen world. This is the only case in which a sacrifice is regarded in this literature as in the nature of an *opus operatum.*

The writer of the Testaments Additions teaches that Israel obtains mercy by God's regard to the merits of ancestors, and that He is gracious to sinful men because they are deceived. In the Psalms ignorance is said to be a ground of mercy with God.

Three writers—the authors of the Psalms, 3 Esdras, and the Song of the Three Children—ascribe importance to sacrifices, offered by the living for their own benefit. But the latter expresses the hope that penitent Israel may be accepted even in the absence of these. Only in the Psalms of Solomon is there insistence on the importance of fasting in the penitent who seeks mercy. In that work alone we meet with the idea that God blots out transgression by His own chastisements.

It has been shown in Chapter II. that, among those who taught in this age the doctrine of the forgiving God, it is only the writer of 2 Maccabees who limits His mercy to Israel.

In Enoch 91–104 the teaching is that the final judgment of God will be strictly according to desert; but in the Enoch Interpolations it is taught that there will be mercy as well as judgment in the great Day, and in the Psalms of Solomon the righteous who are said to inherit eternal life are faulty men whose confidence could not be wholly in their own merits. The clear implication there is that God will be forgiving in the Day of Judgment. The same must be said of the Enoch Similitudes. In 2 Maccabees, again, the faithful look for mercy in the unseen world, and, as we have seen above, apostates also obtain mercy through the prayers of their surviving compatriots.

(2) *God's Redeeming Grace.*—Probably we have the idea of helpful grace from God in Enoch 37–70, where it is said that the works of the righteous are wrought in dependence on God. In the Song of the Three Children and in the Psalms of Solomon the doctrine is that God aids men to do the right in answer to

20

their prayer. In 2 Maccabees the hope is expressed that He will do this.

In the Enoch Interpolations He is said to strengthen the spirits of the righteous.

(3) *The Love of God.*—The Psalms of Solomon teach that God has kindness for all mankind and love for the house of Israel, to the righteous among whom He will be a Father. The Song of the Three Children refers to God's love for Abraham. In no other work in this century is there mention of the love of God. But in 1 Maccabees, Bel and the Dragon, and the Enoch Interpolations it is said that He is loved by men.

In Judith, however, He is described as the sure helper of the afflicted, in Enoch 37–70 it is said that He is of great mercy, and in 3 Esdras He is conceived of as grieved by Israel's sin. Only in Enoch 91–104 does the unworthy idea occur that He rejoices over the ultimate downfall of sinful men.

(4) *The Righteousness Acceptable to God.*—In 1 and 2 Maccabees, Judith, and 3 Esdras righteousness is loyalty to Judaism. This duty is also strongly insisted upon in Enoch 91–104 and the Psalms. But these latter writers, unlike the first named, include other elements in the conception. They insist, as do the authors of the Enoch Similitudes and Interpolations, that righteousness means justice between man and man. In the Enoch Interpolations and the Story of Susanna impurity is condemned. In Enoch 91–104 truth is insisted upon.

It is a remarkable fact that none of the writers of this period even hint that the righteousness which is acceptable to God must include kindness to one's fellows. Unworthy elements appear in Enoch 91–104, 2 Maccabees, and the Psalms, whose authors were

very far from supposing that the spirit of revengefulness would be displeasing to God, and in Judith, where
He is conceived of as not disapproving of lies.   In
one work only—the Enoch Interpolations—does the
idea appear that God is hostile to man's advancement
in knowledge.   In one passage of the same work, and
in the Psalms, asceticism is regarded as conduct
pleasing to God.   The psalmist, and possibly the
author of the Song of Judith, discerned the need of
an inward righteousness.


## THE FIRST CENTURY A.D.

### WISDOM

#### Part 1

There is only one allusion to God's pardoning grace.
This is in 6⁶: "The man of low estate may be pardoned in mercy."   Here perhaps, as in Proverbs 6³⁰,
the thought is that " necessity presses on the humble
with an insistence special to their case, for which
the Judge makes allowance."   This is the view of
Mr. Gregg.*   Dean Farrar's interpretation is similar :
" The temptations of the poor may assume acuter
forms, and therefore may receive greater allowance." †
In 3⁹—" The faithful shall abide with Him in
love "—the thought appears to be that they will abide
in God's love.   The righteous man is described as
" pleasing unto the Lord " and " beloved of Him "
(4¹⁴, ¹⁰).   " Nothing doth God love," says Ps.-Solo-
mon, " save him that dwelleth with wisdom " (7²⁸).
He is the Father of the righteous individual (2¹⁶, ¹⁸,
5⁵).   But a broader love seems to be implied when

* Op. cit. in loc.                    † Ibid.

it is said of Wisdom, His mirror ($7^{26}$), that she is
φιλάνθρωπον πνεῦμα ($1^6$, cf. $7^{23}$), and when Ps.-Solo-
mon says : " It is He that hath made small and great
and alike He taketh thought for all " ($6^7$).   In $4^{18}$,
where Ps.-Solomon prophesies of sinners that " the
Lord shall laugh " them " to scorn," he seems to
present God as unlovable.   But allowance must be
made for the writer's rhetorical style, and the passage
may mean no more than what is said in Proverbs $1^{26}$.

The author apparently teaches that God graciously
assists men to do right, when he says that in all
generations Wisdom passes into holy souls and makes
men friends of God and prophets ($7^{27}$).

Righteousness, in this work, is not at all Judaistic.
The conduct which brings down penalties is deceit,
blasphemy, impurity, injustice ($1^{5f.}$, $3^{16}$, $6^4$).   Single-
ness of heart is called for ($1^1$).   " Crooked thoughts,"
it is said, "separate from God " ($1^3$), and He " bears
witness of the reins " ($1^6$).   The soul of the righteous
is pleasing to Him ($4^{14}$).   In striking contrast to
Ecclesiasticus, there is no insistence on benevolence
as an element in righteousness.


### Part 2

Passages cited in Chapter II. show that this writer
taught God's willingness to forgive the penitent, and
that not within Israel only ($11^{23}$, $12^{10,\ 20}$).   Others may
here be added.   God chastens Israel, it is said, that
when they are judged they may look for mercy ($12^{22}$).
" Thou didst make Thy sons to be of good hope,
because Thou givest repentance when men have
sinned " ($12^{19}$).

Only in $18^{21f.}$ is allusion made to any other means
of obtaining the divine forgiveness besides penitence.

THE GRACE OF GOD

By " prayer and the propitiation of incense " Aaron " withstood the indignation " and " overcame the anger."

It is clearly taught in chapter 10—but only there —that God helps men to do right. It was Wisdom that kept Abraham " strong when his heart yearned over his child " (5), and " from sin she delivered Joseph " (13). In this latter passage the Vulgate has " a peccatoribus "; but this is probably incorrect, for it is not in harmony with the preceding statement that "the righteous man was sold." Of Adam, also, it is said in this chapter that " Wisdom rescued him out of his own transgression " (1). To quote Farrar's comment : " Wisdom (i.e. the redeeming power of God), working in the penitent heart of man, rescued Adam, as Tirinus says, ' inspirando pœnitentiam et indulgendo veniam.' " * Gregg says it is out of the question to suppose that there is here any suggestion of the final salvation of Adam. " Such a discussion . . . has no place in a pre-Christian work, the Incarnation being the indispensable presupposition for such a restoration." † But, as we shall show below, Slavonic Enoch contains the doctrine of the restoration of Adam ; hence Farrar's interpretation must not be set aside on à priori grounds.

Israel is God's son (18$^{13}$), and Israelites are described as, " Thy sons whom Thou lovedst, O Lord " (16$^{26}$). But God is also described as He " that careth for all " and " loveth all things that are " (12$^{13}$, 11$^{24}$). He is the lover of men's lives, gracious and true, long-suffering, and in mercy ordering all things " (11$^{26}$, 15$^{1}$). All this is painfully marred when it is added that God hates the wicked Canaanites and that the idolater is hateful to Him (12$^{4}$, 14$^{9}$). It is possible

* Speaker's Comm., in loc.      † Op. cit., p. 96.

to argue that the contradiction is merely rhetorical, and that, if the author had written more accurately, he would have said that God hates, not the sinner, but the sin. But, as we have seen in Chapter II., the book contains contradictory statements elsewhere as to God's attitude to the Gentiles.

As in Part 1, there is no insistence on a ritual righteousness. The sins condemned are idolatry, murder, unholy rites which provoke God's hatred, impurity, perjury, theft, deceit, and ingratitude ($14^9$, $16^1$, $12^{4-7}$, $14^{23}$, $14^{24, 30}$). Positively, the will of God is that the righteous should be a lover of men and ponder His goodness when he judges ($12^{19, 22}$).

## THE BOOK OF BARUCH

### $1^{1-14}$

Here the exiles beg the Palestinian remnant to pray on their behalf for God's pardon and charge them to offer the sin-offering (12, 10).

### $1^{15}$, $3^8$

In this section there is repeated prayer for forgiveness. In one perplexing passage the suppliants say: " Hear now the prayer of the dead Israelites " ($3^4$). Does the writer conceive of these as suppliants for the living ? It is possible, for the idea of such human intercessors occurs in the Assumption of Moses, in 2 Maccabees, and in Slavonic Enoch. Since, however, in $2^{17}$ this writer says that " The dead . . . will give unto the Lord neither praise nor righteousness," it is improbable that this is his thought. Most likely, the Greek translator misunderstood the original.

מְתִי, "the men," probably stood in the original, and
he has apparently mistaken it for מֵתִי "the dead." *
Sometimes prayer for pardon is based on the idea
that God will have regard to His own glory. "Remember not the iniquities of our fathers, but remember Thy power, and Thy name" (3⁵). "Deliver us for
Thine own sake" (2¹⁴). This may be an appeal in
which the basis of hope is God's character, as it
clearly is in 3⁸: "Hear, O Lord, and have mercy; for
Thou art a merciful God." This hope is strengthened
also in the suppliants by God's promises to Moses :
"I will give them a heart and ears to hear," and they
"shall return from their stiff neck and from their
wicked deeds" (2³¹, ³³).

The writer recognises God's kindness and mercy
toward Israel, but He does not attribute love to God.

### 3⁸–4⁴

Israel, sinning and exiled, is exhorted to turn and
take hold of the law. For "all they that hold it fast
(are appointed) to life, but such as leave it shall die"
(4¹ᵇ).

In 4⁴ Israelites are counted happy in that the
things which are pleasing to God are made known to
them; but the writer does not indicate what those
things are.

### 4⁴–5⁹

This section is full of the conviction that God will
have mercy on Israel, when they cry unto Him,
despite all their sins (4²¹ᶠ·, ²⁷, ²⁹, 5). The only indication of the ethical ideal is in the fact that the writer
is not hindered by it from rejoicing in the approaching
ruin of his nation's foes and comforting his readers

* Speaker's Comm., p. 268.

with the thought that Israel will shortly see their destruction and tread on their necks (4²⁵, ³¹⁻⁵).

### THE ASSUMPTION OF MOSES

This writer looks for God's forgiveness for Israel in the great day of repentance, when He will visit them (1¹⁸). Moses, who was of old their intercessor, " propitiating the Lord with the oath " (11¹⁷), is constantly exercising that function in heaven for Israel. He is appointed " to pray for their sins and to make intercession for them " (12⁶).

God's kindness to Israel comes not of the deserts either of the people or of Moses, but of His own grace. " Not for any virtue or strength of mine was He pleased to call me," says Moses ; . . . " it is not on account of the godliness of this people that thou shalt root out the nations (12⁷ᶠ·). The idea of divine compassion for Israel appears, and Israelites are called sons of God ; but there is no suggestion of His love even for the chosen people (4⁵ᶠ·, 10³).

There is insistence on a life blameless to God and on the divine anger against bribed judges, gourmands, and " devourers of the goods of the poor " (1¹⁰, 5⁵, 7⁴, ⁶). Yet the ideal is low, for, although the writer was apparently a Pharisaic Quietist, who preferred to leave the punishment of Israel's foes to God (9⁶ᶠ·), he nevertheless declares that Israel in heaven will see their enemies in Gehenna and will " recognise them and rejoice " (10¹⁰).

### THE APOCALYPSE OF BARUCH

### A¹, A²

In each of these, as we have seen in Chapter II., God's mercy at the last is only for Israel in the land. A¹

gives no indication of his conception of the nature of
the righteousness which God desires in man, and A[s]
gives nothing on the subject except what is implied
in his denunciation of Rome's lust of conquest and
lack of compassion as conduct which will involve her
in penalties (36[8-11]).

## A[s]

As has been shown in Chapter II., A[s] teaches a judgment of God purely by works (54[21f.]). While in
2 Chronicles 33[12f., 19], it is taught that penitent
Manasseh was forgiven, this writer says that " his
prayer was heard with the Most High," but yet " his
final abode was in the fire . . . for he did not live
perfectly, for he was not worthy " (64[7f.]). Charles
thinks that the writer believed Manasseh to have been
no true penitent.* But it is doubtful if this is what
he means ; it is certainly not what he says.

A[s] speaks of the multitude of God's goodness, the
glory of His beauty, the suppression of His anger,
and the multitude of His long-suffering (55[2], 54[8], 59[6]).
But clearly he has the idea that a man may have trust
in his works and hope in his righteousness in a time
of need (63[3, 5]), and it is not manifest that he believed
in any other standing before God than that of merit.

The only allusion to God's love is in the statement
in 61[7] that, when the nation was sinless, " the land
was beloved."

The writer's idea that Israel was sinless in the
golden age of David and his son leads us to expect no
high ethical ideal from him ; but he gives us slight
material. It was impiety, injustice, adultery, and
sacrilege that made wrath to go forth from God against

* Edition of Apoc. Baruch, p. 108.

Manasseh (64²⁻⁴). It was in the restoration of the religion of Israel and the slaying of the impious that Josiah, his ideal king, showed the righteousness for which he is to receive an eternal reward (66¹⁻⁷). In the nation's ideal age, " the holy festivals were fulfilled in goodness and in much joy, and the judgment of the rulers was then seen to be without guile and the righteousness of the precepts of the Most High was accomplished with truth (61⁵ᵗ·).

## B¹

B¹ exhorts his compatriots to pray " that the Mighty One may be reconciled unto you, and that He may not reckon the multitude of your sins, but remember the rectitude of your fathers. For if He judge us not according to the multitude of His mercies, woe unto all us who are born " (84¹⁰ᵗ·). In the judgment of God, then, according to B¹, ancestral merits are taken into account. But, as we have already seen, God's mercy has other conditions. His people must return to their loyalty.

To Israel He has love. " I bear in mind . . . the love of Him who created us, who loved us from of old, and never hated us, but above all educated us " (78³; cf. 5¹).

There is no teaching as to the nature of righteousness.

## B²

B² did not believe in the forgiving God. His clear teaching is salvation by works. He appears to emphasise this doctrine against current opposition. The righteous, he says, die full of hope, because conscious of their store of good works which are preserved in God's treasuries (14¹²ᵗ·).

It is in chapters 48–52 that he makes the clearest statement of the truth which he believes he is divinely commissioned to proclaim. He describes Baruch as pleading for men. Baruch prays that God will not be wroth with man and not take account of his works (48¹⁴). He adduces arguments. Man, he says, is nothing. He did not choose to be born; he does not choose to die. He has no strength to bear the wrath and judgment of God. Let God protect man in His compassions. Israel is His chosen. No people is their equal. They have not mingled with the Gentiles. God's law will aid them, and the surpassing wisdom which is in them (Ibid. ¹⁵⁻²⁴). But the answer to all this—the answer which embodies the teaching which the author wishes to insist upon, and which, therefore, he gives forth as God's speech—is exceedingly stern : "Thou hast prayed simply, O Baruch, and all thy words have been heard. But My judgment exacts its own, and My law exacts its rights " (48²⁶ᶠ·). The wise and the intelligent will be few (Ibid. ³³). The divine Speaker rejects the appeal of the suppliant. Strict justice will be done, and few will be able to abide it. The co-religionists, whose feelings Baruch expresses in this prayer, were not destitute of a consciousness of their need of God's mercy. Nevertheless, they express themselves as men who are very sure that, at any rate, to some considerable extent, they merit His favourable regard. It seems to have been part of the purpose of this apocalyptist to urge upon them the doctrine of the God who deals stringently with mankind and whose judgment, accordingly, means ruin for the imperfectly righteous—that is, the great majority of men. The blessed will be " those who have been justified in My law, who have had understanding in their life, and

who have planted in their heart the root of wisdom"
(51³). They are saved "by their works"; the law
is their hope, and wisdom their confidence (Ibid. ⁷).
Those not justified by works will depart to torment
(51⁶, ¹⁶). Very fittingly, the section is concluded
with a great burst of lamentation over the pitiable
fate of those for whom woes are reserved (52¹⁻⁴).

In 75⁶ Baruch says to God: "If, assuredly, Thou
didst not have compassion on men . . . they could
not come to these things." Charles regards this as
belonging to B², because Baruch here addresses God,
whereas in chapter 74 the speaker is Ramiel. But
why should not Baruch thus address the angel? In
4 Esdras the angel is repeatedly addressed as God.
It is thus doubtful if this section does not belong to
B¹. It certainly agrees better with his doctrine. If
we remove it from B² this writer is consistent in his
stern doctrine throughout.

He has only one allusion to God's love. "On account of Thy name, Thou hast called us a beloved
people" (21²¹).

Oppression, ingratitude to God, craftiness, and
lying are the sins condemned in B². They are the
sins which God will punish (13¹¹ᶠ·, 83¹⁹⁻²²). Wicked
thoughts are to come under the purview of the judge
(48³⁹, 83³), and He will examine all the hidden works
of men (83²).

## B³

B³ impresses on his readers the doctrine that there
is no divine forgiveness after death. There is no
"place of repentance nor supplication for offences
nor intercession of the fathers" (85¹²). But now
timely action will obtain God's favour for Israel. "If
we direct and dispose our hearts, we shall receive

everything that we lost and much better things than we lost " (85⁴). God " will preserve those to whom He finds He may be gracious, and at the same time destroy those who are polluted with sins " (Ibid. ¹⁵). He is long-suffering (Ibid. ⁸).

## 4 ESDRAS

*The Salathiel Apocalypse (S).*—The doctrine of this writer is that of a final salvation by works. This is clearly enunciated in 7¹⁷ : " Thou hast ordained in Thy law that the righteous should inherit these things, but that the ungodly should perish." Esdras himself will not be amongst the tormented in the unseen world, because he has " a treasure of good works laid up with the Most High " (Ibid. ⁷⁷). The blessed will be those of whom their Maker testifies that " while they lived they kept the law which was given them in trust " (Ibid. ⁹⁴). Esdras desires to know " whether in the day of judgment the just will be able to intercede for the ungodly," and he learns from Uriel that they will not. That day is " a day of decision." " Never shall one pray for another in that day, neither shall one lay a burden on another, for they shall bear every one his own righteousness or unrighteousness " (7¹⁰²⁻⁵). True it is that God has heard intercessory prayers in time, but in that dread hour " no man shall be able to have mercy on him that is cast in judgment " (Ibid. ¹⁰⁶⁻¹⁵). This pronouncement causes a great outburst of lamentation from the prophet. He cries out that it means the damnation of " all that are in this present time " (Ibid. ¹¹⁷), and Uriel confirms that view in his reply : " This is the condition of the battle which man that is born upon the earth shall fight that, if he be overcome, he shall suffer as thou hast said, but, if he get the victory, he shall receive the thing that I say " (Ibid. ¹²⁷). Esdras then celebrates the mercy of the Most High, who is compassionate to them that turn to His law, and long-suffering to sinners; who shows Himself the forgiving God, multiplying mercies, for if He did not the ten-thousandth part of mankind would not remain alive ($7^{132-40}$). He seems to be arguing with himself, hoping against hope, seeking to derive from the fact that God is now merciful the assurance that He will be merciful in the great Day of His judgment. But once more the reply of the messenger of God is stern and hard: " There be many created, but few shall be saved " ($8^3$). And now Esdras is moved to the most passionate supplication. Oh that God would help men to do right! Strange it is that He should take so much pains to nurture His creature and then slay him lightly and suddenly. Why was man made only to be destroyed in the end? Oh that God would look on those who have been faithful to Him, and not regard the sinners! The just have no need of His mercy, but indeed there are no just men; all that be born are defiled with sins. Man is a slight creature. Why should God be bitter against him? His goodness and righteousness will be declared if He will have mercy on those who have no share of good works ($8^{4-36}$). Alas, the reply to all this is stern and sarcastic. Esdras has pleaded that the good deeds of the righteous should incline God to have mercy. Let Him think, not of the sinners, but of the faithful. And the answer is: " Indeed I will not think on the fashioning of them that have sinned, or their death, their judgment, or their destruction. But I will rejoice over the framing of the righteous . . . the salvation and the reward that they shall have " (8³⁸). Still, despite this blank and utter denial of his hopes, Esdras continues to plead. Like Esaias, he is exceeding bold. Perhaps man has needed help which God has not granted him. " Be not wroth with us, but spare Thy people" (8⁴⁵). It is, however, only to be denied once again and to be rebuked. It is man's own fault. Judgment is at hand (8⁴⁶⁻⁶²). Only the righteous will be saved, says the angel (9¹³), and once more Esdras raises his bitter cry. The blessed will be only a small minority (9¹⁴ᶠ·). That Uriel confirms (9¹⁷ ᶠ·).

H. M. Hughes remarks that the " teaching as to retribution is modified by Ps.-Ezra's appeal to the forgiveness and mercy of God. He sees that, if the law of retribution is to operate remorselessly in accordance with the standard of the law, very few will be saved. He therefore turns from the cast-iron Pharisaic view of retribution and declares that judgment will be with mercy, according to faith no less than works." *

This is certainly not the doctrine of the Salathiel Apocalypse. It is rather the fact that the author was one who intensely realised the need of God's mercy, but who utterly despaired of it and designed in the name of God to teach his compatriots that, if they would be among the blessed, they must merit it by coming up to the standard of righteousness. Hughes cites 8³²⁻⁶, 9⁷, 13²³ in his support ; 9⁷ and 13²³ may be disregarded here as not belonging to S, and 8³²⁻⁶ is not a declaration that judgment will be with mercy, but only a fervent prayer that it may be so, which is a very different thing. That prayer, moreover, is immediately followed by a speech of Uriel in which he gives denial to the hopes expressed there-

* Op. cit., p. 307 f.

in. Hughes also says that " Ps.-Ezra's doctrine of the divine forgiveness shows a marked advance on Pharisaism in the direction of Christianity. Although good works are stored up ($7^{17}$, $8^{33}$), the doctrine of merit is not taught, neither is that of the vicarious merits and intercession of the saints " ($7^{102}$).*

The latter statement is unquestionably correct, but, as to the former, the precise contrary must be maintained so far as S is concerned. The doctrine of judgment by merit is precisely what he insists on. Rabbi Kauffmann Kohler sums up the teaching of the whole book in the following terms : " The author recognises God's love for all His creatures ($8^{47}$), in spite of the fact that greater is the number of those lost than of those that are saved ($9^{15}$) ; but for him the end must be unrelenting justice and no mercy nor any intercession of the saints ; truth and righteousness must prevail ($7^{102-15}$). The author differs from the Hillelists, who teach that those souls whose merits and demerits are equal are saved by the mercy of God (who inclines the scale towards mercy), and sides with the Shammaites, who claim that these souls must go through the purgatory of the Gehenna fire before they are admitted into Paradise." † It will be seen that Kohler takes much the same view of the teaching of the book as to God's principles of judgment as that for which we have argued in the preceding pages. But, bearing in mind such a passage as $6^{56}$ and the racial narrowness of the plea of Esdras in the preceding context of $8^{47}$, we are scarcely entitled to affirm, with Kohler, that the author recognised " God's love for all His creatures," nor is there any hint in the book of such an idea as that the Gehenna fire is preparatory to a final admission into Paradise.

* Op. cit., p. 132.          † J.E., art. " Esdras," p. 221.

We have noticed in Chapter II. that S saw the need
of God's helpful grace for sinful man, and that he
questions in one of the conversations whether that
help has been adequately given.

Righteousness is keeping the law, fasting, chastity,
faith, gathering a treasure of good works ($7^{89, 94}$, $9^{32}$,
$6^{31, \text{etc.}}$; Ibid. $^{32}$; Ibid. $^{5}$; $7^{77}$, $8^{33}$). S does not dwell
on the need of benevolence or of an interior righteous-
ness. The one fact which argues in him a lofty ideal
of what God requires is his strong consciousness of
his own and his compatriots' demerit before Him.

Since the foregoing account of the teaching in S
was written Mr. G. H. Box has published a valuable
commentary on 4 Esdras. The view adopted by this
scholar as to the teaching of S on the subject of God's
forgiveness is widely different from that set forth in
this chapter, and therefore calls for examination here.
He considers that $7^{20 \text{ ff.}, 72}$ teach that the Gentiles have
been put outside the pale of the divine mercy because
they rejected the law which God had offered them.*

"It is important," he says, "to remember that, in
the theology of S, it is the acceptance of the law that
is the standard by which men must be judged at the
last, not the observance of it." † "The sin that
dooms is rejection of the law ; salvation consists in
accepting it. Judged by this standard, Israel, on
the one side, is accepted, and the heathen world, on
the other, is condemned." ‡ He considers that in
$7^{17 \text{ f.}}$ the question is raised whether the felicity of the
future world is "destined for Israel, as such, or only
for the righteous members of the nation." The angel,

* "The Ezra Apocalypse," p. xxxv.
† Ibid., p. xxxix.
‡ Ibid., p. 129.

in his reply in 20 f., according to Mr. Box, "ignores the distinction between the righteous and transgressors within Israel" and "proceeds to emphasise the heinous sin of the heathen world in openly despising and scorning the divine law." * Still, in Mr. Box's view, the significance of the indirect reply is that Israel "is destined to participate in the future blessings." † But to this it must be replied that in 7¹⁷ Esdras is not raising any question at all. He is simply stating what he conceives to be a fact and protesting boldly against the hard fate of transgressors in suffering both here and hereafter for their sin. Moreover, it is by no means clear that in 7²⁰⁻²⁴ Uriel is not making a direct reply to Esdras. It is probable that it is of unfaithful *Israelites* that he is here speaking. Stronger language is used of these in 8²⁵⁻³¹. They are described as those who "have lived like cattle," those that "are deemed worse than the beasts." Mr. Box admits that this passage undoubtedly refers to Jews.‡ There is, therefore, no valid reason against interpreting 7²⁰⁻²⁴ in a similar manner. It seems much more natural to understand it so than to regard the angel as only making an indirect reply to the point raised by the prophet. Moreover, Esdras himself is far from understanding the angel as Mr. Box does, for he is still most painfully distressed about the approaching evil fate of Israelite transgressors. Uriel's reply has not brought him the smallest degree of consolation. He laments in general terms the fate of mankind, but he expressly includes his own people amongst those over whose destiny he sighs (7⁶⁴⁻⁹, ¹¹⁷ff., 8⁴ff., ¹⁶⁻¹⁸). He desires to know if "*we* shall be kept in rest" until the judgment, or if "*we* shall be tormented forthwith" (7⁷⁵). He is

* Op. cit., p. 98.        † Ibid.        ‡ Ibid., p. xliv.

commanded not to include himself among the lost, but this is not because he is one of the chosen people who have accepted the law. It is because he is righteous ($7^{76\ t.}$), and it is not Israel as such who are to share his blessed estate. That is for those who are like himself ($8^{51}$). Moreover, when he prays for mercy to Israel through regard being had by God to the merits of the nation's saints ($8^{26-36}$), the divine reply is a denial of this hope ($8^{37-40}$). " The divine reply," says Mr. Box, " makes it clear that no such hope can be entertained." * In fact, this passage is really a distinct and emphatic contradiction of the idea that Israel as such will be blessed in the hereafter. The denial of mercy applies, as Mr. Box suggests, to those " who repudiate the divine law with a high hand and live as the very heathen." † But it does not apply to these only. On the contrary, the rejected supplication is a plea for others besides these —for sinners of a less flagrant character.

In a note on $7^{77}$—" Thou hast a treasure of good works "—Mr. Box again refers to his thesis that in this work " it is faith in the law (i.e. open acknowledgment) of its divine character and obligation) which will save most of those who are to be saved " ; and on $6^{5}$—" They were sealed that have gathered faith for a treasure "—he remarks that faith here seems to be " the righteousness which comes from fidelity to the law." But the fact is that it does not accord with the express teaching of S to interpret such a passage as a prophecy of ultimate blessing for all those who do not apostatise from the law. There is, according to S, no saving righteousness in merely holding by the national religion. We should give " faith " its full value. It is faithfulness. Salva-

* Op. cit., p. 176. † Ibid.

tion comes of loyalty in conduct to what the law requires.

*The Esdras Apocalypse* (E).—E affirms that in the great Day judgment will be according to works, and God will not show compassion to the nations raised from the dead to face the dread Assize ($7^{38}$). But he declares also that the saved will be those in the holy land who are able to escape by their works or by faith, while the condemned will be scorners of the law who have neglected the opportunity of repentance ($9^{7, 11}$). In $13^{23}$, which is apparently an insertion by the editor, it is works *and* faith that save. Here significantly it is works *or* faith. It seems that E held the doctrine which Mr. Box attributes, as we think wrongly, to S. God is here apparently the forgiving God of apostate Israelites who make a timely repentance and bow to the authority of the law. Works do not merit their salvation, as they do in the case of some, but they are saved in God's mercy by faith.

*The Vision of the Eagle* (A).—A's teaching, as we have seen in Chapter II., is that, after the destruction of the Roman Empire, God's kingdom will be established and it seems to be his idea that all surviving men may expect to be recipients of the divine mercy.

There is no teaching as to the righteousness which God requires, save the statement that injustice in rulers brings down punishment ($12^{32 f.}$).

*The Vision of the Son of Man* (M).—As we have seen in Chapter II., the teaching of M is that mercy in the last times will be only for Palestinian Jews. His God is one whose Son and representative taunts the wicked ($13^{38}$).

*The Additions of the Editor* (R).—R taught God's mercy for Gentiles converted in the times of the End and His acceptance of Israelites surviving at that period, if they have works and faith. This has been shown in Chapter II.

### 3 MACCABEES

This writer teaches that God is the forgiving Lord of Israel. " Out of love to the house of Israel, Thou promisedst truly that if we should fall off from Thee, and distress should overtake us, and we should come to this place and pray, Thou wouldest hear our supplication " ($2^{10}$). " Blot out our sins and disperse our errors, and send the light of Thy mercy at this hour " (Ibid. $^{19}$).

The writer goes, indeed, apparently to the opposite extreme from his co-religionists who regarded God as strict. We are reminded of the light-hearted penitents in Hosea $6^{1-3}$, for the writer's temper seems like theirs. He says nothing of any need of propitiation, or intercession, or repentance. God is "easy to be reconciled " ($5^{14}$). If this is the correct interpretation of his thought, which, however, in view of the scantiness of the data, one hesitates to affirm with confidence, he is unique in this matter among all the writers in this literature.

Toward Israel God is loving. He is their Father, their " merciful God and Father " ($2^{10}$, $6^{3, 8, 28}$, $5^7$).

The author praises those Jews who won a great reputation by adorning their behaviour with the works of the righteous, so that they became " well approved by all men " ($3^5$). Otherwise, he gives no hint of any duty except that of loyalty to Judaism, and he regards the vindictive slaughter of 300 apostate Jews as a deed fitly celebrated by a holy festival ($7^{14 f.}$). Righteousness before God is practically synonymous with faithfulness to the law. They who hold to it are described as "adhering to God unto death" (7¹⁶).

## 4 MACCABEES

There is no teaching in this book about forgiveness save that which has been mentioned in Chapter II., i.e. that God is made propitious by martyr-deaths.

The author's whole position precludes him from realising that man has need of a divinely given strength against moral evil. He teaches that, if a man has religious convictions, he is quite equal to the task of controlling evil elements in his nature. That indeed is a *sine quâ non*. "Through all my torments, I will persuade you that the children of the Hebrews are alone invincible in virtue's cause" (9¹⁸). But this suffices. Even the law not to covet can be obeyed (2⁵ᶠ·). In one place only does he seem to acknowledge that God helps man : "By the principle which we have praised they overcame their passions with God's help" (13³).

Of love in God he does not speak, but once he describes Providence as being "just and paternal" (9²⁴).

He teaches the importance of loyalty to God's commands in the matter of unclean meats (5²⁵). He considers that calamities befall the nation through the failure of some to be strict in the observance of the law (3²⁰ᶠ·). He tells how the "divine justice" was provoked by the erection of a gymnasium in the citadel and by the cessation of the temple service (4²⁰ᶠ·). Righteousness throughout the book is loyalty to Israel's God-given religion; but it includes also the Greek virtues—justice, fortitude, temperance, and prudence (1⁶). The revenge for Dinah is condemned as "contrary to good principle" (2¹⁹).

### SLAVONIC ENOCH

In this book God is described as implacable toward sinners. If one " does an injury to the soul of man, he does an injury to his own soul, and there is no salvation for his flesh nor forgiveness for ever. He who kills the soul of a man kills his own soul and destroys his own body, and there is no salvation for him for ever. He who prepares a net for another man will fall into it himself, and there is no salvation for him for ever. He who prepares a weapon against a man shall not escape punishment in the great judgment for ever. If a man acts crookedly or speaks evil against any soul, he shall have no righteousness for himself for ever " ($60^{1-5}$). This is the reading of A supported in the main by Sok. But the whole paragraph is omitted in B except the first sentence. That sentence, however, is altered radically in B by the omission of the words " nor forgiveness " and by the addition at the end of this sentence : " But when a man is in Paradise he is liable to judgment no more." The logical conclusion of the paragraph as it stands in A is, of course, the damnation of all men, since it is not murderers only who are doomed, but every one also who " acts crookedly or speaks evil against any soul." The MS. B is here more in harmony than A is with other teaching in the book which both MSS. contain. The writer anticipates the day " when all the just (who shall escape the great judgment of the Lord) shall be gathered together in eternal life " ($65^8$).* He also asserts his belief in the acceptability of repentance and offerings. " Blessed is the man who in patience shall bring his gifts before the face of the Lord, for he shall avert the recompense of his

* B omits the words in brackets.

sin. If he speaks words out of season, there is no
repentance for him ; if he lets the appointed time
pass and does not perform the work, he is not blessed ;
for there is no repentance after death " (62$^{1t.}$). In
the second of these sentences B substitutes for the
protasis at the beginning the words : " If he remem-
bers the appointed time to utter his prayer " ; and Sok
has, " If before the time he recalls his word." Charles
remarks that " the text is hopeless here " ; and this
is true, so far as B and Sok are concerned, for their
reading makes nonsense.* But A gives us a fairly
clear sense. The meaning seems to be that this life
is the time for repentance, but words of confession
spoken after death are words out of season, which
therefore are not acceptable.

Sacrifices and gifts are, however, acceptable, according to this writer, upon certain conditions which are
partly ceremonial and partly ethical. Clean beasts
and birds must be offered (59$^{2}$). The creature given
for food must be bound by the feet. A beast must
not be slain without a wound (Ibid. $^{3t.}$). A gift must
be the work of the offerer's hand and must be made
without murmuring. If the conditions be not fulfilled, the giver " cannot gain advantage from the
work of his hands " (61$^{4t.}$). But a sacrifice rightly
made " is an atonement : he acts righteously (therein)
and preserves his own soul " (59$^{3}$).†

The work also contains a remarkable prophecy concerning the fate of the fathers : " At the last coming
they will lead forth Adam with our forefathers and
conduct them there (i.e. into Paradise), that they may
rejoice, as a man calls those whom he loves to feast
with him ; and they, having come with joy, hold con-

* Edition of Slavonic Enoch in loc.
† B omits 59$^{3t.}$ and 61$^{4t.}$.

verse before the dwelling of that man, with joy
awaiting his feast, the enjoyment and the immeasurable wealth of joy and merriment in the light and
eternal life " (42⁵).* This is an important contribution to our knowledge of this writer's doctrine of God,
if it be from his pen. God is regarded as holding the
sinning fathers for ages in Hades bearing " the yoke
of that place " (41²), and as intending to restore them
at last to favour when the long penalty is fully paid.

The idea of intercessors in heaven for sinners is
denounced. Osterley says : " In the Slavonic Book
of Enoch 7⁵, we read of angels interceding for men." †
This passage, however, contains only Enoch's refusal
to intercede for angels. " Lo, the angels made obei-
sance to me and said unto me, ' O man of God, pray
for us to the Lord.' But I answered them, ' Who am
I, a mortal man, that I should pray for angels ? Who
knows whither I go, or what awaits me, or who prays
for me ? ' " Moreover, in 53¹ Enoch says : " And now,
my children, do not say, ' Our father stands before
God and prays for us (to be released) from sin,' for
there is no person there to help any man who has
sinned." ‡ But it must be added that in 64⁵, according to A B, Enoch is described as " one who removes
the sins of men." Possibly the doctrine is that Enoch
is an intercessor in the heavenly world. There is,
however, another reading : " An avenger of the sins
of men."

" Forgiveness," Charles says, " is not the message
of this book. For most sins there is no pardon." §
Still, for *some* sins there is pardon, according to our

---

* A and B omit.
† " The Jewish Doctrine of Mediation," p. 42.
‡ B omits the sentence, " for there is . . . sinned."
§ Edition of Slavonic Enoch, p. 78.

author, and that pardon is obtained by timely repentance, by duly made and willingly offered sacrifices.
And while this author teaches that God will not accept
a *post-mortem* repentance, he also declares, if 42⁵ is
from his pen, that God receives offending men into
favour again after a prolonged period of penalty in
Hades. The ultimate divine remission of further
penalties is evidently regarded, not as an act of God's
free grace, but as obtained because a *quid pro quo*
has been duly paid by the offenders. Moreover,
despite his doctrine of the divine strictness, he illogi-
cally expects that some men, by their merits, will
escape God's judgment.

In the title, omitted in B, Enoch is called "a man
wise and beloved of God," and in the introduction, also
omitted in B, it is said that "God loved him." These
are the only allusions in the work to love in God,
but in 63⁴ we have: "The Lord hates every contemptuous man."

In 2³ Enoch says: "May God make confident your
hearts in the fear of Him"; and the passage is possibly
an echo of Proverbs 14²⁶: ביראת יהוה מבטח־עז. It is
the only passage in Slavonic Enoch which at all looks
like a recognition of the fact that God will help man
in his conflict with sin.

The idea of the righteousness which pleases God is
far from being Judaistic. Sacrifices are only acceptable to Him when they are the expression of inner
loyalty. "God does not require bread, nor a light, nor
an animal, nor any other sacrifice, for it is as nothing.
But God requires a pure heart, and by means of all
this He tries the heart of men" (45³). Just as no
king will accept a gift from a subject who is disloyal
at heart, and no man will be pleased with the flattery
of one who secretly plots evil against him, so God,

from whom " nothing will be concealed," judges by the
disposition of the heart ($46^{1-3}$). B omits chapter 46 and
has not the words, " but God requires a pure heart."

It is also said that he is blessed " who has love
upon his lips and tenderness in his heart " ($42^{13}$),*
and that there is no reward for him who gives to the
poor grudgingly ($63^{11}$). God is concerned about
man's conduct. He hates the contemptuous man
and the lying word ($63^4$). What He is most implacable
against is injury done to man by man. What He
most approves in man is kindliness to his fellows :
" Whoever of you shall spend gold and silver for the
sake of a brother shall receive abundant treasure in
the day of judgment " ($50^5$). For the just and the
benevolent the third heaven is reserved, while the
terrible place in the North, with all sorts of tortures
in it, is for those who do not know God and who fail to
be benevolent to their kind (9 and 10). " When you
might have vengeance do not repay either your neighbour or your enemy," says Enoch, " for God will
repay as your avenger in the day of the great judgment " ($50^4$). In B this is narrowed by the omission
of the words " or your enemy," but Sok has substantially the same thought—" one who is near you
or afar off." According to one reading, unsupported
by A or B, the writer teaches that righteousness includes kindness to the dumb creation. " The Lord
. . . will judge the soul of man on account of the
souls of beasts in the world to come " ($58^4$).

## THE APOCALYPSE OF ABRAHAM

Omitting the undoubtedly Christian passage in
chapter 29, we find nothing either said or implied in

* Here, however, B has " upon whose lips are tenderness
and mercy."

this apocalypse about God's redeeming grace for sinful men.

God is said to love Abraham because Abraham has loved to seek Him (9, 10, 14). Abraham is called God's lover. But there is also a broader statement. God is the "lover of men, the good, the charitable, the free giver . . . patient and very pitiful" (17). In the song of Javel He is the object of love. "Thou art He whom my soul has loved" (17). All this is marred by the statement in chapter 23 that God hates some among those that do evil.

### THE SIBYLLINE ORACLES

As we have seen in Chapter II., the Sibyl's thought is that God forgives penitents who expiate impiety by praise and who practise piety in their hearts.

Pious men are described as those who "love ($\sigma\tau\epsilon\rho\gamma\omega$) the Mighty God" (25), but, while God is said to be angry, and is even described as "gnashing with fury" (51, 135, 169; 160), nothing is said of His love.

Unjust gains, murder, theft, adultery, idolatry, and the oppression of Israel are condemned (31 f., 27–34, 135 f.).

### THE ASCENSION OF ISAIAH

There is nothing here to our point except what is implied in the fact that the Messiah is called "the Beloved of my Lord" (1⁷).

### THE PRAYER OF MANASSEH

God is here addressed as "the Lord Most High, of great compassion, long-suffering, and abundant in mercy," who repents of bringing evils on men, and who has promised repentance and forgiveness to sinners. It is said that there are just men who do not need to repent, but even Manasseh, great transgressor that he is, may hope for mercy. God will save him, though all unworthy.

## SUMMARY

(1) *Forgivingness in God.*—The Ascension of Isaiah, the Esther Additions, and the Apocalypse of Abraham contain nothing which is to our purpose.

In 3 Maccabees, B$^1$ of Apoc. Baruch, and the book of Baruch in all its parts, the teaching is that God forgives the sins of repentant Israel. In 4 Maccabees there is only the doctrine that His wrath is turned away from Israel by martyr-deaths. Wisdom (Part 1) refers to His readiness to forgive the man of low estate. Wisdom (Part 2) has many allusions to His willingness to pardon all penitent men, whether they are Jews or Gentiles. This is also the teaching in the fourth book of the Oracles, and, notwithstanding its author's sternness, in the Slavonic Enoch.

A number of writers in this century deal with the principle upon which God will act in the great consummation of all things, and these fall into four categories.

(1) Some teach that, when the Messianic kingdom is set up on earth, God will act simply as the great Partisan of Palestinian Jews. These are A$^1$, A$^2$ of Apoc. Baruch, and M of 4 Esdras.

(2) Some who deal with the fate of men in the unseen world teach that there is final forgiveness with God for those who repent in time. This is the hope expressed in the prayer of Manasseh. B$^3$ assures Israel that God will so act toward them. The Sibyl declares that He will thus graciously treat all peni--

tents.  In 4 Esdras, E teaches the acceptance by
works or faith of apostate Israelites.  In the Assumption of Moses the doctrine is that God finally receives
all Israel in the day of national repentance.  They
go in a body to heaven.

Wisdom (chapter 10) seems to imply the ultimate
salvation of the penitent in the unseen, for apparently
the author teaches the salvation of Adam.

(3) Slavonic Enoch stands by itself.  Its author
teaches the ultimate salvation of the sinning fathers
after an age-long sojourn in the house of doom, where
they have paid the penalty of their sin.

(4) S of 4 Esdras teaches that there is no hope
for those who fail to come up to the required standard
in the great Day.  He has much to say of God's mercy
to sinners in this world, but solemnly warns his readers
that judgment will be at the last strictly according
to each man's desert.  The same stern doctrine is
given in B² of Apoc. Baruch.  B² has indeed a passage in which he affirms the future blessedness of all
proselytes.  But it is his emphatic teaching that
Israelites are to be stringently judged by conduct.
If, then, this passage about proselytes be his, he has
probably failed to make clear statement and means
that all *faithful* proselytes will be saved.

A³ of Apoc. Baruch also teaches that man's final
justification must be by works, and R of 4 Esdras
declares that accepted Israelites will be such as have
works and faith, while yet he implies that God will
have mercy on converted heathen in the times of the
end.

No writer of this century teaches that angels intercede for sinning men, but that departed saints do
this is asserted in the Assumption of Moses, and perhaps in one passage of Slavonic Enoch.  This passage,

however, is of dubious authority, and the work contains vigorous denial of the notion. B³ of Apoc. Baruch teaches that saints on earth are powerful intercessors with God for sinners. Even S of 4 Esdras admits that their meditation obtains mercy in time, though he denies that it is of any avail for men in the settlement of their final fate. Baruch $1^{1-14}$ also witnesses to the belief that men may help their fellows by intercessory prayer and sacrifice for pardoning grace, and Wisdom (Part 2) teaches that Aaron was Israel's mediator.

The idea that the merits of the righteous help men appears. According to B¹ of Apoc. Baruch, God is disposed to have mercy on Israel by ancestral merits. 4 Maccabees contains the teaching that martyr-deaths atone for the nation.

Less is said by these writers than by their predecessors of what offenders may do on their own behalf. The Sibyl in Book 4 says that piety will expiate sin, and in Slavonic Enoch the acceptability of sacrifices offered by the loyal-hearted is taught. We have nothing else.

It is, however, to be observed that no writer implies that intercession, or sacrifice, or vicarious merit affects a man's position in the final judgment of God.

(2) *God's Redeeming Grace.*—The writer of Baruch $1^{15}$-$3^8$ believed that in the future God would change the hearts of Israelites by His grace. According to Wisdom (Part 1), God's Wisdom passes over into holy souls, and in the tenth chapter of the book it is taught that Wisdom redeemed Adam.

There is also a passage in Slavonic Enoch in which the teaching seems to be that His help is available for men. Apart from that passage, the idea of such grace as being in normal operation in the world is found in no work of which we can be sure that it belongs to this century. The writer of the Salathiel Apocalypse complains indeed that such grace, though deeply needed by man, is not supplied.

(3) *The Love of God.*—Some affirm the love of God for Israel. Such are A³, B¹, B² of Apoc. Baruch, S of 4 Esdras, and the writer of 3 Maccabees. A³, however, declares that that love goes out to Israel when the nation is righteous, whereas in B¹ it is an unchanging love. S stands alone in expressly limiting God's love to Israel. Slavonic Enoch only affirms His love for the patriarch, and in the Ascension of Isaiah the Messiah is called the Lord's Beloved.

Wider views are taken by other writers. In Wisdom (Part 1) God is the loving Father of all the righteous. In the Apocalypse of Abraham He is the lover of men. In Wisdom (Part 2) He loves all things that are. Perhaps also this is the idea in the first part of Wisdom, where God's Wisdom is styled φιλάνθρωπος. There is thus much more said of the love of God for men by the writers of this century than by those who wrote in the first century B.C. Moreover, in Wisdom and the Apocalypse of Abraham there appears for the first time in this literature the doctrine of God as loving all His creatures. Unhappily, the fair picture is marred by the passages in Wisdom (Part 2) and the Apocalypse of Abraham in which God is said to hate sinners. That conception of Him is found also in Slavonic Enoch, and in M of 4 Esdras His representative, the Messiah, is said to taunt the wicked.

The idea of God as loving appears in no writer of the century save those named above, not even in the Assumption of Moses, though God is there called the Father of all Israelites. The Sibyl only has an allusion to men who love God.

(4) *The Righteousness Acceptable to God.*—Writers who insist on the importance of loyalty to Judaism are the authors of 3 and 4 Maccabees and the A³ section in Apoc. Baruch. But this is regarded as only a part of the idea of righteousness. According to both parts of Wisdom, the Assumption of Moses, 4 Maccabees, A of 4 Esdras, A², A³, B² of Apoc. Baruch, the Oracles, and Slavonic Enoch God condemns injustice to man. The last writer asserts that He will judge men for injury to the beasts. In Wisdom, Apoc. Baruch (A³), and the Oracles impurity is censured as displeasing to Him. B² and Slavonic Enoch insist on the duty of truthfulness.

There are three writers who declare that God requires an inward righteousness from men — the authors of the first part of Wisdom, Slavonic Enoch, and Apoc. Baruch (B²). There is little insistence on the idea that an element in the acceptable righteousness is benevolence toward men. It is in Slavonic Enoch only that this is emphasised, though it is also implied in Wisdom (Part 1), and in Wisdom (Part 2) we have the statement that the righteous should be a lover of men. On the other hand, the writer of Baruch 4⁵–5⁹ did not think it inconsistent in a righteous man to rejoice over the miseries of the foes of his race, and the author of the Assumption of Moses conceived that even in heaven Israel would joyously behold their enemies in the Inferno.

## CONCLUSIONS

(1) *Forgivingness in God.*—(A) As the foregoing Summaries have shown, a number of these writers conceived of God as being made propitious to offending men by a variety of influences. It will be con-

venient to state here in order their different doctrines so as to show clearly the extent to which these ideas prevailed.

(1) It was the doctrine of some that God has regard to intercessions offered on behalf of sinners, or to the merits of the righteous.

(a) There is intercession made for them in the heavenly places. This idea appears only in Enoch 1–36, the Testaments, and Enoch 37–70. Interceding angels are mentioned indeed elsewhere, but not as acting on behalf of sinners. In place of this, we have in 2 Maccabees and the Assumption of Moses the doctrine that great departed saints intercede for men. In the latter certainly, in the former probably, the idea is that of an intercession for offenders. One passage in Slavonic Enoch implies the same conception, but the author elsewhere stoutly opposes it, so that probably the passage in question is not his. The doctrine of intercession for sinners in the unseen world appears therefore in each of the three centuries, and it is not peculiar to Palestinian writings, since it is found in two works emanating from Egypt. But it is of no wide range in our books. It is confined to half a dozen writers, and finds place in only one of the works commonly called " Apocrypha."

(b) Prayer may be offered on behalf of sinners by their fellows on earth. This teaching is found mainly in works of the last period. Prior to that time it appears only in the Testaments and 2 Maccabees. The latter work is unique, teaching that living men may offer prayer and sacrifices for the dead. This doctrine, therefore, like the previous one, was only taught by a few of our authors, yet it appears in each period and in two non-Palestinian writers.

(c) God is rendered propitious by the merits of the

righteous. In the Testaments Additions and in B[1] He is regarded as taking into account ancestral merits. In 2 and 4 Maccabees martyr-deaths are regarded as making Him propitious. The notion of mercy through the merits of others is therefore peculiar to the two later centuries, and only appears in four writings, two of which are Palestinian in origin while two belong to the Dispersion. It finds place in one work —2 Maccabees—whose author teaches the value of intercession for sinners made by beings on earth and in heaven. He is thus the writer most insistent on the doctrine of help for sinners by what is done on their behalf by their fellows.

The idea of help for sinners with God appears, therefore, in a variety of forms. No one form of it has many advocates. It is not at all in evidence in a considerable number of the books. Nevertheless, the idea that in some way or other help was available was evidently widespread, appearing as it does in each period and among both Palestinian and non-Palestinian authors.

(2) Some taught that God has regard to sacrifices offered by men on their own behalf, or to their penance, or to their righteous deeds.

(a) That sacrifices offered by offenders for themselves avail is the teaching of Jubilees, Oracles (Book 3), the Psalms of Solomon, 3 Esdras, the Song of the Three Children, and Slavonic Enoch.

(b) Penance is regarded as of importance in the Testaments and the Psalms of Solomon.

(c) Righteous deeds cancel sin, according to Ecclesiasticus and Tobit, and a similar idea appears in the Oracles (Book 4). The teaching as to the value of penance and the power of righteous deeds to atone for the past is thus purely Palestinian, but the doctrine that sacrifices avail appears also in non-Palestinian writings.

(3) The doctrine that sin is cancelled by the sufferings which God inflicts appears in the Psalms of Solomon, where the thought is of sufferings in this life, and the author of Slavonic Enoch, who stands alone in this matter, implies the doctrine of purgatorial pains in the unseen world.

The great majority of the writers who teach the doctrine of the forgiving God either assert or else distinctly imply that repentance on the part of sinners is a *sine quâ non*. Some few do not suggest this, but only the author of 2 Maccabees teaches the value of sacrifices for those who die in an impenitent condition.

On a survey, however, of the very various ideas which these writers held, we have evidence of a persistent and widespread idea among them that God is inclined to be propitious to sinners by other considerations in addition to repentance on their part.

(B) We have next to consider the question whether God was conceived of as being merciful to men in His final judgment, and, if so, upon what terms. Our answer, as the foregoing Summaries show, must be that the great majority of those who treat of eschatology teach that the ultimate fate of men turns on their own righteousness or unrighteousness, but that they did not conceive of a judgment untempered by mercy. This is the all but unanimous teaching of those men who wrote in the pre-Christian period, and the same doctrine appears in several works of the first century A.D. But a far sterner idea took possession of some writers, and these are mainly of the latter period. One apocalyptist of the first century B.C. enunciated the doctrine of a rigid judgment of

God according to desert, and his work contains no suggestion that God ever forgives. This writer—the author of Enoch 91–104—was the forerunner of several others. S of 4 Esdras, A³ and B² of Apoc. Baruch teach the same stern doctrine.

In our Summary of the first century A.D. we have noted also two other views—that in the three writers who maintain that God's mercy when the Kingdom is established will be for all Palestinian Jews and these only, and that in Slavonic Enoch where the teaching is the final acceptance in the unseen world at least of some offenders who will have endured age-long punishment.

It must be added that these writers did not apparently conceive of intercessions, sacrifices, or merits of others as affecting the ultimate judgment of God. There is one exception to this statement—the writer of 2 Maccabees ; but the general idea is that intercessions, sacrifices, or merits of saints incline God to be gracious to men in His attitude toward them in this life only.

(C) As to the question whether the divine forgiveness was conceived of as being extended to Gentiles, reference may be made to the Summaries and Conclusions in Chapter II. under the heading : "The justice of God in His attitude to Israel and the Gentiles." The question has been unavoidably anticipated. It must suffice here to summarise the facts briefly. With the doubtful exception of Jubilees, no work of the earliest of the three centuries contains the doctrine that all Gentiles are excluded from the scope of God's mercy. Jubilees *does* teach that the bulk of them are excluded, but perhaps its author thought that some would be saved at last. In the second period 2 Maccabees limits God's mercy to Israel, Enoch 91–104 teaches no doctrine of God's forgiveness, and the Psalter appears to limit mercy to the saints in Israel; but, if the Syriac be correct, there is also broader teaching in that work, as there is in other works of the period. In the third period there is a great increase in the number of writers who teach the utter exclusion of all Gentiles; but, even in that period, the larger thought is by no means altogether without its advocates.

(2) *God's Redeeming Grace.*—Two writers prophesy that grace to change the hearts of men will be given in the future, but they do not suggest that such grace is available for men prior to the great consummation of all things.

To the idea of such grace as in present operation some writers make brief allusion. These are the writers of 2 Maccabees, the Song of the Three Children, and Slavonic Enoch. Wisdom, in chapter 10, tells of redeeming grace given to Adam. There are writers, however, who have much more to say than these on the subject. In the Similitudes and Interpolations of Enoch and in Wisdom (Part 1) the teaching is that grace is given by God to all the righteous. But the chief exponents of the doctrine of divine help for good men are Ben Sira and the writers of Jubilees, the Testaments, and the Psalms of Solomon. They teach that such help is to be obtained in answer to prayer. They recur to this truth repeatedly in their writings. It was evidently a deeply rooted and cherished article of belief to them.

It is notable that the thought of such grace as available now finds its clearest and most frequent expression among the earlier writers. Apart from slight allusions to it in Wisdom and Slavonic Enoch, it is not in evidence in the first century A.D., and S of

4 Esdras complains that badly needed help is not given to men by God.

It must not be forgotten that the very foundation of the work of the apocalyptists is that they are the inspired and commissioned servants of God, whose duty it is to urge men to do right by warnings or counsels or to hearten the pious for loyalty to God by their revelations. The presupposition, therefore, of their work is that God is seeking to influence men to do right. Naturally, it is to Israel that they conceive themselves called to speak; but the authors of the Books of Oracles regard themselves as commissioned to address the Gentiles in the name of God. The case of the books of the Apocrypha is different. It may be that some of these writers took the same view of their own function, but the claim is never expressly made as it is in the apocalypses, unless it be that Ben Sira means this in his Prologue.

Ben Sira is unique in his fine teaching that God acts directly upon all men, as a Shepherd seeking to bring them back to Himself. There is nothing like this elsewhere in the entire literature. But reference to the Summaries and Conclusions in Chapter II. under the heading, "The Justice of God in the Allotment of Prosperity and Adversity," will show that a number of our authors held that God so orders human fortune that chastened men may be led into the way of duty.

(3) *The Love of God.*—Some writers give us nothing on this subject save the inference which may be drawn from the statement that men do or should love God, and some only predicate of Him love to great individuals.

But an often-expressed idea is that He loves Israel. The thought sometimes is that He loves Israel as such, but sometimes it is that He loves the righteous among them. Sometimes there is the thought of a wider love, a love to all the righteous. This noble conception appears in Ecclesiasticus and the Additions to that work. It was the faith also of the author of the Testaments. But after the close of the second century B.C. it finds no place in the literature save in Wisdom (Part 1). There is, however, a still broader thought in Wisdom (Part 2) and the Apocalypse of Abraham, perhaps also in Wisdom (Part 1). In these alone does the idea appear of a love of God to man without restriction of class or character. Unhappily, in Wisdom (Part 2) and the Apocalypse of Abraham inconsistent doctrine is taught. Here, as in Slavonic Enoch, God is said to hate sinners. In three other works there are statements in which God is made to appear unlovable.

One is in Enoch 83–90, where God beholds unmoved the awful sorrows of His people; but this writer is here inconsistent with himself, for elsewhere He pictures God as deeply interested in men generally, rejoicing over their conversion. In the other two—Enoch 91–104 and M of 4 Esdras—there is nothing to modify the impression that the writers represent God as unlovely and unlovable.

A few writers call God Father. The thought is not usually that God is Father of Israel, but that He sustains that relationship to all righteous Israelites. In 4 Maccabees His providence is described as of a paternal character. In the third book of the Oracles God has a unique title—" The All-Father."

(4) *The Righteousness Acceptable to God.*—Naturally, emphasis is laid upon loyalty to Judaism and the due observance of its ceremonial worship by some of the writers, though there is less said about it than might have been anticipated. It is chiefly in works

like Jubilees, Tobit, Judith, and the Psalms that disloyalty to the national cultus is regarded as a deadly sin. On the other hand, in a considerable number of works there is little or nothing on the subject, and it is only a very small number of writers who fail to lay stress on the fact that there are other elements in the righteousness that pleases God.

In the earliest century almost every writer lays it down that he who would please God must be kindly to his fellows; but—though justice is demanded and oppression is denounced by many of the later writers —the idea that God requires man to be benevolent toward men is conspicuous by its absence from the pages of most of those who wrote in the two later centuries.

Three authors—two in the earliest period and one in the last—insist that God requires compassion towards the dumb creatures.

Other elements in the conception of righteousness insisted upon by some are truth-speaking and sexual purity. Only one writer appears clearly to teach that God is hostile to advancing knowledge, but there are many whose conception of what God allows is mean, in that they suppose Him to tolerate the spirit of hatred and revengefulness, or do not think of Him as requiring perfect truth. The latter fault is only to be found in two writers—one of the second and one of the first century B.C. The former defect is to be seen in some of the writers of each period—a considerable number in all. But, almost exclusively, this failure is in Palestinian writers.

The idea that God requires from men an inner righteousness was not entirely wanting in the authors of this literature. There is reference to the idea in some works of each century, and in both Palestinian and Hellenistic writings ; but in a considerable number of books it finds no expression, nor does it in the process of time become an idea more in evidence.

On the whole, it must be maintained that the conception of God implied in the notions of these writers as to what He requires from men is not a lofty one. It is often supposed that He tolerates feelings and actions in men which are unworthy, judged by a true ethical standard. It is not insisted upon that kindliness to man is required by Him save by a small number of the authors, and these mainly in the earliest period.

# APPENDIX

## DR. CHARLES'S NEW EDITION OF "ETHIOPIC ENOCH"

SINCE the completion of this thesis Dr. Charles has published a new edition of his "Ethiopic Enoch," in which he makes some modifications of his critical views. He would now assign chapter 71 to the author of the Similitudes. He will not now call chapters 43 and 44 interpolations, though he says that their presence deranges the context. He thinks that $41^{3-9}$ is alien to its setting and may belong to the Similitudes. For our purposes, the question whether chapter 71 is an interpolation or a part of the Similitudes is of no moment. It makes no important difference to the doctrine of either section.

The chapters 43 f. are negligible so far as we are concerned. If $41^{3-9}$ is the work of the author of the Similitudes there is here an important change, for in that case it is he who propounds the doctrines of predestination and grace in verse 8. The authorship is, however, a moot point.

Two alterations in the translation in the new edition should be noted. In $27^3$ Dr. Charles formerly had this rendering of the Ethiopic Version : "Here will those who have found mercy bless the Lord." He now renders this : "Here shall the merciful bless the Lord." If this is to be accepted as the true reading it is the only allusion in Enoch 1–36 to the idea that the righteous who are accepted at last by God are characterised by benevolence. But the Gizeh Greek fragment has the word εὐσεβεῖς (godly).

In $84^3$, according to the new translation, we have the doctrine of Omnipotence, which did not find expression in Enoch 83–90 according to the older rendering : "Nothing is too hard for Thee."

# INDEX

## (1) PASSAGES CITED FROM THE BIBLE

23

## (3) PASSAGES CITED FROM APOCALYPTIC AND OTHER WORKS

## (4) SUBJECTS

24

## (5) AUTHORS CITED